CRACKER TIMES
AND PIONEER LIVES

CRACKER TIMES
AND PIONEER LIVES

The Florida Reminiscences of
George Gillett Keen and Sarah Pamela Williams

EDITED BY

JAMES M. DENHAM
CANTER BROWN JR.

UNIVERSITY OF SOUTH CAROLINA PRESS

© 2000 University of South Carolina

Published in Columbia, South Carolina, by the
University of South Carolina Press

Published 2000
First Paperback Edition 2003

Manufactured in the United States of America

07   06   05   04   03   5   4   3   2   1

The Library of Congress has cataloged the cloth edition as follows:

Keen, George Gillett, 19th cent.
    Cracker times and pioneer lives : the Florida reminiscences of George
Gillett Keen and Sarah Pamela Williams / eds., James M. Denham and
Canter Brown, Jr.
        p.   cm.
    Includes bibliographical references (p.   ) and index.
    ISBN 1-57003-346-3 (alk. paper)
    1. Keen, George Gillett, 19th cent.   2. Pioneers—Florida—Biography.
3. Williams, Sarah Pamela, 19th cent.   4. Women pioneers—Florida—
Biography.   5. Whites—Florida—Biography.   6. Frontier and pioneer life—
Florida—Anecdotes.   7. Florida—Social life and customs—19th century—
Anecdotes.   8. Country life—Florida—History—19th century—Anecdotes.
9. Florida—History—1821–1865—Anecdotes.   I. Williams, Sarah Pamela,
19th cent.   II. Denham, James M.   III. Brown, Canter.   IV. Title.
F315 .K44   2000
975.9'83016—dc21   00-008313

ISBN 1-57003-512-1 (pbk.)

With love, to my children,
Margaret Grace and James Bennet Denham
J. M. D.

To my friend Stephen Prine, a most worthy
legacy of the Keen family in Florida
C. B.

CONTENTS

LIST OF ILLUSTRATIONS

Illustrations

FOLLOWING PAGE 64

Maps

ACKNOWLEDGMENTS

Numerous individuals are due our heartfelt appreciation for their many kindnesses and contributions to this volume. David J. Coles of the Florida Archives suggested to us that we examine bound volumes of the *Lake City Florida Index* in the Florida Collection of the State Library of Florida, which led to our discovery of George Gillett Keen's reminiscences. Aleene M. Havird of Lake City, who provided us with personal information on several families mentioned in Keen's stories, also suggested that we contact Helen Ives, then of Branford, concerning Sarah Pamela Williams. Mrs. Ives, in turn, graciously permitted us to publish the Williams memoirs and shared with us related materials and family notes. Jimmy Keen of Columbia City, Wanda De Montmollin of Plant City, and Mrs. Doyle Chancey of Palmetto lent their notes and suggestions concerning the Keen family and their relations. David J. Coles and Rusty Alexander of the Florida Archives and Elaine Dickinson, Randi Bailey, Margaret Pugh, Nan Currence, and Cynthia C. Wise of the State Library's Florida Collection all went far out of their way to provide research assistance and helpful suggestions. Peter A. Krafft, director of cartography at Florida State University, prepared the beautiful maps for this work. Karen Ostojic of Lakeland wonderfully transcribed both sets of reminiscences, an extremely difficult task from the poor microfilm copies with which she was provided.

Others to whom we are indebted for their contributions and assistance are, in alphabetical order: Joseph "Pat" Adams, Tampa; Elizabeth Alexander, P. K. Yonge Library of Florida History, University of Florida, Gainesville; Holmes Alexander, Tampa; Nancy Aumann, Florida Southern College; Patrick Anderson, Florida Southern College; Nancy Bartlett, Bentley Historical Library, University of Michigan, Ann Arbor; Harold B. Bennett, Live Oak; John E. Brown, Fort Meade; Patricia Coate, Columbia, South Carolina; Tracy Danese, Tallahassee; J. Allison DeFoor, Tallahassee; Nancy Dobson, Florida Supreme Court Historical Society, Tallahassee; Ann Douglass, Houston, Texas, Public Library; Robin Ede, Hernando County Public Library, Brooksville;

Julius J. Gordon, Tampa; Kathy K. Greenberg and Mark I. Greenberg, Jackson, Mississippi; Patton Hash, South Carolina Historical Society, Charleston; Leland M. Hawes, *Tampa Tribune*; Alice Heisch, Bellville, Texas, Public Library; Bill Hill, Florida Southern College; Virginia Jackson, Brooksville; Janice Mahaffey, archivist for the Clerk of the Circuit Court, Palatka; Marcia Martin, Columbia County Public Library; Kevin M. McCarthy, University of Florida, Gainesville; Randall McDonald, Florida Southern College; Tom Muir, Historical Pensacola Preservation Board; Andrew Pearson, Florida Southern College; Vernon Peeples, Punta Gorda; James M. Perry, Amelia Island Museum of History, Fernandina Beach; Samuel Proctor, University of Florida, Gainesville: Virgil E. Raulerson, Jacksonville; Thomas L. Reuschling, president of Florida Southern College; Taryn Rodriguez-Boette, St. Augustine Historical Society Research Library; Warren Rogers, Gainesville College, Gainesville, Georgia; William W. Rogers, Florida State University, Tallahassee; Marvis Snell, Palmetto; Joe Spann, Polk County Historical and Genealogical Library, Bartow; David St. John, Baker County Historical Society, Glen St. Mary; Bill Stein, Archives of the Nesbitt Memorial Library, Columbus, Texas; Dana Ste. Claire, Museum of Arts and Sciences, Daytona Beach, Florida; Donna M. Stephens, St. Augustine Historical Society Research Library; Kyle S. VanLandingham, Kerrville, Texas; Weatherly D. Whitestone, Texas Newspaper Project, University of Texas at Austin; Nathan Woolsey, Milton; Freddie Wright, editor, *Polk County Historical Quarterly*, Bartow; and Lloyd T. Wynns, Bartow.

INTRODUCTION

George Gillett Keen and Sarah Pamela Williams shared in the adventure, thrill, hardship, and tragedy that embodied the world of Florida's pioneers. During the nineteenth century they and other men and women erected and then slowly moved the line of frontier settlement from northeast Florida down into the peninsula toward Tampa Bay, the Peace River Valley, and beyond. In the process they endured hurricanes, floods, droughts, freezes, heat, plagues, wars, lawlessness, and all manner of other challenges. Still, they persevered and eventually succeeded, leaving their marks on the state. Many descendants of these pioneers yet influence Florida; the state's economy remains tied in part to the communities and the cattle and citrus industries they developed; and its society often reflects its frontier heritage.

That is not to say that George Gillett Keen and Sarah Pamela Williams were essentially similar or that Florida's pioneer settlers as a whole reflected the same characteristics. The state owes a great debt to the diversity of its residents, past and present. Men and women—rich and poor—played their parts. Similarly, blacks, whites, Indians, Hispanics, and others helped to make the state unique by their contributions.[1] Keen and Williams reflected this diversity. They, of course, differed first as man and woman. One received the barest of educations, while the other was tutored by one of Florida's most erudite men. Finally, they inherited markedly distinct positions in frontier society, as their reminiscences record.

The Keens' story typified that of many other "Cracker" families, as the less-affluent plain folk of the southeastern frontier were called.[2] Born in Georgia in the 1820s, George G. Keen soon moved into Florida Territory with his parents and siblings seeking land and a better life. Hundreds of other families made the same trek. Keen thereafter matured in a frontier society that was rough, dangerous, and exciting. As he tells us, he yearned for the trappings of high social standing while realizing that Florida provided opportunity for those who were resourceful enough to take advantage of the varying circumstances offered by frontier life.

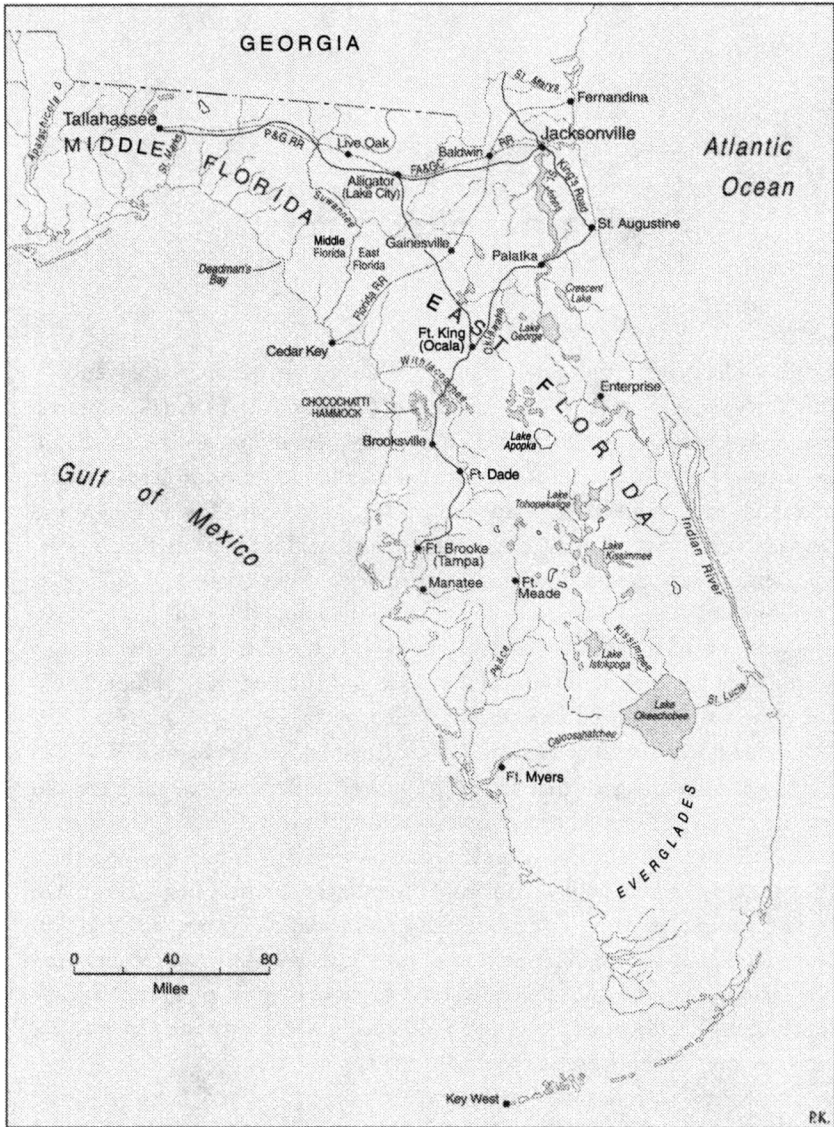

Florida in the mid 1800s

Sarah Pamela Williams admittedly could not be considered a Cracker. Her father, John Lee Williams, occupied a high rung in Florida society and public affairs, and she married into one of northeast Florida's premier planter families. Vivacious and well read, she enjoyed widespread social contacts and the benefits of travel to sophisticated locales such as antebellum Charleston, South Carolina. Nonetheless, the frontier touched Williams as it did Keen. She matured in a community that retained frontier conditions, and she inter-related constantly with Cracker men and women whose lives intermingled with her own. She saw and remembered her world differently than did Keen, but that fact permits us by comparison a rich in-depth glimpse at the multi-faceted world of frontier Florida.[3]

The locale shared by Keen and Williams centered on northeast Florida's Columbia County and its seat at Alligator (later, Lake City).[4] Three-score miles to the east lay the port and trading village of Jacksonville in Duval County; north and west over the Suwannee River was Hamilton County; and south could be found Alachua County and its seat of Newnansville (present-day Alachua). Beyond Hamilton County to the west emerged a rich cotton-growing belt, focused on the capital at Tallahassee and encompassing the counties of Madison, Jefferson, Leon, Gadsden, and Jackson. In those counties an affluent and sophisticated life thrived that eventually rivaled some of the finest areas boasted by the Old South. The plantation region was called Middle Florida.[5]

East of the Suwannee River and on the peninsula a different kind of society developed. Known as East Florida, the area contained most of the remnants of Florida's Seminole, Creek, and Mikasuki populations with their African and African-American vassals. Fiercely determined to protect their Florida homes, these earlier inhabitants found themselves pressed further down the peninsula as the line of frontier settlement encroached on their lands in the 1820s and 1830s. By 1835 the tensions erupted in the seven-year-long Second Seminole War, which arguably also comprised the largest slave rebellion in United States history. The conflict resulted in bloodshed throughout East Florida and, as related by Keen's reminiscences, forced frontier settlers to "fort up" at fortified homesteads and military outposts.[6]

The location in East Florida of armed Indians and blacks, coupled with the presence of less-advantageous soils, retarded development there of the kind of plantation economy that emerged in Middle Florida. After the Second Seminole War, though, planters expanded operations in Columbia and surrounding counties. Partly in response, the frontier at the same time crept southward. Some area families journeyed down toward Hernando and Hillsborough Counties, although others made a shorter trip southwesterly to that portion of Madison County that would become Lafayette. As a whole, East Floridians depended until well after the Civil War upon subsistence farming, hog raising, and cattle grazing, supplemented by the exploitation of natural resources in the form of timber and naval stores. Few improved roads graced the land, and the railroads' steam whistles would not be heard until the late 1850s—and then only just barely. The region, for the most part, remained frontierlike.[7]

When Florida became a possession of the United States in 1821, some American families already lived in the northeast corner of East Florida. The line of frontier settlement had been advancing for generations into the southern interior, with many immigrants—notably hardy Scotch-Irish families—following the Great Valley south through the Piedmont of Virginia, the Carolinas, and Georgia. Some of the settlers remained loyal to the king during the American Revolution and found refuge in Spanish Florida. Others arrived in the 1790s and early 1800s, attracted by generous land grants. They set down roots primarily south of the St. Marys River and east of the St. Johns. On many occasions individuals and families moved back and forth across the national boundary, victims of the fortunes of war or economic pressures.[8]

With the transfer of possession to the United States in 1821, groups of Georgia and South Carolina families began relocating to Florida, looking for opportunity and a new start. They filtered into the northeast interior, prompting the territorial council in 1824 to create Alachua County, followed by Hamilton in 1827 and Columbia in 1832. Slightly fewer than 2,800 persons comprised the total population of these counties in 1830, a figure that doubled during the next decade. When 1850 census takers polled Columbia County alone, they discovered 4,808 residents.[9]

Sarah Pamela Williams did not move to Columbia County until the late 1840s, but the Keen family arrived on the scene in October 1830. Carving out a simple but adequate existence, the Keens and the area's few other families grew corn, herded their cattle and pigs, hunted, and fished. As settlers became more numerous, Columbia's principal village of Alligator grew into a relatively urban magnet for the vicinity's people. Roads running east and west connected the town with Jacksonville and Tallahassee; those to the north linked it with the Withlacoochee, Alapaha, and Suwannee Rivers; and those leading southward led ultimately to Fort Brooke and its small civilian community of Tampa.

By the eve of the Civil War, Alligator's progress had been marked. Renamed Lake City, it had taken on greater regional importance. The Florida, Atlantic, and Gulf Central Railroad brought it swifter and more dependable transportation, which fostered the growth of nearby cotton plantations. In 1860 it achieved the distinction of being Florida's tenth largest town with 332 white and 327 black residents. That year it contained seven dry goods stores, two hotels, two livery stables, two blacksmith shops, three schools, two print shops, two bars, and one eating establishment.[10]

The Civil War and its aftermath saw continued growth for Lake City and Columbia County, but as rural economic conditions deteriorated in much of Florida and the South beginning in the 1870s, the vitality of earlier years eroded. The conditions compelled Sarah Pamela Williams to leave the state for Georgia and a new marriage. George Gillett Keen remained, but the county's 17,000 residents by the century's turn could only vaguely recall the great expectations and exciting times of earlier years. It was during that period—1899 to 1902—that Keen penned his reminiscences, recording for posterity a life and times long gone but which remained alive and immediate in his brilliant storyteller's mind.

Keen's reminiscences, coupled with those of Williams, touch upon numerous important subjects and themes of frontier and rural life. As already mentioned, one important foundation of frontier life for Keen and many other East Florida Crackers consisted of subsistence farming and cattle grazing. This cattle culture was a migratory one, as families pioneered the movement of the frontier southward in search of newer and better grazing lands. Keen's frequent trips to the Tampa Bay area from northeast Florida well symbolize the journeys made, often permanently, by his friends, relations, and counterparts during the 1840s and afterward. Indeed, many of the individuals and families about which Keen and Williams wrote became the first settlers of southwestern Florida's interior, including Hernando, Pasco, Hillsborough, Polk, Hardee, DeSoto, Highlands, Glades, Charlotte, Manatee, and Lee Counties. Some of them—the Summerlin family provides a good illustration—came to dominate the area cattle industry in subsequent years.[11]

While relating stories of his early life, Keen presents insights on themes such as the violent nature of frontier life, the brutalities (on both sides) of Indian warfare, the consequences of such brutality when it impacted upon kinship and friendship networks, the meaning of life and death, issues of social gradations in a frontier setting, law and order, criminal justice, and customs of romance, courting, and marriage. One currently popular line of inquiry into rural southern culture concerns—of all things—nose biting, and Keen gives us a colorful example.[12]

Along the way the old Cracker pioneer explores the ethics, values, and daily lives of Florida plain folk within the traditional milieu of southern humor, a genre that he shared with many of the leading southern writers of the time.

Beginning with antebellum authors such as Augustus Baldwin Longstreet, Joseph G. Baldwin, and Johnson J. Hooper and continuing with postbellum writers such as Joel Chandler Harris, these creative artists made us laugh, but their characters also possessed the wisdom, insight, and sense of direct, straightforward morality common to the society in which they lived. Keen would have been familiar with Capt. Simon Suggs and Uncle Remus, and though he wrote his accounts as the nineteenth century ended and the twentieth began, one can discern the influence of these earlier writers while still sensing that Keen has spoken to us in an authentic Cracker voice.[13]

With Keen, though, the reader gains a dimension often lacking in the works of Longstreet and his fellow writers. Keen tells stories with the same verve and vernacular as the others. On the other hand, while Longstreet and fellow observers of the southern social scene often mask the identity of their characters and key details of events, Keen reveals them. This permits tracing of the stories through newspapers, court records, and other available documentation. In turn, their remarkable accuracy is revealed. Keen's tales— though evidencing a Cracker license for exaggeration—all are based upon verifiable fact.

Mention should be made about the timing of Keen's writing and its implications. The stories were committed to paper at a time when Keen's north Florida frontier world had vanished due to a number of factors—including, of course, emancipation, population growth, railroads, and the mechanization of agriculture. Consequently, much as did his counterparts who wrote a generation earlier, Keen reflected through his reminiscences a sense of "urgency to get on paper something of a unique cultural significance that was rapidly disappearing."[14] The tales reflect a touch of romanticism for days gone by, but Keen nonetheless writes with sensitivity and poignancy of the society that witnessed his passage through childhood and adolescence into adult maturity.

The Keen stories omit reference to the Civil War, a difficult and complicated time for Floridians, including those who lived in Columbia County. Williams steps in to help fill that gap, offering reflections on the responsibilities and hardships faced by women and on conditions she and other planters dealt with following the peace. In a larger context, she shares a woman's perspective on a time and place—pioneer-era Florida—that has been sadly neglected, due in large part to the unavailability of accounts such as hers.

As to the men, women, and children mentioned by Keen and Williams, we have included as an appendix to this volume a "Cast of Characters" that provides basic personal information and, where appropriate, validation of events discussed in the reminiscences. We have avoided excessive footnoting of the text, opting instead for the inclusion of the appendix and correction of mistakes in brackets within the text. Otherwise the text appears as it does in the original, with only a few exceptions. In a limited number of instances long paragraphs have been broken down into two or more shorter paragraphs. In very few instances a part of one paragraph has been joined to the next paragraph for clarity. Periods have been added at the ends of sentences where it appeared clear to the editors that the symbol had been omitted erroneously by the printer. The use of *sic* has been avoided.

The language used by George G. Keen and to a lesser extent by Sarah Pamela Williams reflects social and cultural attitudes typical of rural southern whites, including recourse to racial epithets. These statements and references may offend some readers, a situation deeply regretted by the editors. Still, they accurately convey racial attitudes and assumptions of their authors' time and place.[15] As such, any attempt by the editors to change this wording would have undercut the usefulness of the reminiscences as historical documents. Therefore, we have chosen to present them in their unaltered state.

Within a broader regional context, the life experiences and beliefs articulated by these reminiscences typified the South's most ever-present, yet elusive, social group—a sort of southern middle class without commercial roots. Frank L. Owsley referred to them as "Plain Folk," although numerous other labels have been applied.[16] The themes of their lives have received consideration by historians, anthropologists, sociologists, and even folklorists. The characters brought back to life by Keen and Williams bespeak the independent, self-reliant, sometimes violent, simple, and direct folks who pioneered the southern region. These people seem to have possessed a kind of "pleasure ethic and not a work ethic—a value system based on the enjoyment of life instead of the accumulation of property."[17] The accumulation of wealth, the right way to get ahead, and ethical dilemmas regarding such things are major chords for those who populate Keen's and Williams's memories. Sometimes our narrators' ambivalence about such concerns speaks in greater volume to us than do their certainties.

PART ONE

George Gillett Keen

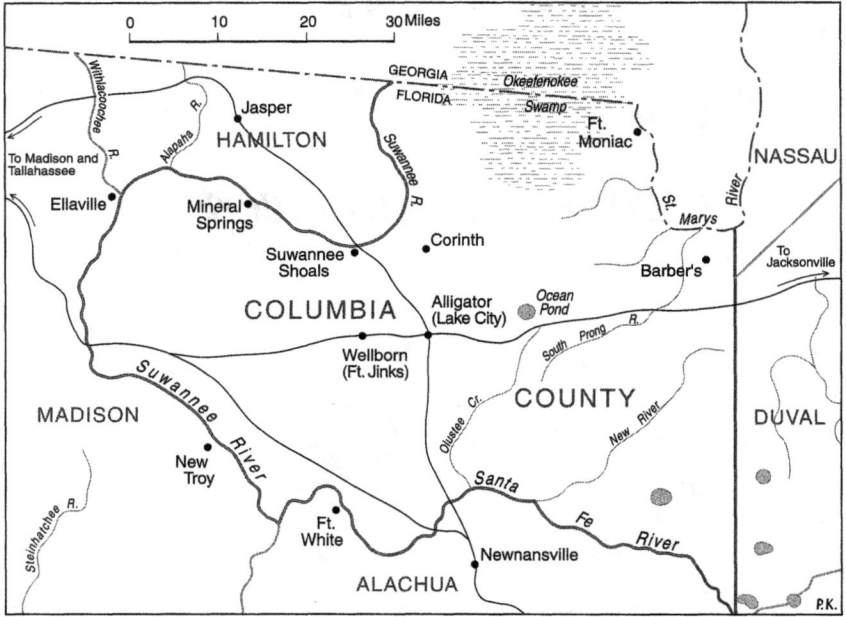

Old Columbia County, Florida, circa 1850

I

Remembrance of a Crime Most Foul

On Friday, June 16, 1899, veteran Florida editor John M. Caldwell launched publication of a newspaper, *The Florida Index,* at Lake City, the long-established seat of northeast Florida's Columbia County. One week later he published an item of historical reminiscence, probably written by him, that clearly appealed to readers who remained conscious of the area's exciting and often tumultuous frontier history. It concerned an apparent homicide that stirred Lake City in the late 1850s.

From *The Florida Index,* June 23, 1899.

REMEMBRANCE OF A CRIME MOST FOUL.

Many years ago, before the sound of locomotive whistles had ever reverberated across our lakes, and when our town was known by the commonplace name of Alligator, two choice spirits had their home here. One was Jack Smiley, a noble, whole-souled fellow who once sold goods on the corner now occupied by the post office, and the other was Abe Ellinger, a Dutchman who kept a saloon just opposite where the Ganey house now stands.

Abe was a social, jovial, fellow of convivial habits who had the goodwill of everybody in town, and between him and Jack Smiley there existed the closest intimacy and warmest friendship.

Charlie Hall in those days kept a saloon, billiard hall and ten-pin alley, where [James Edward] Henry's livery stable now stands, and thither Jack and Abe often resorted to play billiards and, incidentally, to assuage their thirst with the many liquids displayed at the saloon bar.

One night they were there playing billiards together as usual, but on this particular occasion they seemed to have been drinking more than common and appeared to be irritable and out of sorts. Finally a dispute arose between them about some trivial point concerning the game and in the argument which followed Smiley, with much warmth, called Ellinger a liar, and quick as thought Ellinger resented it with a blow. Smiley grabbed up an old pepper-box pistol which lay near by on a shelf and thrusting it directly against Ellinger's body fired. Ellinger fell to the floor and Smiley standing over his prostrate body began snapping the pistol at him which, finally, again fired off. The horrified crowd seized Smiley, disarmed him and procuring a piece of large rope tied his hands behind his back and bound him to one of the pillars of the porch. Another Dutchman by the name of [Joseph] Rosenthal lived in the town, and as he was not only a fellow-countryman, but also a warm personal friend of Ellinger's, messengers were despatched to inform him of his friend's untimely decease. Rosenthal was in bed, sound asleep, when he received the sad intelligence, and it excited him to such a degree that he forgot all about such a small formality as putting his clothes on, but with the exclamation, "Mein Gott in Himmel!" he dashed to the scene of the tragedy clad only in a long, loose-flowing night robe.

In the meantime a large number, for such a small village, had collected and some urged that the proper thing to be done was to take the corpse of Ellinger up to Col. [Matthew] Whit Smith's residence and there hold an inquest. Col. Whit Smith was at that time one of the most prominent lawyers in the State and lived in a double-penned log house where Col. [Rufus T.] Boozer now resides. No sooner was this suggestion made than it was promptly agreed to. For want of a litter a door shutter composed of three thicknesses of inch plank, in which manner shutters of public houses were usually constructed in that day, was lifted from its hinges, the dead body of poor Abe Ellinger was carefully placed thereon, and then about ten strong men laid hold of the ponderous door shutter and started with the corpse on it to Col. Smith's. As the procession was about to depart, Jack Smiley, who had all this time remained tied to one of the piazza posts, begged piteously to be taken along with the crowd. He declared that Abe was the best friend he ever had, that he wouldn't have killed him for the world, &c., and so he was loosed from the post and, with his hands still tied behind him and one or two men holding on to the rope that bound him, the procession took up the line of march. In the meantime the messenger was despatched to acquaint Gen. [William B.] Ross, who was justice of the peace and resided in the house now occupied by W[illiam] F. Watts, with the sad news and that he was needed at Col. Smith's residence to hold an inquest on the body of Abe.

The procession bearing Abe's dead body on the heavy door shutter, and leading Jack Smiley by the rope which bound him, like a prize calf at a country fair, duly arrived at Col. Smith's; the door shutter with the body of Abe reposing on it were duly deposited under a tree in the yard; Jack was taken off to one side of the yard and tied to a mulberry tree and Col. Smith and his family were aroused and made acquainted with the awful tragedy of the evening. Mrs. [Martha Jane] Smith and her daughter, Miss Jennie, on learning the awful news burst into flood of tears and utterly refused to be comforted, for Jack and Abe were two of Mrs. Smith's favorites, and she almost regarded them as her own children.

As soon as Col. Smith appeared Jack, who was still tied to the tree at the edge of the yard, shouted out, "Col. Smith, I don't care what it costs, I want you to defend me, I shot poor Abe like a dog and the Lord knows I wouldn't have done it for a million dollars." "All right, Jack," replied Col. Smith. "I'll defend you, but don't say another word about it; you're incriminating yourself and you had best not talk."

At this juncture Gen. Ross arrived with a copy of the Digest of Florida under his arm and a pen and ink bottle in his hand and proceeded to empannel a jury of inquest. While this was going on Jack again shouted to Col. Smith not to forget that he wanted him to defend him and again proceeded to upbraid himself for having killed Abe, to which Col. Smith replied that he wouldn't forget it and for Jack to keep his mouth shut and not incriminate himself. To this Jack plaintively responded by upbraiding himself for permitting liquor and passion to betray him into the murder of a friend, when Col. Smith, in a voice that could have been heard all over town says, "Jack, you are an infernal fool; I've told you several times to keep your mouth shut and not incriminate yourself and now I don't want to hear another word from you; keep your mouth shut, keep your mouth shut."

Just as the jury were sworn and testimony was about to be introduced, somebody cried out that Jack was loose, and sure enough he had slipped his hands from the rope which bound him and was climbing a fence some fifty yards away, but which in the bright moonlight appeared as plain as day. The entire crowd, including Col. Smith and Gen. Ross gave chase, but Jack got into an oak thicket west of where J[ames] A. Barnes lives, effectually eluded his pursuers and made good his escape.

Tired down and almost completely out of breath the crowd returned to finish holding the inquest on Abe, when upon reaching the door shutter Abe, too, was gone.

It was several minutes before the crowd took in the real situation. Finally it dawned on the mind of Gen. Ross that it was nothing but a practical joke that Jack and Abe had played on the entire crowd, and as it did he remarked with a grunt of fearful disapproval, "well, I don't like any such jokes." [T]hen it worked through the roots of the hair of the balance of the crowd that the fearful tragedy was nothing but some more of Jack's and Abe's devilment and their revulsion of feeling and action was instantaneous. Mrs. Smith's tears ceased to flow; Col. Smith retired to his room; Gen. Ross mysteriously disappeared; the crowd dissolved like sugar in a cup of hot coffee and nothing, in a few minutes, remained of all that excited throng. A heavy door shutter in the yard and a piece of large rope tied to a tree, were the only evidences that court had that night been in session.

Poor Abe, years after when the civil war began, enlisted in the Confederate army in the first company which went from Columbia county—the Columbia rifles, commanded by Walter R. Moore—and was killed at the battle of Williamsburg, Va. Jack Smiley died at Lake Butler and his body was brought back to this place and buried here.

II

Black Eye at Ketch All

Four days following publication of "Remembrance of a Crime Most Foul," one old Columbia County pioneer, George Gillett Keen, set pen to paper to congratulate his friend John Caldwell upon his newspaper.

From *The Florida Index,* July 7, 1899.

LETTER FROM AN OLD TIMER.

Ketch All, June 27th, 1899.

Editor of FLORIDA INDEX:—Dear brother in the faith, please let me say to you that I made the reglet for the first newspaper that was ever published in Columbia county. It was edited by the Rev. H. G. Townsend, then a Methodist preacher; now a lawyer; and, I had like to have said a d—l.

You see I was here during the dark ages, when there was neither law nor gospel. My citizenship dates to the 15th day of October, 1830, (I know it all.)

We never should speak well of a man's virtues to his face, nor speak of his faults behind his back; thus we avoid flattery which is disgusting, and scandal which is criminal. Without flattery, I must say that I am the best pleased with the FLORIDA INDEX that reached my fireside. It gives all the news, both domestic and foreign. . . . What more does anybody want.

Two copies of the INDEX have reached Corinth, my post-office, saying that I was not down as a subscriber, but I was wanted as such. Mr Editor; you put me down as a subscriber, printer's devil, silent partner, agent, or anything, so I get the INDEX. The paper only costs one dollar a year and if I never pay that, I will be owing a long time.

Clearly pleased at receiving such compliments from Keen, Caldwell added a postscript: "We hope that Mr. Keen will write up some of the occurrences of long ago for the benefit of the INDEX readers." More than a month then passed, as Columbia County's hot summer of 1899 persisted. Having not heard again from his friend, the editor (or else an associate) paid Keen a visit at his rural home north of Lake City. Afterward there appeared in *The Florida Index* a story, written under the nom de plume of "GEM," that revealed to area residents something about George G. Keen and his connections with Columbia County.

From *The Florida Index,* August 11, 1899.

THE OLD COUNTRY HOME—
"KETCH ALL," ITS OWNERS, AND THE
HISTORY OF THE PAST.

One of the principal charms of all country homes is their local history, their unknown legends and traditions, and the personal side of their owners or the persons who lived with them. No country home, no matter how humble but shelters memories of a past gladdened with the light of some joyous event, or saddened with a sorrow. The walls may be bare and sightless, the roof low and leaky and covered with moss, the out houses gone to wreck and the yard palings broken down, but the history and the memory of those days that little log hut was but the beginning of a mansion to be built bye and bye—are as fresh as if they but happened yesterday. I love to delve into the history of these old farm houses, and to associate present impressions with the past. I love to trace the genealogy of the people through all the generations. To muse on the half forgotten stories of romance, to fill in missing links and make the stories real. But I want the "skeleton closet" locked. No need now to be shadowed with the sorrows of the past, we have troubles enough of our own.

If there are others similarly inclined let them follow me in the present series of letters written for the INDEX, for a clever better view of the home life of the farmer, and especially the history and personality of those farmers whose life work it has been to make of North Columbia the section it is today.

Did you ever hear of "Ketch all?" Well, the place and name dates back to the time our first settlers drove their cattle thither and reared their habitations in the wilderness. "Florida crackers" they called themselves, but the name originated not as the Georgia crackers did, from cracking corn on a hand mill, but from the cracking of whips in driving their herds to pasture.

"Ketch all" was like an Oasis in the desert, with this difference: it was a high and dry spot of land in a world of mud and water. Some one in the early days erected a cabin there, but grew tired perhaps and left it. Anyhow for years and years there was no regular owner nor inhabitant, but just a structure built—an asylum in the wilderness.

The flatwoods were immense stretches of low lands covered with gall berry and palmetto, and travelers in their peregrinations often found trouble in securing a spot of high and dry land on which to camp. But "Ketch all" was such a spot, and here the traveler would rest for a day or a week and then pass on, to be followed by some one else. And so the name "Ketch all" was given because it caught them all even as did the darkies' coon trap "a gwine and a comin'."

Settlements began to spring up everywhere about this time, and it wasn't long before "Ketch all" had an owner. One who lifted it out of the common place and gave it individuality, who though he founded it and beautified it into a home, left it to other hands to desecrate, but through the vicissitudes of life has returned in old age, and it continues his home today.

Familiar indeed as "Ketch all" is, the name of its owner is more so, and "Black Eye" from "Ketch all" is known even in those remote corners where the knowledge of his home and hospitality have never come. "Black Eye" was only a pseudonym, selected on account of the owners jet black eyes, which even now though dim with age flash with hidden fire. George G. Keen is the name in full, and to those who recognize the office of Justice of the Peace which he has held for years he is known as ["]Justice Keen," and to others "Blackeyed George." There were many curious names in the old days, such as "Big Man Box," ["]Acre Foot Raulerson," "Hominy Jim Keen," "Panter Lewis" and others that added a peculiar charm to the nomenclature of that period.

"Ketch all" was an ordinary farm house, well built and ceiled throughout. The shade trees were its chief beauty. Standing close by the roadside it appeared almost hidden in the evergreen trees around it, and a combination of other trees—maple, and bay, and cherry—to give it all the colored tints of autumn and the crowning glory of spring. But these trees are not all there now, and the house is growing old. When Justice Keen a few years ago sold his home and went away it fell into other hands that lacked the ideal touch. First the trees one by one were cut down "because they shaded the house and would cause it to rot" while other trees far up in the field were left standing to "cool under" during the heat of summer, and this same utilitarian spirit tore the ceiling from overhead in front of the piazza to floor the home of his son who had just married, and was too poor to buy lumber. "A man who would do that" to quote from Black Eye "was born the wrong time of the moon, and neither God Almighty nor the Devil can ever make anything out of him."

Justice Keen was married in the years agone and his wife [Arkina Lane Keen] still journeys with him. No children of their own have ever brightened that home, but others have, and with goodness and charity they have reared several who had no homes of their own. Justice Keen is a rare character in his way. He has a remarkable memory, and never gets tired of talking of old times. He has a wonderful fund of anecdotes that he has promised to write for the INDEX, and I hope he will keep his promise. He is back to his first love.—"Ketch All," the house of his youth and age. His wife is with him and

"As they totter down John,
Baith hand in hand they go—"

I saw them both not long ago and they are happy. May they ever be so. The memories of "Ketch All," old and new, resting on them like a benediction.

III

1830s Florida Frontier Life

Editor Caldwell's reiterated hopes that George G. Keen would share with *Florida Index* readers tales of his experiences as a Columbia County pioneer bore fruit. On August 12, the day following publication of the story of Ketch All and Black Eye, Keen authored the first of a score or more of letters, usually signed "Black Eye," that would run intermittently in the paper until early 1902. To initiate his history of olden times, Keen chose the same subject reflected in "Remembrance of a Crime Most Foul," frontier violence and its close association, at times, with frontier humor. Still, he managed to touch upon family interrelationships, the paucity of educational opportunities, marriage customs, greed, primitive medical practices, legal and judicial procedures, economic factors, and other aspects of frontier life in the early 1830s. Keen began the story with the coming of his family to the raw northeast Florida frontier as the decade opened.[1]

From *The Florida Index,* August 18, 1899.

THE FIRST FIGHT.

Ketch All, August 12th, 1899.

Editor Fla., Index, Dear Sir:—You wanted me to tell you a story five years long. Please let me say that I cannot do it, and for this reason; when I was a boy, little boys were seen and not heard, and knew better than to speak when old people was talking, that accounts for my being a man of few words now—don't you see?

You wanted me to tell a long story about old time happenings. I am willing to tell you a short story. but not a long one, for I heard all my life that long story Kotch Runaway Nigger and I don't won't long story to Kotch me.

And again, I don't want to bring in preliminaries, nor tell of prevailing circumstances, but come to the point at once.

So much for prefatory remarks.

On the 15th day of October, 1830, my father [William Henry Keen] poured me out with the rest of his children down at the root of a pine tree seven miles north of Lake City. That was the first night in my life that I slept with the earth for my bedding and the sky for my covering. I enjoyed lying down and looking up at the stars. Next morning father said "children, you are now in the territory of Florida." During the day he built a camp, covering it with pine tops which was quite an improvement on the preceding day.

Game was plentiful, so he killed one deer and two turkies, then went in search of corn, obtained the corn, hauled it home and commenced building a dwelling house. The material used was green pine sapling poles with the bark on them; the covering was clab boards five feet long and held in place with weight poles; the flooring was dirt, but it was quite an improvement on the camp.

We are now in the middle of a wild Indian territory with at least fifty Indians to one white man, and we without Law or Gospel, that is what I call living in the dark ages. As to provisions that was no scarsety. We had all the corn and potatoes we wanted. So far as meat was concerned we got that from the forest. We had, beef, pork, venison, turkey and fish all that we needed, and it was summer one eternal day.

We had a perfect union of society, one man was considered just as good as an other if not a little better, it was just so with women.

The whites and Indians was on the very best of terms, all was lovely and run as smooth as pond water. No one had any right to complain, for every one was enjoying the best of health and never had time to get hungry.

This state of affairs continued for the space of one year, and then old Mister They-say, and his old half sister, Gossip moved into our midst. I did not know them nor don't know them now, nor never will know where they came from, but I do know that they raised a world of trouble.

Joseph B. Keen [brother of William Henry Keen] was thought by some to be the best man physically in Columbia County. Others thought William Locklar [Locklier] was a better man than Keen.

In steps old Mr. They-Say and old Sister Gossip and took up the subject and in a few days Keen and Locklar was fighting mad with each other. James Douglas[s] gave a social, inviting all the neighbors. Keen and Locklar went among the rest. Douglas had began digging a well; it was about 25 feet deep and as dry as a powder house, with a sand rock bottom. They met commenced talking and two minutes agreed to fight a fisticuff fight. Keen pulled off his shoes as well as his coat. Look out, they go together; Keen knocked Locklar down and went to jump on him and fell down with his feet in Locklar's face. Locklar took one of Keen's feet in both hands and bit him on the big toe. Keen kicked like a mule, jumped, took Locklar on his shoulder, and if he had not been prevented would have thrown him in the well. That would have called an inquest. After the fight was over the combatants went to the well and took a wash. After the washing was over they looked for the extent of the damage. Keen's toe had bled about a teaspoonful and Locklar had not lost one drop of blood. Their friends told them they were not hurt, and no cause to be mad with each other. Nor never would have had any hard feelings if you had not paid any attention to old Mr. They-Say and his old half Sister Gossip. Now make friends, shake hands, kiss and do better for the future. They did so—no they didn't kiss each other but they did kiss the black bottle.

Now the difficulty is settled but the neighborhood is badly confused and there was as much talk about that fight, according to the population as about the battle of Manila during the Spanish war.

Time defaces all things and this fight has gone down into history and the people have all come to one conclusion which was this: We hope for the best, prepare for the worst, and bear with equanimity anything that may happen. Everything is harmoniously going along.

Now comes up new questions. What is it? To have a school and educate our children for education is the balance of power, between the civilized, and uncivilized man, and we feel confident that no more trouble awaits us. Oh, what a sad mistake! Worse trouble is in our own ranks, is even at the door if we had of known it. Next thing in order is to consult the teacher. Who is the teacher? Daniel Gillett, of course, for he was the only man in the settlement that could read and write except my father. Gillett said he would teach if he could get ten scholars. Seven children was all that could be raised and the school died out for the lack of children. It's not so now. Us children had to wait for emigration but time brings all things to bear, so in due course of time there was plenty of children.

Other troubles come on us before our school commenced, but I havn't time and space to tell you what it was, but will tell you in my next. So take this as an incipiency.

From *The Florida Index,* August 25, 1899.

THE FIRST MAN SHOT.

Brother Caldwell, I intended to redeem my promise. To do that I will have to give names.

When we arrived here we found a few families that had been here from one to three years. Among them was one man named Burress Brewer and another named William Raulerson, more commonly called "Old Billie Raulerson."

Brewer lived on Big Creek at the place where the Rev. T[homas] J[efferson] Greene was living at the time of his demise [in October 1898].

Raulerson lived where Corinth church house stands [eight miles north of Lake City]. They were neighbors living three miles away from each other.

Brewer was a sharp man and could see away down the stream of time, and at the beginning of the war of 1812, men was very scarce and wouldn't volunteer, and had to be drafted and made to fight their country's battles.

Brewer was subject to the draft, and he put Capsicum in his eyes, (red pepper you know,) and was rejected, and remained at home, and never did fully regain his sight. His eye balls was as red as fire, and the lids sore till the day of his death yet he could see how to get round pretty well, any way he could see well enough to execute his nefarious plans.

If you doubt my word, you just keep your eye on him till the second Sunday in June, 1834, and let me hear from you again.

Columbia county was the finest cow range I ever saw in my life, the panhandle of Western Texas to the contrary not withstanding.

Nearly every man that moved here fetched a few cattle. Brewer being one of the first settlers had as many cattle as his neighbors, but wanted to be the biggest toad in the puddle, and have it said that Brewer was the richest man in the country in the cattle line. Now comes a problem; he wanted the cattle but didn't have any money.

How he put his wits to work and hit the nail on the head as the sequel will show.

Daniel Stewart was an orphan boy, raised by Tasset Douglas. When he was twenty one years old he went to work for himself. He is now twenty three years old. He had bought and paid for a whole stock, brass mounted, flint and steel, snapping, plantation rifle, powder-horn and shot bag; that covered his mundane affairs. He was the man Brewer was looking for and said to him, "Daniel, I want you to farm with me next year and we will run two plows. You and Edward to do the plowing and I will give you one-third of everything made on the place, also furnish you board, lodging, making and mending." Let me tell you who Edward was; he was an orphan boy that Brewer had raised; his name was Edward Mobly [Mobley] and he was about 18 years old.

The bargain is made and Stewart was to commence work on the first day of January and did so. At the end of the first week Brewer says, "Daniel, how would you like to have a pretty little wife and three hundred head of cattle?" Daniel says, "I would like that proper well." "Do as I say," said Brewer, "and you will have a wife and the cattle." "How is that Mr. Brewer?" "You Marry Nancy Emery, you know her, she has three hundred head of cattle; she is an orphan raised by Martin Hair, and he has the cattle. The cattle is to be delivered to her when she is twenty one, and in the event she should marry before she is twenty one, the cattle is to be delivered to her at the time of marriage. Now is the time for you to take a wife." "Mr. Brewer I never talked with a gal in my life, and don't know what to say." "Turn the case over to me and you will be married in two weeks." "I'll do it," said Daniel.

Brewer goes to see Nancy Emery, "Nancy, I am a friend to you, also I am sorry for you and I want you to marry so you can have a protector." "I never talked to a young man in my life nor never went to church, nor to school. Now who could I marry?" "Marry Daniel Stewart, of course," said Brewer. "I would, if he will have me," said Nancy. Brewer says, "leave it with me and I will have you married in two weeks." Nancy says, "I will be governed by your advice for I believe you are a friend to me." Brewer says, "I am." "Goodby Nancy." "Goodby Mr. Brewer."

Brewer goes home. "Well Daniel, she says she will have you." "Good," said Daniel, "its all in luck if you fight a goose." Brewer has both sides of the question and is master of the situation.

The next day is Tuesday. Brewer goes back and tells Nancy that Daniel is ready to marry her at any time and set the time for Thursday at high twelve; returns home and tells Daniel to be in readiness, and be at the time and place appointed to receive his bride.

Daniel says, "Mr. Brewer, I am not ready to marry just now." "Why not?" said Brewer. "Because I have neither money nor sustenance to take care of a wife. We must put it off." "No need of that. I only have four in family and you can bring her here and she shall have her board and lodging without money and without price, and she can assist the old woman in cooking, &c., and then its only five in family."

The last objection is overruled by Brewer and there is no alternative but to marry. (Watch Brewer.) Thursday 12 o'clock Mr. Stewart and Brewer put in appearance, and the twain was made one flesh.

Dinner is the next thing in order. After dinner Brewer said, "Daniel, get up your pretty little wife and let us go home." He did so.

Now I will give a discription of Mrs. Stewart. She was about four feet ten inches high, weighed about one hundred and thirty pounds, eighteen years old, blue eyed and looked like she was made one-half tallow and the other half bees wax, and was bald headed. Notwithstanding all that, she was the prettiest wife Daniel ever had.

Friday Brewer said, "Daniel let's go and fetch your cattle home." "Allright," said Daniel, and done so. Imagine Brewer's feelings when he saw three hundred head of cattle shut up in his pen. You know what he thought.

Everything ran smooth till the second Sunday in June. Now the crop is made, the fodder housed and the corn nearly ready for gathering.

Men in them days done their own tanning and shoe making. Deer skins when taken out of tan were relieved of the ooze, rolled up and placed in the shade till nearly dry, then they were dressed up ready for use. That was the way in this case. After breakfast, second Sunday in June, Daniel took one of the skins out and was picking the pelt [off of] it.

Brewer says, "Daniel to day is Sunday and I don't work on Sunday, nor allow it done on my premises." Stewart says, "Mr. Brewer, I don't call this work, but I will quit and put up the skin." Brewer says, "you have violated the Lord's day and got to leave the place." Daniel offered an apology. Brewer says, "no excuse will do and picked up a hand spike took it in both hands, saying, 'leave at once, or I will kill you.' (Could not have the Sabbath day violated, but could afford to glut the earth with human gore. Oh, consistency thou art a jewel.) Daniel took his gun, powder horn and shot bag and said "Nancy let's go." "Go," said Brewer, "or I will kill you."

About twenty yards from the door there was a rail fence, about four rails high, that was the going out place from the house. Before they got to the fence Daniel saw Brewer was following him with the hand spike in a striking position, saying, "I will kill you if you don't leave." Brewer was bare headed, Stewart told me afterwards that he took aim at Brewer's forehead and the gun snapped. He lowered the gun and thought as I haven't killed him I won't do it, he crossed the fence about twenty feet and says, "If you cross the fence I will shoot you." Brewer knew Daniel to be a good shot and had just seen him snap the gun at him. Why he didn't stop was a mystery to me, but he crossed the fence and when he did Daniel fired upon him, the bullet entering a little to the right of the center of the breast, passing direct through his body. To quote Daniel he said that "Brewer fell and hollowed very loud, 'Oh, God, Oh, God, Oh, God,' like he thought his God was a long way off and if he did not call loud his God would not hear him." Daniel left.

Mrs. Brewer and Edward Mobly ran to Brewer. He couldn't walk and they couldn't carry him, so they dragged him to the house.

Now we return to Old Billie Raulerson. Edward went for him. He went notwithstanding he never had seen a wounded man in his life. After examining the front wound, "now let's se[e] your back, oh, yes, I see where the bullet is, get the whetstone Ed." He whetted his knife. "Now Ed, you set down on his legs and help me hold him still till I cut the bullet out." Ed done as directed. Old Billie commenced cutting as though he was cutting up a beef. Brewer screamed and begged for mercy and tried to get up. Old Billie would say, "hold him down Ed, I will get the bullet directly." At length he got the bullet and then said, "all right Brewer, I got the bullet and you will soon be well." The next thing was to dress the wounds, so he took equal quantities of pine gum and tallow and dressed his wounds.

To be continued in our next.

From *The Florida Index,* September 8, 1899.

THE FIRST MAN SHOT.

(CONTINUED.)

Ketch All, September 1, 1899.

Raulerson gave Brewer his undivided attention for four days, then quit using the turpentine and tallow plasters, using nothing but bandages and cold water.

In fifteen days Brewer was again about the premises saying he was all right. Raulerson discharged his patient, saying he was all right with good care. In sixty days Brewer was driving nearly five hundred head of his own cattle to the cow pen, saying they were his own.

Now, lets look after Daniel. He done like the fellow's bullock, he broke the impannel of the impound exlofisticated all over the forest and landed in Ware county, Ga., nearly seventy five miles from home. That distance appeared as far to the people of that day as the Indian Territory [of Oklahoma] does to us now.

He remained for several months, but not hearing from home he came back on the sly, expecting Brewer to be dead and buried. Instead of that he found him in good health.

In a few days Brewer and Stewart met and spoke friendly to each other. Brewer says, "Daniel you hurt me very bad when you shot me and for my suffering and loss of time I charge your part of the crop and Nancy's three hundred head of cattle." "All right," said Daniel. Brewer said "we have always been friends, except that little trouble, and that wasn't worth falling out about, so lets continue to be friends." "Good" said Daniel, and they remained friends ever afterwards.

The compromise made by Stewart and Brewer went over Columbia county as though it went on the wings of the wind. The fall of Richmond, Virginia, [during the Civil War] didn't create any more excitement, according to the population, than the Brewer-Stewart compromise did.

The commotion was great and the excitement ran mountains high. Give us law, give us law, was all that we could hear. We have had one rough and tumble flight, one man shot, and another robbed of $250 worth of farm products and one woman robbed of three hundred head of cattle, worth $1500, and not a scrap of law in the Territory of Florida. We have no protection for life, liberty, nor property; we must and will have code of laws and routine of officers.

In a few days Isaac Daniels, the father of the great [J. E.] Berry Daniels [a desperado in the 1870s,] was appointed Justice of the Peace and Robert Payne was appointed constable. The people were as wild as rabbits, no fighting, shooting, nor stealing going on; Squar [Squire] Daniels was called and notified to be at Andison [Anderson] Gilletts the next Thursday at 12 o'clock to discharge some of his official duty in a matrimonial point of view.

Ransom Par[r]ish and Sookie Morgan were to be married at 12 oclock. The hour has arrived and all parties interested was present. We were called into the house, every one except Bill Locklar [Locklier] went in, (Watch Bill Locklar.) He took a position in the door way. Now the happy couple stand before Squar Daniel, as he was called. He throws himself back on his dignity. "My beloved friends; we have assembled here in the sight of God and in the presence of these witnesses to unite in the holy bond of matrimony, Ransom Parrish and Sookie Morgan, and if you, or any of you have, or can show just cause or impediment why this couple should not be lawfully jointed together, after Gods ordinance in a holy estate of matrimony, you will now speak or else for ever hereafter hold your peace. (All is silent) I charge you as you will have to answer at the great day when the secret of all hearts shall be made known if you or either of you know just cause why you should not be joined together in wedlock you will now make it known. As there is no objections join your right hands. Do you take this woman who you hold by the right hand to be your lawful and wedded wife, to love, cherish, honor her in sickness and in health, forsaking all others, cleaving to her only so long as ye both shall live?["] "I will." "Do you take this man that you hold by the right hand to be your lawful and wedded husband, to love, cherish, honor and obey him in sickness and in health, forsaking all others cleaving to him only so long as ye both shall live? Answer, 'I will.' Bill Locklar shook his head at her. She says, "Mr. Locklar, if you will have me I won't have Mr. Parrish," and jerked loose from Parrish and went out of the house.

Several of the women followed her and in a few minutes they returned, saying she said that she never would marry Parrish as long as water run and grass grew; and she kept her word, for she married Joe Wilkinson [Wilkerson], and you bet she made him pay for eating rags.

After the women made their report Parrish busted out in a big boo-hoo cry and he cried like he had the contract to cry for the neighborhood, and left the place, and if I ever saw him again I never knew it. We ate the wedding dinner and each one went home.

A LAWSUIT.

A man by the name of Allen came here; he was a stranger. He made a trade with Henry Smith and left the country. In a few week[s] he returned saying Smith had put a ten dollar bill of counterfeit money on him and wanted to give him another ten dollars. Smith denied the charge and wouldn't do it. Allen took a warrant for him. [Thomas] Williford Smith was a State witness. Court is now in session. Allen is called to the witness stand and swears that Smith did as accused. ["]Where is the bill," said the court. Allen says it was no good and he threw it away. Williford Smith is sworn and says that was a counterfeit bill that Henry Smith put on Allen. The court says, "Mr. Smith, can you read and write?" "No sir, but I can tell money." The court hands him a bill saying, "please tell me what kind of a bill that is!" Witness says, "that is a leven dollar bill." "No," said the court. "I was mistaken," said the witness, "it's a twenty five dollar bill." "Mistaken again," said the court, "we don't have leven dollar bills, nor twenty five dollar bills, so Mr. Smith, this court cannot take your sworn testimony as moral truth. As the Territory of Florida has failed to make a case, Mr. Constable, you will discharge the prisoner and adjourn court." The prisoner is discharged and the court adjourned.

From *The Florida Index,* September 22, 1899.

BLACK EYE'S LETTER.

Ketch All, September 9th, 1899.

My Brother in the cause: I am as true to my trust as the Needle is to the pole and I promised that you should hear from me again. Now listen, don't you hear me?

We have gone down in the year of our Lord 1835, and fathers are whooping up for our school and have gotten up nine children, but we are short one boy. Old Billie Hair said he would have that scholar if he had to make him out of a lightwood knot, so he went to Georgia to hunt him. When he returned he fetched a young man by the name of Fennel Aughtrey. Now the requisite number of scholars. The 1st, Monday in September the exercises of the school was to begin which was sometime in the future. ★ ★ ★ ★.

A CROSS-INDICTMENT.

Now let us go back to the law and the testimony. Columbia county at that time embraced, Suwannee, Bradford and Baker counties and covered more

territory than the State of Rhode Island. Law and order had ruled supreme
for some time. About this time a man by the name of William Hart [William
Bartola Hart?] came into the neighborhood. He was twenty three years old,
six feet and two inches high and weighed two hundred and twenty five
pounds and was the most perfect model of man that I ever looked at. All the
men liked him, and the girls loved him; that was the difference between the
girls and boys.

Pretty soon Bill Hart was in the mouth of every body and he was called
the best man on the muscle that lived in the territory of Florida. Notwithstanding he never had been in an angry mood. This state of affairs was of
short duration. Silas Overstreet lived near Ellaville, on the Columbia side of
the [Suwannee] river. His height, weight and fighting qualifications were the
same as Hart's, only in age, he was twenty five while Hart was only twenty
three.

Overstreet said Columbia county was too small to afford two Bullies and
he would go down and take the bell off him. The first day after leaving home
he did not find Hart. He stopped with Daniel Gillett that night and got the
desired information where he would find Hart and after riding six miles he
found him at Bill Locklars [Locklier's]. He introduced himself, took a drink
of whisky and told Hart his business. Hart told him no, he didn't want to
fight. Just then Overstreet dealt Hart a terrible blow in the face. Hart went at
him like a Bengal Tiger. Now the fight became general. They knocked and
kicked for the space of five minutes. Hart knocked Overstreet down and
jumped astride of his breast and began pounding him in the face. Hart, was
choking him, he now quit beating him and done just like he was going to
kiss him, and it would have been better if he had. Instead of kissing him he
bit off part of Overstreet's nose, which disfigured him for the balance of his
life. Overstreet says, "boys take him off." They done so. They were both badly
hurt and Overstreet forty miles from home and his nose bit off. He was good
[and] mad and Hart appeared to be happy. He was one of those jolly, good
fellows. He proposed friendship to Overstreet but he would not drink nor
make friends with Hart, but went to Squar [Squire Isaac] Daniels and took a
warrant out for Hart for biting off part of his nose. Hart was arrested and carried before Squar Daniels and he called for a warrant for Overstreet for striking him. The Squar did not use the words, mayhem, assault and battery, but
as above stated.

The court is in session, Hart arraigned, the charge explained, and the
question, "guilty or not guilty" asked by the court. The answer was, "guilty."
"Well," said the Squar, "that stops all further investigation, for you have plead
guilty to the very thing that the court was going to prove, stand aside."

"Overstreet stand up," he done so, and the charge was read. The question asked as was in Hart's case. Overstreet says, "I am guilty." Stand aside, "no need of any further investigation."

The court says, "Mr. Hart, stand up," he did so. The court says, "Hart what have you got to say why the judgment of this court should not be past against you?" "Nothing," said Hart. The judgment of this court is that you pay a fine of fifty cents for biting off Mr. Overstreet's nose, take your seat, Mr. Hart."

Mr. Overstreet is ordered by the court to stand up and the questions is asked him as was asked Mr. Hart, and the same answers given. "This court imposes a fine of one dollar on you for striking Mr. Hart. Now gentlemen, we hope you will be more considerate in the future than you have been in the past and not let your passions get the upper hand of natural good sense. Adjourn court Mr. Constable and discharge the prisoners." He done so for the last time in his life for Squar Daniels resigned, and so did constable Payne.

Now we are without law and without officers. We don't need them. In a short time after this Daniel Gillett and Joe [Joseph B.] Keen started for the Land Office which was kept at St. Augustine. They were going to buy land and had to pay for it with gold or silver. In them days men carried their guns and shot bags wherever they went. Keen and Gillett had theirs and went by the way of Aligator (Lake City.) A man by the name of Jas. Johnson, more commonly called old Fitterfoot [Flitterfoot], kept a rum shop at Aligator. When there was ten men there at one time it was considered a big crowd; if there was twenty five it was called a universal turn out. And there is yet another man, his name was Loram Brown. He was called Loram P. the Ranter, and Ranter he was. He was at Alligator that particular day. The boys got to jumping. Keen being very active pulled of[f] his shot bag which contained a good sum of money and hung it on the corner of the store house, which was a log house. When Keen went for it, it was gone—stolen of course. Lets see what man is gone. Loram P. the Ranter is gone. He is the man. There being only one road they knew how to pursue him and did so and soon overtaken him. He had the shot bag. They carried him back[,] examined the shot bag and the money was in it. Now, what shall we do with him? Punish him of course.

What kind of punishment shall that be? Tom Goolsby says, "Loram P. the Ranter is a thief and has broke the law of stealing, and is now a rogue and will be till he dies, but if he don't never steal any more he will be a reformed rogue. Boys, my plan is not to be too hard on him as it's the first offense." Tom says, "I'll do it. Loram P. the Ranter, are you sorry that you stole that shot bag?" "I am," said Loram P. the Ranter. "If we let you off with a light punishment will you ever steal any more?" "I never will as long as I live," said

Loram P. the Ranter. Tom says, "now boys, you have heard the confession of the prisoner and as it's the first crime, and he has promised to do better for the future, I say that Loram P. the Ranter shall treat this crowd to one gallon of the best whiskey that Flitterfoot Johnson has in his store." All hands agree to that and Loram P. the Ranter calls out the whiskey. They all had a good time and parted.

From *The Florida Index,* October 6, 1899.

TRIBUTE OF RESPECT.

Ketch All, Columbia County Fla.

Editor of the Florida Index:—Please give space in your valuable paper for a few remarks in regard to our highly esteemed departed friend, Melton Deese, who departed this life a few days ago. My esteemed friend, whom I loved next to a brother was an orphan boy, raised by Rev. Handen Cheshire in Hamilton County, Florida.

When brother Deese arrived at manhood he married Miss Mary Sistrunk, a perfect little beauty and a lady. In due course of time they located in half a mile of Oak Grove church [in northern Columbia County near the Georgia state line]. They had a paragon of a home. He was one of the most devoted husbands I ever saw. His love was reciprocated by his better half. He was one of the most accommodating neighbors I ever saw. His equal for morality, industry, honesty and truth was hard to find and could not be surpassed.

His untimely demise will leave an aching void that time will never fill.

God knows that my grief for his untimely death is great, and his dear wife has my heartfelt sympathy.

His place as a citizen can never be filled. That man don't live that would look, act, and do as our highly esteemed friend Melton Deese. The old adage is, Death loves a shining mark. God bless his widow.

GEO. G. KEEN,
In sympathy.

Of course the Keen and Loram P. the Ranter case spread over the country like wild fire and every one draw his own conclusions, and the conclusion of the whole matter was this: We must have law, and officers. Up steps Bill Plug Newmans, and says, "what is law, and what is it for"? James Jerkins says, "the first principle of law is to protect the virtuous from the vicious; the weak against the strong; the poor against the rich; the ignorant against the wise, and for many other good purposes." "If that be the case," said Bill Plug, "give us law and officers."

Now comes the question, who will act as Squar [squire; that is, justice of the peace]? Up steps a man and says, "my name is John C. C. Ponch[i]er, I have just moved in to your neighborhood and see the great necessity of law and order and I will act as Squar for the present, that is if you will give me a Sheriff; I don't want a constable; these people are not afraid of a little thing like a constable, but the word sheriff would strike terror to their heart."

Now comes the question, who will be Sheriff? After some delay Charles Fitchet[t] was commissioned Sheriff of Columbia county, in the Territory of Florida.

Now I will give you a minute description of Charles Fitchett. He was twenty five years old, four feet two inches high, and weighed one hundred and twenty five pounds. After Charles was commissioned Sheriff, he walked the streets of Alligator with as much pomposity as ever old John Quincy Adams did the streets of Philadelphia. If you could have bought Charles at his real worth, and sold him for his imaginary worth, as Joe Collier says, it would have been an everlasting fortune to you.

Squar Poncher says he is reduced to a solid lump of sense and knows exactly how to deal with these people.

Now the authorities are ready for business, and business is ready for them, for Elam Daniels and John Gipson have disagreed and Elam used some ten pen alley talk to John. That is to say, Elam used curse words. As Gipson wouldn't fight Daniels left him, thinking no more about it, but Gipson goes to Squar Po[n]cher and gets a warrant for Daniels for cursing him.

What did Charles Fitchett say? He said if a warrant was put in his hands he would arrest the party, or shoot him [d]own like a dog. Now Sheriff Fitchett has a warrant against Elam Daniels, one of ex-Squar Daniels sons. Now let's watch developments.

Just about this time there was a knife, called the Bowie knife introduced in this vicinity. It was about one and a half inches wide and about eight inches long, and had a dangerous appearance. It was carried in a case attached to a belt, worn around the waist. Elam, was said to have one and carrying it to keep the Sheriff at a proper distance. Charles, as we called him was an unmarried man and boarded with [John] Wesley Low[e] in the Western part of the town of Alligator.

In a short time Elam Daniels went to Alligator equipped for war or any emergency. Sheriff Fitchett saw him; now for the fun. (Notwithstanding he was a little tenderfooted.) He got within about twenty feet of Elam and says, "Elam Daniels, I arrest you in the name of the Territory of Florida." Elam said nothing. The sheriff walks up in about six feet of Elam and says, "Elam, you are my prisoner in the name of the"—Elam drew the Bowie knife, raising it in a striking position, and said, "yes, and you are my meat in the name of Alligator." Charles changed front to rear and burnt the wind, and Elam after him. The race continued for fifty yards and Elam stopped, but Charles ran till he entered the door of Wesley Low his boarding place. "What is the matter Charles," said Low. "Elam Daniels is trying to kill me with a Bowie knife," said sheriff Fitchett. "What for[?]" said Mr. Low. "For trying to arrest him," said the Sheriff, "and I just saved my life by the skin of my teeth. What must I do Mr. Low.["] "Resign, Charles, or some of these piney woods Devils will kill you." "I'll do it," said Charles, and he did so. Now, Squar John C. C. Poncher resigns. That ended civil law for nearly ten years.

Now let us go back and examine Elam Daniels Bowie knife. He had seen one of these Bowie knives and he placed the knife down on a piece of white pine box, scribed round, and got the shape of the knife and made a perfect imitation. Then he rubbed the knife with a bar of lead, and that give it the coloring, and to an excited man it looked just like a Bowie knife, and that knife abolished the civil law in the eastern part of the Territory of Florida and it remained so until some time in the early part of the 40's.

I said in the beginning, that the people lived the best in them days that I ever saw people live in my life—I am going to explain how it was.

The man made all the corn, fodder; potatoes, rice, sugar and syrup they wanted. They tanned cowhides and deer skins and made their own shoes. From the buds of the palmetto they plaited and made their hats. In connection with all this, they planted one acre in cotton; that was for spinning purposes. That acre of land would yield one thousand pounds of seed cotton, This cotton was ginned on a hand gin, and afterwards was manufactured into cloth and made into clothing by the lady folks. But you say, "that don't say something to eat." "I know that. Don't you know that its mark of low breeding to disturb a man in the midst of a discourse?" "Yes" "Please don't disturb me any more." "I won't, go on," "Now see that you don't."

We have all the bread stuff and clothing that we want. We want salt, coffee, tobacco, ammunition, flour and whiskey. We made no farm produce for market, still we had plenty of money. I expect you would like to know how we got it, but you don't know, but you shall know, for I am going to tell you. Cow hides were worth 25 cents per pound, tallow the same, deer skins and beeswax was 75 cents per pound, and buck horns was worth 50 cents a pair.

Our place of trade them days was Jeffersonton, Ga. Went there twice a year, Spring and Fall, and from seven to ten men would go together at the same time. Each one would carry from two hundred and fifty to three hundred pounds of hides, skins, tallow, beeswax and all the way from fifty to one hundred pairs of buck horns and sell at the prices above stated. They got the money and bought their supplies afterwards.

One barrel flour $3; one sack salt $1.50; 20 lbs of tobacco $5; one pound of powder 50 cents; four bars lead 50 cents; four gallons of whiskey $1. Whiskey was worth all the way from 17 to 25 cents per gallon. Don't you see from these figures that the money multiplied on them.

As to meat, we had beef, venison, turkey and fish the year round. We had chickens, eggs, milk, butter and cheese all the time, and did not pay any taxes either.

All of which is respectfully submitted.

IV

The Second Seminole War, 1835–1842

Following the publication of his initial letters from August 18 to October 6, 1899, George G. Keen turned in a series of five reminiscences of Florida's Second Seminole War and its catastrophic consequences. The conflict began in December 1835 and lasted until the late summer of 1842, the result of pressures for westward Indian immigration by the presidential administration of Andrew Jackson. During most of that time interior northeast Florida residents were confined to "forted up" settlements or risked sudden death by returning to their homesteads. Although Keen confused the timing of certain incidents, his words otherwise agree with available accounts or else supplement them. His passion particularly flares as he recalls bloody incidents in the Corinth neighborhood of northern Columbia County, where his family lived. Readers should keep in mind that many of the individuals mentioned were related to the author, especially members of the Gillett family.[2]

From *The Florida Index,* October 13, 1899.

TIMES OF LONG AGO.

Ketch All, Oct. 9th, 1899.

Brother Caldwell:—I want to tell you that the first Monday in September, in the year of our Lord one thousand eight hundred and thirty five, has opened up bright and lovely. So has our school, with Daniel Gillett as teacher and the following named parties as pupils: [Liberty] Franklin Raulerson, William Gillett, Sherod S. Keen, John T. Rutledge, William R. Keen, Riley Blount, Maria [Molcy Mariah] Hair, Fennel Autrey [Otray], Pelester Harrington, and Geo. G. Keen.

Everything went along lovely for nearly two months. The patrons visiting the school and was well pleased at the way the children was progressing; saying, if the school run the full term, what they did not learn wouldn't be worth knowing. My brother, stop and consider for a moment. Man proposes, but God disposes of events as he chooses; this case was not an exception to the general rule.

The Indians in them days were as thick here as spatter. The nearest Indian town to us was on Sandy Drive, three miles from our house. The next one was on Big Creek, where Sugar George Grime lives, five miles away. Third one was the Spice Pond ridge, seven miles distant. The fourth, and last one, was a half mile South of Oak Grove church house, nine miles. Notwithstanding they numbered hundreds, they did not molest our stock and was on the most friendly terms with the whites and every thing ran as smooth as pond water for the space of five years.

You must recollect that I had entered into my eighth year of age, and my experience was quite limited, but I could hear as good then as I can now, and I heard the men say the Indians was stealing cattle south of Alligator and the cattle that they were stealing belonged to Jacob Summerlin [Sr.] and Jack Hope. This report was current in the northern part of Columbia County. Understand and mistake me not; I don't vouch for the validity of this report.

The next report that reached us was, that Summerlin and Hope killed every Indian that they caught alone in the woods. Pretty soon an other report reaches us that Summerlin and Hope caught two indians butchering a cow of Summerlin's and they, Summerlin and Hope, [on June 18, 1835] ties them up and gave them a dose of Hickory oil.[3] The men in our neighborhood said that would bring war.

Now, let's go back to the school house. The school ran just two months to a day, when a man come running to the school house panting for breath, saying, "every rat to his hole, for the Indians had their hair cut leaving the scalp lock, put on the war paint, slung his shotbag, sharpened his tom-a-chu-chee, (Hatchet) and struck out on the war path, and the last devil of us would be killed if we did not hurry and get home. I did not think I was a devil, nor don't think I am now, but if I did not run [. . .] I made a long step and a follow to it till I got home; also, the other children and teacher done much the same as I did, and not one of us got scalped by the red men of the forest. I am glad of it until this day.

I don't know of my own knowledge that Summerlin and Hope whipped those Indians, but I do know that pretty soon after the report reached us that some Indians come into our neighborhood, calling themselves runners, and said they were from Blounts Town.

Blount, was the great Mogul of the whole Seminole tribe at that time. Our Indians, as we called them, said they were called to Headquarters to hold a counsel of war. They all left here in one and the same night.

They are a people that never carry a second load; they carry their entire belongings every time they move.

I am sure of one thing, they never come back here any more. Only to cut up devilment; they done that often to the great annoyance of us poor creatures. I don't want them to come anymore as long as I stay here, for I have as much sympathy for a pond alligator as I have for a Seminole Indian, and I don't care who hears me say it, for you had just as well try to make a catch dog out of a wolf as to make a white man out of an Indian: Blounts Town was on the Chattahoochee [actually Apalachicola] River in Middle Fla.[4] (I have been there:)

A family had been killed on the Ocilla [Aucilla] river in [Middle] Fla.[5] They said that was a hundred miles away, and there was no danger now, for it would take them a year to get here.

The depredation already committed was so far away that we did not consider that we were in any danger, so we sat down on the stool of do nothing, thinking we had time enough to prepare for war. William Raulerson and James Deese said the surest plan for safety was to move to Georgia and the other men called them cowards. They moved and both of them survived the war and died a natural death, at a ripe old age. Others remained here and them and their families were murdered by the Seminole Indians.

About six weeks after the murder that was committed in [Middle] Fla., there was a family killed in Colum[bia] county. (Now Suwannee county.)[6]

That brought about a commotion in the neighborhood of Alligator which cannot be described.[7] The Indians was all over this county and there was no place of refuge for the whites. Their object was to all gather to one place, unite and protect each other. There were places designated; one place at William Edward's, another one at Joseph B. Keen's, a third one at Elias Walker's. The people were going in every direction and not one of them knowing the way where they wanted to go to.

I can write it, but I don't believe that you, I nor the printer's devil can put it in type. . . . The people were running from the Indians that was in one direction, often times would run into a bunch of Indians that was in another direction. Then and there would be blood and carnage, death and destruction what was to be done? The survivors would escape and get to a place of safety.

But this slaughter was fun for the Indians, but it was death to the whites. The Indians that lived here knew more about the country than the Whites did; that give them an undue advantage over us.

This country was settled up in spots; say, from five to fifteen families in a settlement. As the men did not have any business, only in hen scratch of home, they did not know the way from one settlement to another, consequently it caused a great many people to be killed while going from their homes to a place of safety. We never went to church. Why? Because there was no church to go to. We done our own praying if their was any praying done. We ground our own corn on a hand mill; we never went to court, because there was no court, lawyers, witnesses, nor jurors. We hunted up Shakespear[e] and he was considered the sharpest writer that ever lived on either Continent, if he did kill himself in a rum shop; that was no more than Alexander the Great done. Shakespear[e] says, "if ignorance is bliss, it is folly to be wise," so we were the most happy people in the world.

Brother, you may think from what I have said that we were regular rum suckers. I say not so, for it was considered more disgrace to get drunk in them days than it is to steal a horse now.

A man was better raised than to get drunk, or use cuss words in the presence of ladies; they dare not do it. With these remarks I close.

From *The Florida Index,* November 10, 1899.

OLD TIMES IN COLUMBIA.

Ketch all, Oct. 31st, 1899.

> "Mark the perfect man and behold the upright."—Bible.
> "The best may slip, the careless fall,
> Its more than man that never erred at all"
> —Poet.

My brother, please let me correct you in regard to the name of Osceola Powell, his name was Osceola; that was it in Indian, and in English the word was Powell, Osceola Powell.

I lived among them for twelve years. From 1830 to 1835 we were on the most friendly terms. From 1835 to 1842 we regarded them as our most inveterate foes. All they done for us was to glut the earth with human gore.

Yet there was a portion of the country they didn't invade, that was from Alligator to Blounts Ferry [on the Suwannee River]. Notwithstanding, the people kept bunched up nearly all the time. Robert Sandlin lived more in the center of the neighborhood than any one else and there was the place they congregated for self protection. As no assault had been made on them by the Indians [by the late summer of 1840] some families moved home.

They concluded to build a school house and educate their children, so the day appointed to work on the school house [August 14] came round and the most of the men was working on the house. Bill Locklar [Locklier] had to go to Alligator that day and went by where the men was working.

John Bonnell, sr., and John Bonnell, jr., lived on that road, but lived on opposite sides of the road, living about one hundred and fifty yards apart. When Locklar got pretty close to the nearer house he saw a man on top of it; he goes on and sees a man on top of the other house. He supposed the Bonnells was repairing their houses. He was now in rifle shot of the nearer house, took a second look and saw the top of the house on fire. He was riding a bay mare called Betsey Baker and she was a dandy. He saw both houses was on fire, he looked below and there stood about sixty Indians. He turned Betsey Baker's head towards Blounts Ferry, giving her a squeeze with his knees and Betsey Baker went like she had slipped out of a grease gourd. The Indians failed to see him until he was out of harm's way.

He ran to the school house and told the men of the near approach of the enemy. Joe Howel[l]'s family was between him and the Indians. He mounted his horse. Now we have a race for life. Howell trying to get to his family. As he got within eighty yards of the house he saw the red D—ls in thirty feet of the house. One Indian saw him and took deliberate aim at him. Howell was sitting on his horse, the horse standing perfectly still at the time, the Indians shot but the bullet mis[s]ed its mark. Just at this juncture the savage heathens entered the house and began shooting his family.

Oh! husbands and fathers just think of it. Your poor wife and children being murdered by a merciless set of Devils, and calling on you to help them and you powerless to render them any assistance.

It makes my blood boil every time that I think of Joe Howel's family. If I had my way I would kill every one of Seminole tribe if it want bigger than a chunk bottle, notwithstanding its been over fifty years since this atrocious murder was committed.

Howell sat still thinking some of the family might escape. In a few minutes he saw a little daughter about eight years old, and a colored boy about the same age running from the house. He remained quiet till the children got far enough so he thought he could get to them before inhuman brutes could. He went for them, he took the little daughter in his lap and the boy behind him and carried them to a place of safety.

Now, lets look at the house. Howel had two grown daughters, 16 and 18 years of age. They ran for Suwannee river swamp, which was near by and as they run, the Indians fired upon them. One of the young ladies was hit in the back, the bullet passing clear through her body and coming out in the centre of the breast. They got in the swamp and near the run of the river and the wounded sister gave out and could not go any further. They remained there during the night, The wounded girl called for water every few minutes and her sister carrying water in her bonnet. Through the kindness of an Allwise providence she survived the blow and in due course of time regained her wonted health. We will leave Howel's for a little while and go back to them again.

The Indians after killing Howel's family took the Blounts Ferry road, going on for Sandlin's, but Locklar had got there first and filled every barrel, tub and bucket full of water and carried into the house and made all other arrangements necessary to give them a warm reception when they come. Before dark they all, except a colored man and wife, went into the house; the old darkey said if they fooled with him he would kill them with his ax.

All is ready for battle. One woman opened the door and stood in the doorway for a few seconds and two Indians fired at her; both bullets lodged in the wall just above her head. Then there was one continual firing for two or three hours, the Indians doing all the shooting. Their object was to make them leave the house, and if it had not been for Bill Locklar they certainly would have done so. He stood backed up against the door and when they come he would knock them down, by that means he saved the lives of the whole turn out.

After they failed to accomplish their purpose with the whites then they went and talked with the darkeys. They did not want to hurt them nor didn't.

Now, lets look after the Daniel Boon[e] of Fla., which was Lieutenant Henry Harrington, the father of Cap. [Henry Monroe] and Lib[erty Franklin] Harrington. He was one of the bravest men I every saw in my life and as good an Indian fighter as ever shaded the earth. He was in Hamilton county attending to some official business when all this occurred. He got home at dark and heard of it; he remounted his horse and started out to hunt up men to relieve, or reinforce them that was at Sandlins. He found two men and the three started out to give battle. They got in half a mile of Sandlins and called a halt to listen; everything is as still as the grave.

They had just crossed a branch about thirty yards wide and the water about two feet deep. They heard a horse strike the water; in a few minutes the man rode up, it was Joe Howel; now they are four strong. Just then Howel and the other two men turned and run. He told them to stop and tell him what they were running for, Howell said, "you hear them guns cock?" "No." "There was fifty of them I am sure.["] Now, the Indians are scattered all over the woods, so they held up till day light. Daylight appears. This little scout reinforces during the night till they number ten rank and file. They proceeded to the place where they made the stampede the night before; they discover there was about fifty Indians in twenty five yards of them when they ran.

Then pull up at Sandlins, all is well and nobody hurt, then they go to Howels. Oh! what a sight met their eyes. If nature could have had its course their would have been another member added to Joe Howel's family. There lay Mrs. Howel literally cut to pieces. The feotus was lying on the floor two feet from its mother, the other little ones lying dead all over the house with their brains beat out; only three of about nine children escaped the tomahawk and scalping knife.

The Indians was very successful on this raid, they had a day and night the start of the whites and got into a place of safety without losing a drop of blood. That was encouragement for them to try it over again, which they did but I have neither time nor space to tell you about it, but will tell you later.

Now let's go back to the Bonnels. Neither one of them nor their families was at home when the Indians called on them. Don't you think the Bonnels was glad of that?

The school house was never finished and Sandlin's never was head quarters for refugees any more during the war, they all believed that the Indians would call on them and they were right in their conjectures.

I close for the present.[8]

From *The Florida Index,* November 24, 1899.

A FAILURE.

Ketch All, Nov. 13, 1899.

After the Indians had committed the depredations at Howel[l]'s they came to the conclusion to break up the citizens from Alligator to Blounts Ferry. While they were making their arrangements for a second attack the whites were pulling their freight to old-time, captain Billy Cone's, thinking it a safer place than Sandlins, and it was too. Sandlin went with the rest, leaving several hundred bushels of corn in the crib.

Lieutenant Henry Harrington, the great war horse, kept one eye on the movement of the enemy and pretty soon he caught them stealing corn from Sandlin's corn house and informed Capt. W[illiam] B. North of it. North was Capt. commanding the company and Henry Harrington was second Lieutenant. Capt. North says, "Henry you must rally the company and fight them." Harrington was then a boy seventeen years old, six feet high, weighing 175 pounds. Henry did as commanded by Capt. North, taking first Lieutenant Sam Cannon with him. Now they are in half a mile of Sandlins. Lieut. Sam says, "Henry, how is the attack to be made?" Henry says, "Sam you take half the company and go where they cross the river, and secrete yourselves, and I will take the other half and approach them from the East. They will make for the river and you kill every one of them." Sam says, "I will do it." Lieut. Henry goes a round a bout way and got within two hundred yards of them. The Indians were shelling, sacking and carrying off corn, but they burn the wind when they saw the whites. Lieut. Henry ordered a charge, and kept pace with them till they run into Lieut. Sam, when the fighting become general. As Lieut. Henry and posse arrived at the river bank the firing ceased. Lieut. Henry told me that he saw two men rise up out the water caught breath and disappeared. When they rose again he saw one of them was a white man and Jesse Pennington had his gun raised to shoot them. Lieut. Henry caught the gun, saying "don't shoot, one of them is a white man." They went down again and when they rose a third time he discovered the white man. Lieut. Sam's half brother told Sam to hold him. The Indian had a buck skin belt around his waist and Lieut. Sam had a firm hold on the belt. The fourth time they rose the belt broke and Lieut Sam grabbed him by the scalp lock and says, "Now you are my meat, so go ashore," and the Indian done so.

Now, they commence looking among the dead. There lay twenty dead Indians and one prisoner, so you see they had killed twenty, and captured one, and that was all of the stealing party.

Lieut. Sam says, ["]what must we do now?" Henry says, "remain here till night, and all night, for there will be others here about dark; they will come to hunt them and we will kill more of them if they come." Lieut. Henry told me, that about dark that night that he never heard such screams emanate from man nor beast before in his life. They were looking for wounded braves, but there was not any wounded. Just before day break a dead silence prevailed. About sunrise the whites, by certain signs found out there was about thirty more on an island in the swamp. They made the captive lead the way and they followed. When they got to the place of rendezvous the Indians had left, leaving about fifty bushels of shelled corn on the island and twenty of their braves dead on the river bank and one prisoner.

This expedition proved to be a failure. Now all is lively with the whites and when they could enjoy themselves was the time to do so.

They, the whites, had what we country people call a good time for nearly three months. The majority of the whites saying the Indians never will make another raid on the Blounts Ferry road. Lieut. Henry, says, "about the time that we think that all is peace and harmony death and destruction await us. You all can do as you please, but I am going to watch the movement of the enemy." He suited the action to the word and kept the woods as well as the road hot for nearly a month.

One morning at an early hour he discovered about sixty Indians bearing down hard on the Capt. Cone stockade, but yet some miles away. He ran back, informed Capt. North, who was a disgrace to the company, of the near approach of the enemy. Capt. North says, "Henry, take command of the company and fight them." Lieut. Sam was out of the way but Lieut. Henry put the company in battle array and marched out to do battle with the enemy.

Lieut Henry went to where he saw the Indians, took their trail, followed about three miles where they had come to a proper halt, and might have held a council of war.

From there they had deverged to the East, giving the Cone stockade a wide berth. Lieut. Henry knew that it was not of pure friendship to the whites that caused them to do this; to the contrary it was cowardice. Lieut. Henry says, "take the trail and let's follow them," they done so. The enemy was on foot, so was the whites, they followed the trail till dark and were now getting in the enemy's country. The men became a little tender footed, but Lieut. Henry buoyed them up.

John Thomas says, "Lieut. how can we follow them any further unless we could see the trail?" Before Lieut. Henry could answer, [John] Milledge Brannen says, "I see fire." Lieut Henry says, "that is their camps, now boys, we'll get them," so they marched up in twenty five yards of the Indians. Lieut. Henry was to fire the signal gun and then his men were to fire. Lieut. Henry told me that the Indians was as thick around the fire as spatter and was confident that all the men would fire into the bulk of them. There was one Indian standing off to himself nailing a Tiger's foot to a tree and he took good aim at him and shot him dead as he stood. His men fired into the crowd killing and wounding more than half their number.

He hollowed to his men to charge and he run in among them. His gun was empty. He then commenced shooting the Indians with their own guns. He looked for his men and there was not one of them to be seen. He hollowed to his men to come on and they done so. They quit shooting the Indians and beat their brains out with their gunbarrels. They thought that too slow a way, so they cut their throats with their pocket knives and kept on till the last wounded was dead.

The Indians never fired a gun, but ran and left their guns and packs.

Now the whites commenced counting dead Indians; there were forty dead out of sixty and not a white man hurt.[9]

Add twenty one to forty and you have sixty one of their braves. What have the red brutes done? They have killed one woman and six helpless little children. They looked around and saw that they had paid dear for their whistle, and from that day till this I never have heard of an Indian being seen from Alligator to Blounts Ferry.

Now, lets look after the prisoner Indian. He was sent under the care of a corporal and five men to be carried to Ft. Jink[s].[10] The men were gone about an hour and returned saying the Indian got away; and if he did not get away I know the whites did. As ever, brother.

Having jumped from the opening engagements of the Second Seminole War in 1835 and 1836 to the 1840 attack on Joseph Howell's family in Columbia County, Keen then reversed course and next related earlier incidents, beginning with ones of 1836.

From *The Florida Index,* December 8, 1899.

TALES OF LONG AGO.

The Creek Indians burned the town of Roanoke and murdered all of the people in it but one man, in the year 1837 [actually on May 25, 1836]. Roanoke was a small village in [Stewart] county, Ga., on the [Chattahoochee] river. One man escaped by concealing himself under a large box.[11] People were not so numerous in 1837 in Georgia and Florida as they are now, and not so well prepared to defend themselves against their enemies as they are in the year 1899. Such a thing as burning a town and murdering all the people in it but one man, is impossible now, in either Georgia or Florida. The thing could not be done now. Therefore, you need not give yourself any trouble with doubts as to the truth of my statement. It is the truth. The few people who were here in those days were full of courage; they had grace and grit, a plenty of it and they were making it possible for the present occupants of the country to live in peace and security. At times I am troubled with the belief that those who are here now do not appear to be troubled with gratitude for the old people that come and have gone. No sir. They are not caring anything about them. They can't point out their graves.

The Indians after accomplishing their work fled from that section of country to the Okeefeenokee swamp about eighty miles, the way the crows fly, in an easterly course. They were loaded with plunder and with their women, children and old people they did not get along as fast as the trains on the railroads do now in the same country. The white people, able to fight, were soon organized, in the saddle and on their trail. They overtook the fighting Indians at Cow Creek [on August 27, 1836], and they had a hot time of it for a while. The Indians were decently whipped and scattered to assemble again at some place on their way to the swamp.

I never had any talk with but two of those who fought in the battle of Cow Creek. Barzilla Staten and Angus McAuley were in the fight and both of them wounded. Mr. Staten was shot through the body, the bullet went clean through him. Mr. McAuley was shot through his thigh. They said the Indians didn't shoot well after the first shot was fired, the damage done to the whites was confined to the first volley fired by the savages. They ran off and nothing more was heard from them until the people on the upper Suwannee, in the vicinity of Blounts Ferry, began to suffer from their depredation.[12]

It was ascertained by later searches that the savages had taken refuge upon islands in the swamp, from which they made raids upon the white people who lived near their hiding places. The Hogans family lived on the swamp near Moniac and [in late October 1838] the Indians broke them up destroying everything they possessed.[13] The wife and children escaped by concealing themselves in a palmetto patch in sight of the home. The old lady told me of her experience with these savages many years after the occurrence. She said they come to the house in two rows and marched into the yard when they put their guns down and went to robbing the bee hives. They took the honey and mixed it with milk taken from the dairy and eat a power of it. After filling themselves they went into the house smashed everything to pieces they didn't want to carry off. They took the beds out in the yard and ripped the ticking open and scattered the feathers all over the yard and would laugh, and whoop, and dance around when they saw the feathers fly. They said she never saw the like of feathers. She told me she laid there and saw it all and "I dassent say a word." After satisfying themselves with all they desired they formed again in two rows, under the orders of their head man and marched off, "I laid there, me and the children and I dassent say a word." That was somewhat of a predicament the good woman suffered when she saw the savings of many years toil destroyed and "I dassent say a word." It was certainly a trying time. She was eighty years old when she told me of her experience with these savages.

The Norths, Bryans, Sandlins, Cone's, Summerals, Crews, Bonnells and many others that I have forgotten, had many, and often very sad experiences with this band of savages. When they came upon defenseless white people, it mattered not, whether women or children, they spared none. The nursing infant would have its brains dashed out before its mothers face, despite all of her pleading, and then she would be brutally butchered herself. They would not fight our men if they could well get off unless they believed they had all the advantage in their favor. They were badly fooled on one occasion when they made a night attack upon Mr. Sandlin; they got badly cut up.

Our white people gave them little time to rest. Military organizations were formed promptly, and went in pursuit. Capt. [William B.] North headed a company. George W. Smith headed another company from Hamilton county and had a fight with them, in which Hamp [Henry Monroe] Stephens, a relative of Worth Stephens, of Live Oak, was wounded. General [Charles Rinaldo] Floyd organized a regiment and did good service [during November and December 1838] in breaking up their hiding places in the great swamp.[14] If they had any women or children with them it was unknown to the whites, and there could not have been more than thirty warriors in the bunch from what Mrs. Hogans saw of them at her place. Finally they disappeared and no one knew certainly where they went. They were not Seminoles.

It was a matter of conjecture among the white people, who had suffered so long, as to the destination of this bunch of savages, until they discovered themselves in several attempts to murder Moses Barber whose place was on the South branch of St. Mary's river near where Macclenny is now on the F. C. & P. Railroad. They made several unsuccessful attempts to kill Barber and burn his place but "Old Mose" and his dogs were too much for them every time. They murdered a family and burned their place somewhere near where Baldwin is now.[15] It was on the road to Jacksonville, and was known as the Burnt House until the coming of the railroad, when it was forgotten. This was the last that was known of this bunch of savages, they disappeared and the people they troubled knew of them no more and they have lived in peace from Indians till this day.

The presumption is strong that, they were the fugitive Creeks that burned Roanoke, and fled to the big swamp for security. They had no women nor children with them; if they had any families with them, it has never been made known by those who pursued and fought them. While other bands of Indians had women and children, who were concealed, and their places of hiding known to the whites. It was upon the women the warriors depended for bread. The women and children were concealed far in the dense swamp upon islands where they planted patches of food stuff and took care of the children. There was none of that discovered as belonging to this bunch of savages that harrassed the people of the Upper Suwannee for a period of three or four years.

In the following letter Keen first digresses back to events of early 1838 before jumping ahead four years to the closing months of the Second Seminole War.

From *The Florida Index,* December 22, 1899.

TALES OF LONG AGO.

Ketch All, Dec. 8th, 1899.

Bro. Caldwell:—You have neglected publishing my communications so long that the subject matter has become cold and don't know where to begin.

I will commence by saying the Indians had been defeated in the two last raids with heavy losses and was mad about it. They now change the direction, giving Blounts Ferry road a wide berth. Uncle George Gillett and Mrs. Fanny Raulerson (Frank [Liberty Franklin] Raulersons mother) with their families moved and located on the north side of the Ocean Pond in Columbia county (now Baker county). They had been there seven weeks to a day. Mrs. Raulerson with her son William went to spend the night with Mrs. Gillett, and Miss Lydia Gillett went to spend the night with the Misses Raulerson, they lived half a mile away. Just at first dark [on March 16, 1838,] the Indians made a raid on the house, killing Gillett by shooting two bulletts into his back, passing through his body—he was dead in two minutes. Mrs. Raulerson said to Mrs. Gillett, "come, Tempy lets go." She says, "No, I would not desert my husband in life and I won't forsake him in death." Mrs. Raulerson was so excited till she forgot her 14 year old son in the house. Four colored women was in the yard washing by fire light. They followed Mrs. Raulerson; she going home, and pretty soon the Indians commenced killing the Gilletts. They shot Mrs. Gillett and daughter, also, William Raulerson. The daughter was three years old, her name was Adaline; William [Gillett] was five years old. He was sitting in a rocking chair; they killed him with a tomahawk; he never fell out of the chair. Mrs. Raulerson went home and gathered up her children, their names were Independant [Independence], Polester, Franklin, Adaline [Adeline], David, and Lydia Gillett; with the four colored women, and they started for our house, fifteen miles away. Tried to make a woods route and got lost; walked all night and the next day, till about one hour by sun in the afternoon, trying to make fifteen miles. They were torn up with briers and bushes and they had just clothes enough to say they had on a few rags. Their persons was scratched, I would say in not less than five hundred places.[16]

That morning a party of men started to Jacksonville, intending to take dinner with Gillett, and when they got there they found the family dead. The Indians took all the silver money, but left three or four hundred dollars of paper money on the table, also the pocket book. They won't have paper money for two reasons first, they can't keep it dry, second, they can't tell what amount a bill calls for.

The next day a sufficient force of armed men went out and brought in the dead, and the next day all five of the dead was buried at the same time and place. This is encouragement for the Indians. The whites was mad, and fighting mad, especially Daniel, David and Anderson Gillett, they swore eternal vengance against the Seminole Indians, saying they would have satisfaction or die.

About this time [February 24, 1842] another raiding party went by Fort Jinks, (where Wel[l]born now stands) and a party of whites were on their trail. The Indians were making for Old Town Hammock, but seeing a new road they took that which lead them to Dick Tillises. He was not at home, so the heathens fell on a helples woman and killed Mrs. Tillis, and thought they had killed Miss Mahaly Hyatt and four children. They shot the young lady in the back, the bullet coming out in the breast, and then stabbed her in each side; and they shot little Jim Tillis with a spiked arrow, it entering the back and coming out in the breast, leaving the arrow in him, and then struck him with a grubbing hoe over the left eye, then stuck fire to the building and left the place.

When the scouts found them the house was nearly burned down and Miss Hyatt and Jim had come to life and consciousness, so the whites took up the wounded and the dead and carried them to Fort Jinks, and the wounded recovered.[17]

Two victorys for the Indians and nothing but grief and vexation for the whites. This s[pu]rred the whites to action and while on a scout east of the Ocean Pond they struck trail of a large body of Indians making for Okeefeenokee swamps. "Now for fun," cried the whites, they increased their speed and sighted the enemy just as they entered the big swamp. The Captain ordered a charge; they did so, and halted at the bushes, dismounted, and into the swamp they went for the space of fifty yards. The enemy fired on them; the whites couldn't see any thing to shoot at; the Indians give them a warm reception, so much so that the whites was seized with a panic and ran out of the swamp. John Thomas cursed the Indians for cowardly re[d]legged sons of b—s, saying "come out on open ground and fight us on open ground like brave men." The Indians came out, about four hundred strong, "Holy Wogus, we fight you," meaning, big white man, we fight you, and began shooting holy wogus. The whites numbered sixty, and the enemy four hundred. Capt. W[illiam] B. No[r]th gave orders to mount and to do so quick and leave here. Every white man obeyed that order. Now a race. For the space of three miles, the Indians on foot and the whites on horse back, the Indians doing all the shooting and the whites doing the best share of the running.[18]

Now the Indians have killed our people and whipped our men and they are gloating over their victorys. That was their time.

Col. Robert Brown, (the father of our townsman, E[paminondas] Brown) was Colonel commanding the regiment. He said the cause of our defeat was because we did not have the right kind of men, but he would choose the men, head the company and whip the redskins. Now comes the names that he selected: Rigdon Brown, who was known and called "Old Rawsom the

Bow." (a fiddler.) Jesse Long, Loram P. the Ranter, [John] Milledge Brannen, John Futch, Joe Keen, Daniel Gillett, Jim Brewer, David Gillett, William Markham [Marcum], Steven [Stephen] Sparkman, Jim Osteen, Asa Roberts, David, Joe and Enoch Mizell, and lots of others.

The enemy had been invading our territory, now Col. Brown was going to return the compliment by invading them. The colonel had the utmost confidence in the Gillett brothers, but he regarded "Old Rawsom the Bow" as his right bower, for he feared no man nor set of men. He would drink whisky and fight when necessary, and no man could whip him, and he did represent the people of the county of Columbia in the State legislature, but to the point.

Col. Brown, with one hundred picked men, went in pursuit of the Indians. They found their trail going south, they overtook a pappoose that had got lost off, but was following the trail. Jesse Long took the little one by both legs and knocked its brains out against a black-jack. They overtook the Indians near Wacahoota and surrounded them, the men closed in on them and fired. The Indians wanted to surrender, but the two Gilletts, Long and old "Rawsom the Bow" ran in among them with their big knives and cut them into sausage meat. Lieutenant Daniel Gillett would chop them down with sword and the others would kill them by piecemeal. This brought about peace for along time. You may hear from me again in the course of human events.[19]

V

Response

By late December 1899 many northeast Floridians eagerly awaited each new installment of George G. Keen's reminiscences, and a few of them, in turn, began writing to *The Florida Index* to share their reactions. As illustrated in William A. Sheffield's letter published January 5, 1900, Keen's letters evoked for some memories of particular people, places, and times past. Others, such as the author of one communication published January 12—he designated himself A.D. 1835—waxed more philosophical, using area history to provide a context and set an agenda for argument on important issues of the day.

From *The Florida Index*, January 5, 1900.

A Welcome Letter.

Alachua, Fla., Dec. 23, 1899.

My Dear Sir:—The INDEX has been received and read of Dec. 22nd, inst. I am 69 years and 4 months old today and my prayer to our Father in Heaven is, God bless you and all your godly efforts to better humanity. When you are 69 the world and everything will have changed. It is all change from the cradle to the grave.

I often think of what my old partner, Joe Price, said of you, that you took your literary turn of mind from your mother. God bless the mothers. I owe all that I am to my mother who died two years ago in her 92nd year. See Mrs. W. S. Cone [Kesiah Cone Sheffield Hagan] and read her obituary for my sake. I may never see you again, but I love you for your mother's sake. God forever bless you. . . .

I have just read Black Eye's article in the INDEX of the 22nd, inst. I knew Milledge Brannen, Henry Harrington, Frank Raulerson and I slept in Rigdon Brown's house repeatedly in 1852, forty miles below Tampa [Brown lived near present-day Bartow], and himself and wife [Esther Howell Brown] treated me as a son.[20] I was all around where Bartow now is when it was woods and saw old man McClintand who Black Eye says tied the line around him that caught 100 geese in the Okeefeenokee swamp. [21] Get him to tell you about it.

As judge [Washington Mackey] Ives would say, thirty five years ago today I left Mosely Hall [in Madison County] with 20 men for Deadmans Bay to guard a blockade runner from the deserters who left the Southern army and finally joined the enemy and are drawing pensions now. . . .

With best wishes for you and yours I am your friend,

W. A. SHEFFIELD.

From *The Florida Index*, January 12, 1900.

"THE SURVIVAL OF THE FITTEST."

In town the other day, I met up with a man I had never encountered until that morning. He was evidently a new comer. I was pleased with his appearance as it was all outwardly decent and tidy, and he had a kind of bookish, knowing look. He was not in the least uppish as some people in town try to be, and fail. I made it convenient to have a talk with him to which he appeared willing, and altogether, well pleased.

He informed me that, his name was Josiah Didwell and that he had come to Florida in order to better his conditions which was not well prepared to sustain any more less than had already been charged up against it. He come for gain. I considered he had a good name, at all events, whether his condition and object fitted it or not, was immaterial to me. I was in for a talk with him anyway.

"So,["] I said to Mr. Didwell, said I, ["]have you any idea who was the first man that come to this country where he come from and for what purpose he came?["] "Well sir," he says to me, "those are very difficult questions to answer correctly. I am satisfied he come just as I did, to better his condition. He thought he could do better here than he was doing back yonder at his old home. I think," he said, "that is the object every man has had in mind that has come to this country from the very first one that set foot here, to the very last one. But as to who he was that came first, and whence he came from, it is a difficult matter to determine correctly." I said, "Yes Sir, that is true, I believe."

He proceeded to state that the most ancient work of men that remains in this country, are the mounds that are to be seen in nearly every State in the United States; they are the work of a people who existed so long since that it is quite impossible to tell who the people were, or whence they came from.

Said Mr. Didwell, "it is written that after the flood in which everything, and everybody, was destroyed except Noah and his family, and the Ark was left on dry land on a mountain in Armenia in Asia, away beyond seas, that Noah went to China and founded the Chinese empire. It is believed that people came from China here to this country and built these mounds. They are nothing more or less than the grave yards of a people long since extinct, gone, nobody knows where."

"Yes sir," I said, "I have read about Noah in the Bible, and I have no right to say it is not true, every word of it, but there are people who dispute the truthfulness of the Bible account. For instance an Irishman will tell you there were no Irish people in the Ark because, in those days, the Irish were very wealthy and had boats of their own. If you contradict him he will get mad, and just as likely as not, want to fight. He will not agree that he is related by blood to Indians and Negroes which he must confess, if he believes in the Bible history of the flood. There is danger in pressing this matter of blood relationship with Indians and Negroes upon the Irish, and some who are not Irish don't like to be considered of kin to Indians and Negroes," "why," said Mr. Didwell, "you are not Irish are you and you don't dispute the Bible do you?" "No sir, I'm not Irish and I believe the Bible account of the flood, and of this time, we are all doing fairly well. I will remember what you tell me about contending for the truthfulness of the Bible with some people, it don't amount to any good to try to convince such of their error." "But," said he to me, "the Bible is a good book, and it matters not how learned a man may be, he will find good and profitable lessons in the Bible. There are those who have tried to disprove its truth but they failed. God has made no mistakes that man has been able to find out." I told Mr. Didwell I believed in the truthfulness of the Bible and that no man had ever been able to shake my faith in its teachings.

But to return to Noah. He said, "Noah was one hundred and twenty years engaged in building the Ark, and said he, it was not impossible for him to have accomplished the work in that time under the direction, and with the help of the Supreme being. See what wonderful things our people have done in a hundred years despite of all opposition. It would require a big book to tell of all the wonderful works that have been made useful to mankind in a hundred years. Therefore it is folly to dispute the truthfulness of the history of what others have done long before we saw the light of day."

"It was not impossible," he said, "for people to have crossed from Asia to North America at Behring Strait, where the sea is very narrow and from their descendants might have come those who built these mounds. They are very old as is proven by the growth of giant forest trees of immense age. The mounds may be more ancient than the Pyramids as we find no metal of any kind in them. They were evidently, built prior to the discovery of metals. I have found nothing more in any I have searched but parts of implements made of stone or burned clay, and pieces of human bones, encased, to all appearances, in charcoal. It is wonderful how long common charcoal will resist the ravages of time, whether or not, the remains of those who are buried in these mounds are the bones of white folks, I can't say; they were very large people it is plain to be seen from the size of the bones.

When the white race invaded Florida they found the Indians in undisputed control of the country. They were divided into tribes and special mention is made of two, via Micosookies [Mikasukis] and Tallahassees. That is now over four hundred years since and they maintain their tribal organization until the present day. The Shawnees were here too, how long, no one knows. They left Florida in the early years of the present century and went into Pennsylvania and Ohio. Tecumseh was one of that tribe, and may have caused their removal, where he formed an alliance with the six nations to make war upon the whites. The Seminoles are not one of the ancient tribes; they were said to be runaways from other tribes that formed a tribal organization of recent date, but old enough to have given a historical name to the seven years war with the United States. In point of fact, the leading spirits of that war, from 1835 to 1842, were Micosookies and Tallahassees. [22]

The white race has given the red man some hard raps but the punishment has been tempered with mercy. It has never been the object of the white man to destroy the red and black races. In the contest, the object of the white man has been to obtain and to hold supremacy over the red and black races, who have brought upon themselves the destruction that has fallen to their lot by their pugnacity and want of good sense. Instead of quietly submitting to the leadership of the white man in peace, they attempt the impossible when they seek to stay his progress in the contest for supremacy. The red man has proven to the world his inability to organize a successful resistance to the progress of the white race. That other tribal race—the negro—thinks he is smart enough, with the aid of corrupt white men, to grab the power of control, it is a question of time only, when he will wake up to realize his weakness and folly." "Yes," I says to Mr. Didwell, "it looks that way, but it is not best to be too rash; you will only make the trouble that is with us nor, much worse by the expression of violent opinions."

You know Mr. Editor, that opinions are plentiful and cheap; they can be had in car load lots F.O.B., for little or nothing, such as are floating about. It is only the opinions that Judge [John F.] White [Jr.], and Judge [Rhydon Mays] Call and Mayor [Robert Furman] Rogers, and Mayor Dave Johnson give out, that have any weight. They bear heavily upon such of our people as chance to occupy the mourner's seat in their court. It is there we learn who is supreme, and the cost of supremacy.

Very Sincerely Yours,

A.D. 1835

VI

Getting Ahead in the 1840s and 1850s

Having enjoyed a two-month respite from writing chores, George G. Keen resumed his reminiscences with a series of letters, the first dated February 12, 1900, that celebrated his own coming-of-age saga. With a good humor that stood in marked contrast to the angry passion of his Second Seminole War tales, Keen traced his search for the pot of gold at the end of the rainbow as it led through the thicket of courtship and marriage. In doing so, he revealed a more serious insight into the white Cracker's mentality concerning slaves and the importance of their ownership. As readers will discover, Keen's best-laid marriage plans failed of success. Not until January 14, 1856, would he and Georgia-born Arkina Lane initiate the happy union that would last George the remainder of his life.

From *The Florida Index,* February 16, 1900.

WANTED AN OVERSEER!

Ketch All, February 12, 1900.

Brother Caldwell:—I have been pouting with you, but am all right now.

I am going to take you on probation, like [Jackson] Tharp Raulerson said the Methodist's did him. He said he joined the Methodist church and they took him in on six months probation and if his daily works at that time was that of a christian, they would have received him in full fellowship in the church. But he got drunk twice and had three fights and the church thought they could afford to let him off at three months, and done so. Brother, take notice and govern, &c. So much for prefatory remarks.

We are now in the latter part of the 40's. There was deer by the dozen and turkeys by the bushel. We had a crowd that hunted more than we worked. Their names was as follows: J. T. Goodbread, Garret Vanzant, J. W.

Jones, John Goodbread, G. W. S. Waldron, [Adam] Sowder Goodbread and Jack Peeples. All of them were rich men. I was poor, but a natural born pioneer with a thorough knowledge of the woods, and was a crack shot, together with a pack of hounds as good as ever give tongue on a deer trail, all that considered, put me in the swim.

We would go for three or four days on a camp hunt, having a nigger to drive the wagon, carry the grub and haul in the meat. When the day's hunt was over, supper eaten and all seated around the fire, the subject of farming was introduced. One would say, Iv'e got the best overseer I ever had; another would say, my overseer is a worthless fellow, a third would say I am pretty well satisfied with my overseer, and so on. I would sit there like a bump on a log. You bet I never wanted anything worse in my life than I wanted a plantation of niggers so I could talk about my overseer. I had some niggers, but not enough to have an overseer; that's what worried me. When hunting time come round I was in but when overseer talk was the topic of the day I was ten feet above high water mark on dry land.

I wanted niggers. How to get them was the question. I come to this conclusion; I will marry a rich widow, then I can talk overseer talk as big as any of them. I put on my best clothes, mounted my fine horse and went to Tampa, in Hillsborough county, South Florida.[23] When I got there I didn't find any rich widows, but found one of the prettiest girls I ever saw in my life. She was so pretty that it took my best to look her full in the face ten minutes at a time without fainting. So I made eyes at her and she made eyes back at me. That was woman like. The next thing was a private conversation; them days I could say as much in the same length of time as the average man. Its not so now as you know. She was a daughter of Capt. William B. H[ooker]— and he was worth $250,000; her name was Martha, and pretty soon I got to love her better than all the world besides and thought of marrying her. On a second consideration I saw that wouldn't do for he had two sons-in-law and only give each one $2000. I couldn't hire an overseer on that; again, he looked to be good for thirty years and I knew that a rich father-in-law, in one sense of the word was like a fat hog, he never was any advantage to his son-in-law till after he was dead. I come to this conclusion, I will keep her in duress until I see that I can't do any better, then I will marry her, but I didn't tell her that.

There was a campmeeting coming off at Suwannee Shoals, so I told my gal good bye and come to campmeeting. There I found the widow that I was looking for, but I did not have the pleasure of her acquaintance. I got it for a fact, that she was rich, and that filled the bill.

In the course of a few weeks I wrote her; silence was my only answer. In about four weeks I wrote again and got the same answer. I didn't see any overseer in that kind of business, so I went to Geo. W. French, who was acquainted with her and he gave me a letter of introduction. Now I am solid. Goose like, I went into Col. A. J. T. Wright's store (the father of our towns-man [Mitchell] Ed. Wright) [at Lake City] and gave him $10, for a pair of black broadcloth pants, $7, for a pair of boots and $16, for a saddle, then went to Abe Ellingers store and give $25, for a coat, $6, for a vest, $4, for a hat and $6, for two shirts and went home.

The next Sunday I put on my new clothes. I looked at myself in the glass and I thought I was a Jim Dandy. I had a nigger named Henry. I said, "Henry this way." He says, "Boss what is it?" "Tell me how I look." "Boss you look as bold as a lion." I didn't like that, and said, "where did you ever see a lion?" "In Mr. Arter [Arthur] Daughtrey's new ground field." I says "You fool, that was a Jack ass." "Can't help it Boss, you look just like him."

"As you think that I look like the lion you saw in Arthur Daughtrey's new ground field, go bring out the Bengal Tiger and saddle him." He done so. Now I am ready. I mounted my horse and rode off. I expect that you have heard of things called non-descripts, if so I was one of them.

That night I stopped with Dick Tillis on the dry prarie. The next day noon I took dinner with Arch Carroway. Now I am five miles of the object of my affection. I told him I wanted to reshirt. He says, "old boy, that means something." "It does; it means that I put on this shirt yesterday morning, and as I am going among strangers I want to bear a decent appearance." "It means that you are going to see the widow D—." "Arch, get out, you know there is not one word of truth in that" and I left.

Her name was Rhoda D[ean]—but I won't tell you her name. The pub-lic road ran parallel with her fence, and near the fence, there was two darkies hoeing cotton. I asked who lived there. They said the widow D—"Is she at home?" "You see two [wo]man where dem people plowing?" "Yes." "One am de missus and de udder am de overseer wife." "Thank you uncle." I rode on saying, "there's two of my niggers, I will have an overseer in a few days and can talk overseer talk as good as any man on the camp hunt, and I will do it." I always knew that my looks would pass me over where other mens' money would fail. I am in luck and when she sees me she is bound to love me. After we marry I will treat her well on her own, for she can't live over six years, then the property will be mine and I can marry who I please.

It's now about a mile to the house. I went by the barn and horse lot. There I saw the close carriage, open buggy and the two bay carriage horses. I knew they would soon be mine. I rode to the gate and hailed. A yellow woman come to the front; I knew she was the cook. I was well pleased with my cook, and inquired for the lady. She said she would be in directly, did I wish to see her? I said, yes. She said tie my horse and come in. I did so. She took the [Methodist] Southern Christian Advocate. I picked up one of them and tried to read, but the lines began to wiggle, all went into a black blur and I could not read one word. I tried to speak and had lost my utterance and couldn't speak a word. I felt for my pulse, they were down to about twenty beats to the minute. Now what?

If the lady should have come just then, no doubt she would have took me for an idiot, imbecile, lunatic, or maniac, and would have caught me with the yard dog, made the niggers tied me and the overseer hit me a hundred with the buggy whip. Fortunately she delayed her coming for half an hour.

I tried to read a second time. No sir. No read in that thing. I wanted to be ten miles from there. I felt my pulse again; they were fifty to the minute. Oh! I felt good and I could distinguish the lines and divide the sylables. I began to feel good. I felt my pulse again. They were 72 to the minute, and that was the happiest minute of my life.

I threw myself back on my dignity and began to read. Knowing that I wouldn't be at a loss for a word when the time come for a conversation. Just at that moment the lady put in an appearance.

(To be Continued.)

From *The Florida Index,* February 23, 1900.

WANTED, AN OVERSEER.

(Continued from last week.)
Ketch All, February 20th, 1900.

I jumped up with all manner of politeness and presented her the letter of introduction and we spoke recognizing each other. We were seated and went into conversation.

We began talking about the health of the community and exhausted the subject. Farming was the next thing under consideration and most uppermost in my mind. I wanted to know the dividend that the farm paid annually. I knew the niggers, land, cattle, horses, mules and rolling stock was all right, so we digested the farm thoroughly and found it good.

There is another question to be considered which was of more importance to me than the health of the people. that was the subject of matrimony.

How to introduce the subject got next to me. I will make an effort to tell her . . . my business and done so, but I choked down, coughed and said something else. Talked on for a little while and tried it the second time and done like Dr. [Samuel B.] Todd said he done when they called on him to preach when he was in conference he made a failure—so did I. I said to myself,

I will hit it if it stagnates business from the Pacific to the Atlantic. Now for it. "Mrs. D[ean]—did you ever get a letter, or letters, over my signature?" "Yes sir, I received two." "Silence being my only answer, I have come to ascertain the case. "The case was this, my penmanship was not as good as I would like for a gentleman to see was one reason, and another was, I felt a delicacy in making my son to write for me on as delicate a subject."

So far as the writing and spelling was concerned I didn't care a fig for that, all that I wanted was a favorable reply. "How did my letters meet your approbation?" "Very well." "Mrs. D— I never was favorably impressed with long courtships; they seldom prove satisfactory to all parties interested. as you have met me, I would like to know what objection you have to my looks?" "I haven't the least objection to your looks, (that pleased me) but I do have objection to your age." "In what way?" "You are too young." "How old are you pray?" "38" (She was the mother of nine children, and the youngest was 26.) "How old are you Mr. K—?" "37." (I was only 22.) "Your extreme youthhood is all the objection that I have to you." "The contrast is our ages don't amount to a hill of beans with me, and you must consider that time will make me older, or it does other men, and why not me?" "All that is true, Mr. K—, but where an old woman marries a young man they commonly live very disgreeable and there is no happiness at home."

"Now, I will give you my view of the matter. I don't consider the acts of other people any criterion for us to go by, and again, I think that a matrimonial obligation is the most sacred obligation that man can take and he should make it his daily thoughts to keep that obligation inviolate. Mrs. D— I am a man of few words and don't like to bring in too many preliminaries nor tell of prevailing circumstances, so this case shall not be an exception to the general rule, but please let me say that I have been drifting about in the matrimonial world for sometime and my orthodox tells me that a mans' religious duty enjoins upon him to marry. I am going to speak plain, but no plainer than true. I am a candidate for matrimony and have chosen you from all your sex of people as the only one that I can love with sincerity my whole soul's salvation is based on your beautified charms and if my love is disappointed it will cause me to mourn in solitude. The tongue of Demosthenes, nor the pen of Shakespeare, could not express that love I have for you. Will you be my wife?"

Just at this particular minute the, or our, cook called the missus' attention. She was gone a few minutes and returned. She did not take her seat, but stood in front of me. I rose and walked in front of her and took two dovey little hands in mine and plead for a favorable reply. She said she didn't know what to say. I took both of her hands in one of mine and hit her love taps on the cheek with my other hand and told her how I loved her. "We cannot she said, marry under a month; will that suit?" "Yes." I wish you boys knew the feeling it puts on a feller when a rich woman tells him she will have him.

About this time the overseer and niggers come in from the field; my horse was near the gate; the overseer had him carried to the lot and cared for and the nigger bragging on him. "I say boys, that am de Bosses hoss, but de Madam, overseer, nor niggers, don't know what I done been tinking about." That suited me.

That night we finished our conversation and I didn't sleep much, for I was trying to count how much I was worth. I ran it into near $75,000 and went to sleep. After breakfast the widow and I were seated in the parlor. I thought she was the prettiest piece of mortality that ever grew out of natural philosophy, and I loved her better than any thing that ever wore crinoline. You say why did you? I say because I looked upon her as my wife expectant. "Now Mr. K—the reason I wanted to put off marrying for a month was, I wanted to visit my mother and she lives in Alabama and it will take a month to go and come and make a visit. How does it suit you?" ["]All right, for I have got to go to Tampa to attend to some financial business and I don't think that I can do justice to myself under a month, and after we are married I don't want to be gone a month, at a time from my little Rosenglory, nor I won't do it. Sweet one, can you give me your mothers address?" "Yes sir, Abbeville, Ala." Thank you, dearest, I will write you when I get to Tampa." "All right, Sir, I will be pleased to hear from you and will answer at once." "Thank you, love."

I told her good bye (please don't mistake and say I kissed her good bye.) After I got one mile from the house, I took out my pocket glass and looked at myself and thought I was the prettiest man on earth and had the finest horse. Psalmist David thought Absalom pretty, but what would he have said if he could have seen me and I would have looked to him as I did to myself? No doubt he would have given me the second highest position in his kingdom. And if Lord Cornwallis could have seen the Bengal Tiger, the horse I was riding, what would he have said? Might of said there is the finest horse my eyes ever beheld. He is full sixteen hands high, the eye of a hawk, the spirit of a king eagle, chest like a lion, swifter than a roe [doe?], but as strong as a buffalo. If these men could have seen me and the Bengal Tiger as we were leaving my overseer to look after my interest for the space of a month, we, I and Ben, would have received a compliment, but as it was we received only what I could give us.

(To be continued.)

From *The Florida Index,* March 2, 1900.

Wanted, an Overseer.

(Continued from last week.)

I went home and began making arrangements to go to Tampa to look after my interest, believing there was not a man in the South that could steal my darling's affections from me and I knew that I would have my finger nails trimmed to the quick before I would forsake her. I was easy on that point.

About the time I got ready to start on my journey my Brother Sherod, who was older than I was, says "Black Eye, are you going to bring Martha [Hooker] with you when you return?" "No Sherod, I am not, we are too poor to marry and it never will do to add poverty to poverty." He was acquainted with her. "Look here old boy, they say you are going to marry the widow D[ean.]" "Suppose I do, anything wrong in that?" "A boy like you to marry a woman 60 years old, weighing 200 pounds and not a tooth in her head!" "She will have teeth soon." "Yes, that is so, for I heard her say at camp-meeting that she had the roots extracted and as soon as the gums shrank she was going to have her teeth put in."

"All that is true, but she is worth seventy five thousand dollars." "I don't dispute that, and in five years after you are married, if you go to a party and dance with the girls as you know you will do, the next day she will make you think she is worth a hundred thousand and besides that she is old enough for your grandmother and how will you carry her to church?" ["I will carry her in a two-horse carriage," I said.] "In a two-horse carriage, you had better say a two-horse wagon, and when you get there it will take two preachers and three lay members to lift her out of the wagon and all the old people and young ones too will laugh at you for marrying her and they will call her granny Grampers, how would you like that? Black Eye, I would rather have Martha H—with a second dress than that old lady with all her niggers."

"If I do that I can't have any overseer." "You are worth nearly $4,000 in niggers, land, cattle, horses and money, and marry Martha H—and you will have the prettiest wife that I ever saw in my life." "But I won't have any overseer." "The devil take the overseer, you will have about $6000, to begin with and you are only 22 and she 16; in ten years with industry and good management you will have niggers enough to hire an overseer." "Do you think so?" "I know it, and be a happy man besides." "Well, old boy, I will take your advice."

Now I have delayed three weeks, but will start for Tampa tomorrow.

I told my brother I would start for Tampa next day, and done so, and was six hard days ride to get to my place of destination. I didn't have anything to do but travel and make up new plans from the ground up. I'd give up the

farm, discarded the widow and discharged the overseer and was changed
from a farmer in Columbia county to a stock raiser in Hillsborough county.
I put on my studying cap. I intend to marry Martha the third day after I get
there. If I don't some one will try to break up my plans.

What made me so positive that Martha would stick to me like glue and
molasses in a bushey head of hair, was every time I went there her mother
[Mary Amanda Hair Hooker] would have a conversation with me, and it did-
n't make any difference what the subject was, she always wound up on the
subject of matrimony. And again, to make me more sanguine their first son-
in-law [on April 18, 1850, Eliza Jane Hooker married William W. Stallings] and
I stood in, and he stayed there one night and the Capt. [William B. Hooker]
was on a cow hunt as usual, but at a late hour in the night the Capt. come in.

The family all asleep but the son-in-law, he was listening to the old folks
talking. The madam said, "Capt. I think we are going to have a wedding in
our family soon." "Who with?" "Martha and Black Eye." "Well," said the
Capt. "I had rather have him for a son-in-law than any man in the county. I
have known him since he was a little boy up to manhood and there has not
a nicer man been raised in Columbia county than he is; and was raised by as
good parents as I ever saw in my life. I have known him ever since I kept the
ferry on the Suwannee river. I have been to his father's house many a time;
it was second home for me."

The son-in-law told me of it next day; all these things come fresh to my
mind, and I knew Martha loved me for I was so handsome that all a sensible
girl had to do to love me was to see me.

I was all alone on that long road, but Martha was uppermost in my mind.
My mind wandered back to the widow once in a while but la, my love for
her was fading away like the morning dew before a rising sun and going back
to Martha. This is the sixth day on my journey. Shall I go to the Capt's.
tonight? No, I won't do that, for I may take her on a surprise. I will wait until
she hears that I have come, then she can put on her best looks. When she sees
me she will meet me at the gate. The meeting with the father and the prodigal son will be nothing to compare with our meeting. So I stopped with a
friend that night.

(To be continued.)

From *The Florida Index*, March 23, 1900.

WANTED, AN OVERSEER.

(Continued from the INDEX March 2nd.)
Ketch All, March 12, 1900.

Tonight I am in Hillsborough county, whereas, according to previous arrangements I should have been in Columbia county.

I meet a warm reception. After supper we are seated on the piazza enjoying a pleasant conversation. These people were originally from Columbia county and wanted to hear from their old friends back there. After answering a thousand and one questions a dead silence prevailed. I took the advantage of it, and says, "now tell me all that has transpired since I left here." "Nothing worth relating." "No weddings, nor deaths among the neighbors?" "Oh! yes, old man Gomus is dead and Martha H[ooker] is married." [Martha Hooker married Hillsborough County sheriff Benjamin Hagler on May 27, 1851.] That sounded louder to me than old Ben did when the Yankees opened their biggest battery on us at Fredericksburg in Northern Va., in 1862.

"Who did she marry?" "Ben Hagler." "Great Scot I wouldn't have believed it." "No neither would I, but he is rich." "But he was a widower, and forty five years old, and had an impediment in his speech, and can't tell what he does know, that is the truth, and he gives me the jim-jams to hear him talk." "Mrs. H— was the cause of their marriage. You know Bill Stallings married Jane, Martha's sister, and he was said to be rich, and she said she had two poor sons-in-law, now she had two rich ones and didn't care how the men looked that her daughters married so they were rich.

My brother, don't you think that Black Eye is now where Moses was when the light went out. He was ready to go to his room and done so, and to bed but not to sleep.

Now what am I to do? I have been governed by the advice of my brother who wished me well and have falsified my word, discarded my widow and lost pretty Martha by being too slow.

My dear mother often told me that a proud heart and beggar's purse never did agree and that pride always went before a fall. I began to see where in she was right.

Now the widow is the only chance and I did not love her one bit; and again, I failed to come South as I promised, and the month is up and she has had her visit out and I don't know where she is; I didn't write as I should have done. Now I want to have the wisdom of Solomon so I would know what to do, but you see I didn't have the wisdom of Solomon, and in trouble and no one to sympathize with me.

Imagine my condition and see if you don't think that I was in a similar condition to Elias Walker said he was in when he went to Jacksonville to buy goods and was not acquainted with a man in town, did not have but twenty five cents in money, and lost that. He said he was in a peck of conditions and a half bushel would not of held them. It would have took a two bushel basket to have held mine—all the blunders that I ever made in my life come fresh in my mind.

I began to wish I never had seen the widow nor Martha in my life. I am into this trouble and how to get out of it is the question. I thought if I ever got out of this trouble I never would make eyes at no other woman in my life. The beautiful Delilah wrought Samson's trouble and this woman and girl had put me on a par with Samson.

The next morning I didn't know which one of the boys I was. Martha was fresh in my mind. I said, "they give a big wedding and a universal invitation?" "No, it was rather a private affair; the near relatives and a few special friends" "How was that?" "The Capt. was opposed to the marriage and the madam was in favor of it and they had some trouble over it. You see Miss Edna Deshon[g] [possibly Caroline C. DeShong], she can tell you all about it, for she was first bride's maid.["] "I will go there at once for the Dr. and I are good friends." I done so. After the common-place remarks, I told Miss Edna I wanted her to give me a full detail of Miss Martha's marriage and wedding.

She says I will do it.

It was like this: The Capt. was opposed to Hagler and Mrs. H. was in favor of him and they had some sharp words about it, and he told her that Hagler was an old fogy and besides that there was no business qualifications about him and if she married Black Eye he would turn over all his business to him and be a saving of $2000, yearly, for he would watch the shipping points and keep his books and do all financing, and in ten years he will be worth $25,000. She said all that may be true, but Hagler is worth more than that now. He says he may be, but I don't believe it, and if she marries Hagler you will live to regret it. Well, she has got to marry him.

After Martha was dressed, we [Edna and Martha] were sitting in her room and she began to cry. Her mother came into the room and says Martha, what are you crying for? No answer, I know; you are crying about Black Eye and you will not get him. You are right, ma, for he is the only man that I ever loved in my life. Well, you have got to marry Hagler in a few minutes. Yes, said Martha, and I'd rather die than to do it. At that moment Hagler entered the room, led her out and they were married, and Martha crying—that's all.

Brother, I wish you could experience the feelings that I did during that day; you would want some one to kick you all over.

Now for business, I collected every dollar that was due me, and made my arrangements to go back to Columbia county.

I would not see Mrs. Hagler, nor never have seen her from that day till this. But I thought I would go back and marry the widow "D—," but wanted to see Edna Deshon and get her to keep me posted in regard to Mrs. H—

sons-in-law that was so rich. She said this: Stallin[g]s and his wife went after his property and his wife said he wasn't worth $500, in the world and when they came to find out the truth Hagler wasn't worth $300, and Hagler and wife parted [they divorced in 1866]; also Stallins and his, and they never lived together another day in their lives [Eliza Jane Hooker Stallings died in 1858].

I am now on my way home, and it come to mind what Moses K[een] said to me, why are you so stuck up? You are respected by all your associates, but you are not satisfied. I heard of a bull frog that was as big as any of the frogs, but he wanted to be as big as an ox that was feeding in the margin of the lake, so he drew in his breath and got a little larger he tried it again, but not yet as big as the ox, one more swell and I'll make it; he made a desperate effort and busted, and then was smaller than any toad in the puddle; look out boy—there is a moral in it.

Moses! I have heard of these old saying, also, between two chairs you strike the floor, but I am not that kind of a hair pin.

My brother, I am at home again. Well, Sherod, what's the news? Your widow is married. The d—l you say. Yes. Who did she marry? Old Parson [Cotesworth L.] Carruth. My first thought was between two chairs. I have fell as flat on the floor as a pancake, and blasted all my glory and lost my overseer. You can better imagine my feelings than I can write them. I went to my room, so confused I couldn't sleep. Next morning I looked at the Bengal Tiger, he was so ugly that I couldn't look at him. $30 was more than I could have sold him for. I went back to the house and looked in the glass. I saw that I was the ugliest man I ever saw in my life. Edmond J. Deloch [DeLoach] had wore the belt for four years, but he was a beauty long side of me, and I was a bigger fool than John McClelland, and he was such a fool that he cut down a tree to catch a turkey. I was worse looking than Rid Wop or Ned Gandy, and they were so ugly that no one would let them stay in the house with them. The girls thought I meant harm by looking so bad, but I didn't. Blood is thicker than water, hence nature binds connections together, so ma let the remains in the house with her.

Boys, don't make big improvements on uncertainties. In this case you have the example if not the experience, and there is a material difference between example and experience.

The next day after I went home I took off my boots and fine clothes and put on an old suit of working clothes and a pair of brogan shoes and went to work in the blacksmith shop and decided that Henry was right when he said I looked like the lion that he saw in Arter Daughtrey's new ground field and I didn't want an overseer, nor don't yet.

I told the girls an everlasting farewell, for I knew all women wanted a fine looking man for a husband and I was not the man they were looking for, and I would live and die the death of old Tom B. Fitchpatrick [Fitzpatrick]. He never married, neither would I.

With these remarks the scene closes, the curtain drops, I tip my beaver and quietly retire.

VII

Alligator's Transformation

Six months elapsed after publication of the final installment of "Wanted, an Overseer" before George G. Keen's tales of frontier fortune and misfortune again graced *The Florida Index*'s pages. Still, his essays' influence persisted, as interest in local history remained a topic of conversation and consideration. On March 9, 1900, editor John M. Caldwell had interrupted the "Overseer" series to print a short letter from Keen regarding the town of Lake City's name. On May 18 he followed with another letter on the same subject from the author of "Survival of the Fittest," who now addressed himself more formally as "ANO DOMNI 1835."

From *The Florida Index,* March 9, 1900.

SEEKS FOR KNOWLEDGE.

Ketch All, February 26, 1900.
My Brother:—Knowledge is power. I write this to please a pretty little blackeyed school girl.

She wanted to know when Alligator (this town) was changed to Lake City.

Others may want to know why it took so omnious a name as Alligator when the original is the ugliest thing that I ever saw crawl—I will tell you why.

The chief commander of the Seminole Indians in 1830, was named Alligator and his town was situated two miles south of the Whit Smith lake.

In the year of 1843, James Johnson, better known as old Flitter foot, put up a little store where Col. [Bascom H.] Palmer's office now stands and James Pearce, a Methodist preacher, named the place Alligator, in honor of the brave red man of the forest.

In the year of 1858, James M. Baker, a lawyer, came here from North Carolina and to practice in his profession. Recollect, he come here prior to

1858, but it was at that time that he made a move which was sanctioned by others to change the name of this town from Alligator to Lake City and it was changed, and remains so till this day, and I think it a very appropriate name, don't you? Now, if the desired information is obtained, and one more link added to the chain of knowledge—I am satisfied.

From *The Florida Index,* May 18, 1900.

CONCERNING NAMES AND PEOPLE.

Why is it that people give their children such unheard-of names as Alligator? Is it not the result of a depraved taste and ignorance? A mother could not be the possessor of good taste and intelligence that would name her little boy Alligator. No sir; she that did this was a rough one sure. It was done once, however, and then to men matters, they called your town Alligator. It held on [to] that name many years until finally Capt. [Jacob] Summerlin [Sr.] named it Lancaster in honor of a whig Judge [Joseph B. Lancaster], of that name, who used to preside as judge of the Eastern circuit.[24] Capt. Summerlin owned the land where the town of Lake City is now and he was a whig in politics, so was Judge Lancaster. In those days whigs loved one another better—much better—than democrats and republicans love each other now days.

It went on, and on, as Lancaster 'till the coming forth of one David Levy [Yulee], a democrat and one James M. Baker, a whig, and they loved one another. David was sent to the U. S. Senate and James M. to the House of Congressmen. When James M. came back to frontier life, full of refined memories, he cast about him for a new name for his home town and then it took very naturally, to the name of Lake City on account of the lakes in Capt. Summerlin's field and the continued presence of the alligators. Joe Smith and the Mormons were about that time building Salt Lake City and there were some objection to calling the place Lake City but these objections were overcome in time and Lake City was adopted.[25]

The war between the North and South came on, in due time, and regular order and, with it great changes. Among the changes was the smashing of the whig party; nearly all the whigs turned democrats and James M. amongst the rest. David changed also in the meantime from Levy to Yulee but he swung to James M. and James M. swung to David and David had James M. made a judge and moved him from Lake City to Fernandina. That is the way it come to be Lake City from Alligator, but as to the motives of the old Indian mother for calling her son Alligator I am at a profound loss for an answer, arn't you?

David died in New York after selling his belongings in Florida for three millions of dollars. His wife died in Washington some years before his passing away. They left some children but Florida knows them no more. Most everybody that dealt with David, come out short of everything but experience. James M. Baker died in Fernandina, and those of the name yet living are solid. Capt. Summerlin died in Lake City on the 15th of January 1848, leaving many children and grand children; lots of 'em and they have managed to keep out of the jails and chain gangs. Some are poor and others wealthy, but all of them respectable as the world goes, and I say truthfully that, not one of 'em is named Alligator.

Very Sincerely yours,

ANO DOMNI 1835.

VIII

How Old Times
Argue against a
New Capital

When George G. Keen recommenced writing for his northeast Florida audience on October 15, 1900, he received inspiration from an ongoing debate—one as old as the state—about moving the capital from Tallahassee to Jacksonville. Like so many East Florida pioneers, Keen resented each and every dollar taken from him as taxes by the government, and it was beyond him to understand why he would be asked to pay to relocate the seat of government. To add force to his arguments he founded them deeply and personally in area history, even finding a connection with the weaving of homespun clothing and the manufacture of rope.

From *The Florida Index,* October 19, 1900.

BROTHER. DON'T DO IT.

Ketch All, Oct. 15, 1900

Brother Caldwell:—A big word is as easy spoken as a little one, as you know.

I can't look down the stream of time as the prophets David, Isaiah and others did, and tell what is going to happen one hundred years hence, so I must speak of the past and the present.

Tallahassee was established as the capital of the Territory of Florida in 1823, the location having been chosen by a commission consisting of Dr. W[illiam] H. Simmons and John L. Williams, who were appointed by the Government for that purpose, and it was the most appropriate place at that time in the Territory of Florida, and for the following reasons, viz:

All the inhabitants at that time were living West of the Suwannee river, and East of said river was a wild Indian Territory; they did not want any capital in theirs.

On the 15th day of October, 1830, my father moved here and settled seven miles North of Lake City in the land of flowers, bringing me, a kid, along with him and I am here yet, (thankful to an all-wise providence) and he was the seventh man living in the vicinity of Lake City; the most happy people on earth.

The people from the older states continued to move in till 1835, when war was declared by the Seminole Indians against the Territory of Florida which ended in 1842.

Now we must be represented in the legislature so Col. Robert Brown of Suwannee Shoals, and Joseph Dyal[l] of Pine Grove neighborhood was elected. [In 1835 Robert Brown indeed was elected to represent Columbia County in the territorial council. Joseph Dyall was not; however, he likely accompanied Brown to the capital to secure his commission as county judge.[26]] Going to Tallahassee was to be thought about; they had to go on horseback, and the distance was considered 150 miles, and they knew there was neither hotel nor boarding house to be found when they got there, and the chance to sleep was to camp out, but they were willing to do that, they were accustomed to that kind of a life.

Now for their dressing. Their coat, pants, vest and shirts was made at home out of their own raising of cotton. The cotton was gathered, and the seed picked out with their fingers. Next, their wives carded, spun, warped[,] wove and made the cloth and then made the clothes that their husbands wore when they went to Tallahassee to make laws for us.

The men had to do something, what was it? Tan cow hides and deer skins and then make their own shoes. Was that all? No, next they done was to get the bud from the cabbage palmetto tree and plait it and sew it together in the form of a hat and it looked nice. Now the clothes, hats and shoes are ready for any emergency.

The next thing to be considered is a pair of saddle bags, a quart cup and a pint cup, one for a coffee boiler and the other for a drinking cup. Next thing that is wanted is cloth enough to make a wallet that will hold half a bushel of shelled corn. Yet there is something else wanted, and that was a rope to tie their horses. They cut the bush off the cattle's tails and threw it into a pile till they got a sufficient quantity and with the aid of a forked stick they formed this hair into a rope that would hold any Buffalo that ever traversed the black hills of Arizona. Now they are ready to start for the seat of Government when the time comes for their departure, which is in the near future. The day before they start their wives cooks up as much provision as they can carry and put it in the saddle bags and roast coffee and beat it in a mortar with a pestle to last them for the term.

The day has arrived for their departure; grub in the saddle bags; corn in the wallet; the rope tied around the horses neck; cup and boiler tied to saddle. Now they saddle their horses, kiss their wives good-bye, mount their horses and off for Tallahassee like a hot shot in a shovel. No tickets in this thing.

Maj. [Joseph B.] Watts is elected from Madison county; they stop with him that night and the next morning the three start together and others join them. [Watts, a prominent Hamilton Countian, was not elected to the council in 1835. Rather, William Miles Hunter Sr. represented Hamilton, and Archibald D. McNeill stood for Madison.[27]]

Now they are in Tallahassee. Do they inquire for a hotel? No, they the members, ride out of town to a convenient place for wood and water, dismount and strike camp. Each one while in Tallahassee buys a black quart bottle full of whiskey, all of those bottles are called Hanner. After looking after their horses one of the men would say, "Boys, let's kiss Hanner and then eat dinner, what you say?" "All right," says every one. Brother how would you have liked that?

Now they lounge around till bedtime. Let's take a look in their bedroom. What do we see? We see the earth is their bedding and the sky is their covering. ($1,000,000 for State capital to be built by a people that's bowing down by a little heavier [load] of taxes than they can carry.) Brother, you know that I am telling the truth. Tax-payers land is sold for its taxes and never has been redeemed by the owners for they were not able to do it, but others was able, and redeemed it and the proper owners lost it. Am telling the truth? If I am telling a fat squirrel, say so, and I will think the more of you.

Oh, great gravy! I had got off the subject, I must go back to my text and see what the Honorable members are doing. When we get to camp the members are rolled up in blankets with their a saddle for a pillow, as sound asleep as if they were in the Central Hotel in New York.

They would rise up and all hands would kiss Hanner to cut the cob webs out of their throats; then for a wash, make coffee and eat breakfast, feed and water their horses, proceed to the State house and to business.

They held short sessions, made good and wholesome laws and no technicalities, as we have now, by which numbers of felons escape the chain gang, received $4, per day and no mileage. (Now its $6, per day and ten cents a mile going and coming and they can go and come for 4 cents a mile, but they put on the other 6 cent per mile just for luck.)

Our present State capital cost the State of Florida $164,000. I was walking the streets of Lake City the other day when I heard a gentleman say, "we are going to move the State capital to Jacksonville." I paid but, little attention to it, for I didn't see how it could be done, for I have seen it and its bigger than the Central House in Lake City. About a week afterwards there was quite a commotion among the railroad employees; I ran out to see what caused the trouble and there stood three engines and about one hundred cars, all headed for Tallahassee.

Oh, yes, now I see, they are going to bring down the state capitol. I was anxious to see how they loaded it. The cars failed to bring it; I inquired the cause why they didn't bring it and one of the boys said: "Aint you go[t] no sense? They can't bring the house, they will change the location thats all." If that be the case where will the legislators meet in April? "At Tallahassee of course." Then what? "Oh, you are a goose. We will build a new capitol at Jacksonville." Who will pay for it? "Stuff, I don't like to talk to a man as stupid as you are." Tell me please for I want to know.

"It will be done in this way. The state will issue, say $1,000,000 worth of interest bearing bonds and with that money the state capitol will be built." Won't we, the citizens, have these bonds to pay? "No, the state pays her own debts, just the same as you and I pay ours. You never will have a dollar of it to pay." But I thought the state was already indebted? "Well, she is in debt a little." How much you suppose? "Oh, I don't know, I suppose a million or so."

That is what I call a lots! "That's not much for a state to owe." But if she issues a million more bonds that's $2,000,000. "That won't be a hill of beans, for the immigration that will come in two years will pay all the state's indebtedness and leave a margin." Look here, what will become of the present state capital? "Leave it where it is, its nothing but an old shack and looks more like an Indian wigwarm than a state capitol." It looks like a waste of money to leave it there and get nothing for it. "Don't let that bother you."

See here, while I think of it. Where does the State get her money from? "From the tax payers of the state, of course." What state do you mean, Florida or Georgia? "You have got the least sense of any man that I ever talked with. Florida is the state." Well, it looks like the people will have the debt to pay, and not the state, like you said. The people pay the state and the state pays the bond holders. Where does the people get the money from that they pay their taxes with? They raise corn, cotton, beef cattle, meat hogs, build houses[,] work in saw mills and any kind of work that they can do to get the money.

Let's make a suppose case; suppose a man has not got the money when his taxes are due, then what: The collector will sell something that he has got, say horse, or a cow that is if he don't own any land. When will the owner get the money that horse or cow was sold for? Never in life. What does the tax payer get in exchange for all this money he has paid out for taxes? He gets the tax collectors receipt. What can he get for this receipt? Nothing. If we move the capital, how long will we have to be paying these taxes? About 25 years. How much would it be on the $1000 worth of property a year? About $20, and the thing lasts 25 years. Yes. It would be a mighty big pile of money at the end of 25 years; I think it will be about $500 on each $4,000 worth of property that a man owns. Don't we ever get anything back for all that we have paid out? No not one cent. I think that would be a poor legacy to leave for our children.

If we don't move the capital will we have these big taxes to pay? No, nothing more than the common taxes that we are now paying. What profit will it be to the poor people of the state of Florida to put this additional tax on them? None in the world.

Now my christian friend, I am going to vote for the State Capitol to be and remain at Tallahassee for the next hundred years, just to keep off the high taxes. I want you to vote so too. St. Augustine, Ocala and Jacksonville to the contrary, notwithstanding.

Editor John M. Caldwell of the *Lake City Florida Index* served as president of the Florida Press Association when George G. Keen died in 1902. (Collection of Canter Brown Jr.)

Frontier developer, soldier, politician, and storyteller William H. Kendrick (Collection of Canter Brown Jr., courtesy of Pat Adams)

Hillsborough County cattleman William Brinton Hooker, who supported George G. Keen's plan to marry Martha Hooker (Collection of Canter Brown Jr., courtesy of Kyle S. VanLandingham)

Florida's Cracker frontier settlers typically lived in log cabins. Often a structure consisted of a single room and was called a "single pen." This "double pen" cabin, built by Polk County's Hill family during the 1850s, offered more living space than many families could afford. (Collection of Canter Brown Jr.)

This drawing, published not long after the Second Seminole War's beginning in late 1835, illustrates the terrible violence perpetrated by all factions during the seven-year conflict. (Courtesy of Florida Archives)

George G. Keen's teacher Daniel Gillett married one of Keen's fellow students, Molcy M. Hair. They are portrayed here together. (Courtesy of Marvis R. Snell)

George G. Keen's friend Benjamin Moody, with his second wife, Lydia Carlton Hendry Moody (Collection of Canter Brown Jr., courtesy of Eugenia Dillon Allen)

Sarah Pamela Williams (Collection of
James M. Denham, courtesy of Helen
Ives)

Sarah Pamela Williams's father, John
Lee Williams, who wrote Florida's first
published history and helped to choose
Tallahassee as the site for its capital
(Courtesy of Historic Pensacola Preser-
vation Board)

Washington M. Ives, half brother to
Sarah Pamela Williams (Collection of
James M. Denham, courtesy of Helen
Ives)

Capt. William Cone, legendary surveyor and Georgia-Florida frontiersman, represented Columbia County's families in Florida's territorial house of representatives during 1841–1842 and in the Florida Senate during 1854–1856. It was said that "no man had more friends than 'Old Billy Cone.'" (Courtesy of the Florida Archives)

James McNair Baker was a native of North Carolina and moved to Columbia County about 1849. An accomplished lawyer, he served in the Confederate Senate and later sat as an associate justice to the Florida Supreme Court, 1866–1868. Baker County was named for him. (Courtesy of Florida Supreme Court)

Gov. Harrison Reed appointed George Gillett Keen justice of the peace for Columbia County on May 23, 1870. (Courtesy of the Florida Archives)

George Gillett Keen's brief and tumultuous tenure as sheriff of Columbia County ended on July 11, 1873, with this resignation letter. (Courtesy of the Florida Archives)

IX

Tricky Politics and Gunfights as Humor

In 1900 George G. Keen celebrated his seventy-third birthday, and his age began to catch up with him. As suggested by his intermittent submissions to *The Florida Index* after March, he suffered increasingly poor health. Still, he could be prodded to exercise his pen when the mood struck him. Two letters, written in December 1900, stemmed from a Jacksonville newspaper's story about one of Keen's boyhood friends, William Harney "Captain Bill" Kendrick. A celebrity throughout East Florida, Kendrick had dabbled in cattle, politics, land development, and public speaking, all with a great sense of humor that Floridians found endearing.[28] When published in November 1900, his short article of reminiscences prodded Keen, first, to offer some corrections and, then, to write further about the nature of antebellum politics and other facets of the rough-and-tumble life of Florida's 1840s frontier country.

From the *Jacksonville Florida Times-Union and Citizen,*
November 4, 1900.

FLORIDA CAMPAIGNS OF THE LONG AGO.

Captain William Kendrick Relates Incidents of Contests
Between Whigs and Democrats Before the
Days of Railroads and Telegraph, and
Candidates Rode Mule-Back Through the State.

Reminiscences of old campaigns and life in the early part of the eighteenth century was the topic of conversation by Captain William Kendrick, better known perhaps as "Captain Bill," when a reporter called on him yesterday. Captain Bill is seventy-seven years old, and has lived in Florida all his life, long before Florida became one of the States in the Union; or, as the aged gentleman puts its, "In the Territorial days."

Born on the banks of the Suwannee river in 1823, his boyhood was spent among the cotton fields, listening to the songs of the plantation negroes and hunting among the hammocks and piney woods, which in those days abounded in game.

"I remember," said Captain Bill, coming through Jacksonville in 1828 with my father. There was only one house in sight at that time, and I guess it was the only house in Jacksonville. It was owned by a man named Hogans. My father blew his horn loud and long, and a farm hand named Hendrick came out and bid us welcome to the house. We were then on our way to St. Augustine, and I remember that when we arrived we found just half a "dozen families living there."

"But talking of politics. Election days then were great times. There were no long tickets with thirty or forty names. Everybody took a piece of paper and wrote the name of his candidate in pencil, and the ballot box was two hats, one inverted and placed over the other. The polls were opened at 10 o'clock and closed at 5. There were only two parties in the State then, the Whigs and the Democrats. My father was a Democrat, and I was born a Democrat and have been one ever since. Well, after election was over, we used to gather around the store and wait for the returns from the local election, and then we always had to have some fights. Everybody fought then with their fists; no knives or guns were used, and after an argument, the talkers would take off their coats and go at it in fine style; while everybody else stood by and cheered their favorite. Then everybody made friends and went away, having had a good time.

The first Delegate in Congress from Florida was Mr. Davi[d] Levy, who afterwards had his name changed to Yulee, which was his mother's maiden name.[29] There were only four State Senators east and south of the Suwanee river. They were Colonel [Francis Littlebury] Dancy, a man named [Erasmus Darwin] Tracey, Q. W. [Giles U.] Ellis and George U. McClennen [George E. McClellan], and in the election they ran against Judge [Joseph B.] Lancaster, Colonel [John M.] Hanson and two other members of the Whig party. I remember this election well. I voted for Judge Lancaster, who was a Whig, on grounds of personal friendship, and when I ran for Legislature several years later, the fact that I had supported a Whig defeated me, but I will tell you all about that later.

CANVASSED FLORIDA ON A MULE.

Candidates had a hard time in those days. I remember David Yulee coming to my father to borrow a mule on which he canvassed the State. Indians were around then, and they were warlike, having been driven away from their regular camps further south, and a man canvassed the State with a gun in hand and his eyes and ears alert for the roaming savage who hated the white man. Judge [Benjamin Alexander] Putnam was the leading Whig in Florida in those days, and it was a hot campaign, which took nearly all summer, and, then, when the vote was cast, there weren't a thousand ballots in the box. But we lived a long way apart in Territorial days. Then there was the wait for election returns. Sometimes it was a week before we ever heard from some of the precincts. There were not many railroads in the United States then, and the returns were coming in on horses or muleback for three of four weeks. It was almost a year sometimes before we knew what had taken place in the States at the elections, and in the Territory, some of the returns had to be brought hundreds of miles in a boat and on foot. Tampa bay was then in Alachua, and the county seat was Noonansville [Newnansville], which is now Gainesville [actually, the town of Alachua].

BILLY BOWLEGS AND THE SIX-YEARS WAR.

"You know that Florida was largely settled by Georgians and North and South Carolinians, and a few Virginians. When the Indian War broke out, in 1835, we all had to fight, and it was not until 1841 that the war ended, and a treaty was made with Billy Bowlegs, who was then King of the Seminoles. He was to move south of Peace creek, which is near Bartow, and all whites were to keep north of the territory granted to him. Benton's armed occupation act was then passed by the Senate, and all persons who were able to bear and carry arms were granted 160 acres of land by the Territorial government. I had 160 acres granted to me, and moved into Hernando County, which was then a portion of Alachua County. The country was still sparsely settled in 1844, and it was during that year that I entered politics. I ran for the Legislature [in 1850] on the Democratic ticket, against [Robert D.] Bradley, Democrat, and [Joel L.] Lockhart, Whig.[30] I was defeated by one vote, getting 51 votes, while each of my opponents received 52. The men that didn't vote for me used the argument that I had voted for Judge Lancaster, who was a Whig, and they wouldn't give me their support. Well, the funny part of that election follows. Both Bradley and Lockhart went to Legislature, and both claimed the seat, and the Governor sent them both home, telling them that neither of them had been elected, and so we were not represented in Legislature that time.

HOME MANUFACTURES IN THE OLD DAYS.

"My grant of 160 acres was within a quarter of a mile of what is now Dade City, and I lived there for nineteen years. Florida was then a cattle-raising State mainly, but we raised in a small way almost everything, and the women folks spun and wove their own cloth. I guess that Florida then produced more of what was consumed at home than she has ever done since, and really all that we had to buy was coffee and salt.

"Then the treaty after the Six-Years War was broken, and another terrible war resulted, which lasted a year. In 1849 a white man named [William] McCullough crossed the Peace river with his family, and was building a log house when the Indians swept down upon him, and massacred the entire family.[31] Hundreds of Indians were killed, and many whites saw the last of Florida at that time. It was not until a year later that peace was again declared, and Billy Bowlegs agreed to take his tribe south of the Caloosahatchee river, which he did, and peace once more reigned.

"Again the white man broke his faith with the Indian, and again war was abroad in the land. Well do I remember that terrible report which came to Fort Myers two days after Christmas [1855]. On Christmas Day word came to the military station at Fort Myers from the Governor ordering Lieutenant [George L.] Hartsuff to take thirty-three cavalrymen and make an examination of the Everglades. The order was contrary to the treaty with the Indians, and the first night out several hundred Indians swept down upon the camp, and massacred all except two and captured the horses. The two who escaped were Lieutenant Hartsuff, who jumped into the creek, where he lay all night among the alligators and the water moccasins with nothing but his nose above the surface of the water and another man, who swam across the creek and escaped in the darkness, bringing into Fort Myers the terrible news.[32]

ONLY TWO ESCAPED THE MASSACRE.

"A large armed relief party was sent out to find the bodies of the massacred soldiers, and bring in any that might have survived. Lieutenant Hartsuff was found, but he alone and the soldier, who had carried the news to the settlement were all that escaped. War followed again, and every man who was old enough to fight went out against the Indians, who were protecting their rights and who never broke an agreement they made.

"When the war was over, I again entered politics, and was the first Democrat elected to the Senate [under the constitution of 1868?], and served there seven sessions [1868–1872].

"I forgot to tell you about my own company of soldiers; I am getting old now, and get ahead of my story. January 1, 1856, I formed a company of soldiers, and we entered the United States service, serving two years and seven months. This was known as the Billy Bowlegs war [or Third Seminole War].

"In 1845, the Territory was taken into the Union, everybody being in favor of the change, and the election was as quiet and as orderly as an election ever was.

"I am getting to be an old man now, but I would like well to live over the Territorial days again.

"Oh, for one month of youthful joy.
Give back to me my thirteenth spring.
I would rather dance a bare-legged boy
Than reign a gray-haired king."

From *The Florida Index,* December 14, 1900.

A CORRECTION.

Ketch All, Dec. 1st 1900.

Brother Caldwell:—I see an article from Capt. Bill Kendrick. It appeared in the Sunday Times-Union and Citizen, Nov. 4, 1900. It was based mostly on facts but not in toto.

Old timers must tell the truth, and write the truth. But I must correct Brother Kendrick in a few instances though they are minor errors.

He says at the time he first went to what is now called Jacksonville, there was only one family living there. He was right, and that mans name was Arch Hogans, and the place was called Cowford, on the St. Johns River.[33] Hogans sold out to Isaiah D Hart, the same man that died in the early 70s while occupying the Gubernatorial chair of the State of Fla.[34] He also was the first man that ever put up a store at the Cowford on the St. Johns River, then the place was of some importance and the name of Jacksonville was adopted and holds it till this day.[35]

SEE THE CORRECTION.

Brother Bill says that Tampa Bay was in Alachua, and the capital was at Newnansville, there is where he makes the first mistake. Newnansville was the Capital of the county, but Tampa Bay never was in Alachua county. But Tampa Bay was in the extreme southwestern portion of this State, at a place called Point Pinallas [Pinellas] and where Tampa now stands was called Fort Brook[e]. In due course of time it was ascertained that Ft. Brook was the most appropriate place of the two, and they drop[p]ed the name of Ft. Brook and called it Tampa Bay and it wears the name yet, and the first Tampa is now called Old Tampa, and is as dead as Tallahassee would have been in fifty years, if the boys had not turned out like men and voted like men to let the Capital be and remain where it is.

(Bless the Lord.)

SECOND MISTAKE.

Brother Bill claims a six years war with the Territory of Florida, and the Seminole Indians. While it was a seven years war. War was declared in Nov. 1835 and ended in 1842. (I was going to school at the time war was declared.) He gives Ellis' name [and] also McClellan['s] wrong. Giles U. Ellis and Geo. E. McClellan was their name.

I write this, hoping Brother Bill will see it. I was visiting Relatives in Hillsborough and Hernando counties. The Mizells was the name of those in Hernando county and while there the election day [October 7, 1850] come off, and the night before election I stopped with Ben Moody who had married a female cousin of mine.[36] Cho-cha-chat-tee Hammock was quite a prominent place at that time and there was a church house on the side of the Hammock called Mount Zion, that was the voting place. There was not as much red tape used at elections them days as is now and I was allowed to vote there and did so.

Capt. Enoch Mizell, Ben Moody and Luke Mo[o]re was the Inspectors and I was sworn in as clerk. Bro. Bill was there, and was a candidate. Every man voted just as he pleased, no man had any right to object, tickets were all put in open. I could not tell how the thing was going. Bro. Bill became excited to a great extent. He was a good talker, and done his talking.

There was a man named Sebe Garrison. Brother Bill did all in his power to get Sebe to vote for him. Sebe would not promise, but convey[ed] the idea that he would do it. This continued till 12 o'clock. Sebe held his vote. Brother Bill said, "Sebe I will bet you five dollars that you don't vote for me to day. Sebe says, "I will take that bet." Now the bet is confirmed. Sebe picked up one of Brother Bills tickets and showed it to every man in the house then past in his vote for William Kendrick and won the five dollars.

I considered that a five dollar vote, and it was more than I made and I worked all day, and till after dark.

Sebe began to laugh and kept it up till the house became uproarus and I couldn't hear the men as they handed in their votes. Capt. Mizell threatened to tie Sebe before [t]he qui[e]t was restored. When all the precincts was heard from, Brother Bill was beaten [by] one vote just as he said, and the other two made a tie.

Brother Bill was raised on Hamilton side of Suwannee river, near White Springs, and I was raised on Columbia side nine miles from said spring.

Brother Bills Father [James Kendrick] was the first man that killed an Indian after war was declared, and it come about in this way. The captain put up a reward of twenty five dollars for the first Indian skelp. While the company was marching on foot, and not expecting any danger Brother Bills Father saw something drop down behind a log and he thought it was an Indian so he kept his secret to himself as he wanted $25, and went for the log. Not thinking the Indian would try to kill him, the Indian rose up and snap[p]ed his gun at him and then run. Now its Kendricks time, and he made use of it and shot the Indian dead in his tracks, and tore of his skelp in a moment of time, claiming the $25, and the Capt. paid it.

Brother Bill, you are right when you say you want to be back in your 13th year of age. I am 73 years old, and if I had ten million of dollars I would give every cent of it to be back in my 13th year with all my faculties that I had then and the experience that I have now. I am sure I would pursue a different course.

No use in talking old boy, we have got to go on, for that is the way of all the world.

Oh, if the age of a man was 150 years how glad I would be, 1st 50 years to learn some sense, 2nd 50 years to make his property and the 3rd 50 to enjoy it. Wouldn't that be nice?

From *The Florida Index,* January 11, 1901.

A MEAN TRICK, BUT A GOOD DEED.

Ketch All, Dec. 29, 1900.

Brother Caldwell:—This will inform you that I ate my 74th Christmas dinner last Tuesday and am thankful that I yet are in the land of the living.

Now I want to tell you that in the 40's and 50's politics ran high.

It was Whig and Democrats in them days and the war with the Seminole Indians was a thing of the past. So was our going to Jefferson, Ga., to do our trading.

Jacksonville was a town of some magnitude and our trade was turned in that direction. I[saiah] D. Hart, [Cyrus] Bisbee, Jake Hickman and John H. Gunby were the leading merchants of the town. John Adams was clerking for J. H. Gunby, who was his brother-in-law. Keep your eye on John Adams.

In them days us boys held together, to insult one meant to insult all. I will give you a few of our names: Jack [Andrew Jackson] Keen, Elam Daniels, Bill Godfrey, Wiley Keen, Aaron Daniels, [John] Arthur Jones, Sherod Keen, Jeff Daniels, William [R.] Keen, Elisha Sapp, A. J. T. Wright, John Keen, Bill Curry, Elijah Hunter, Jack[son] Gillet[t], Frank Raulerson and Dave Raulerson, and I don't know how many more.

We were to remain in the bonds of friendship and no man was to whip one of us. But says you, how did John Adams become one of you? why, in this way: we went to Jacksonville a trading; he made our acquaintance and thought us the most jolly fellows he ever saw, and wanted to be one of us, so A. J. T. give him a clerkship, and he come to Alligator and we took him in and a good fellow he was.

About this time three strangers come in. One's name was A. R. Bexley, he was a Doctor; second one was N. M. Nostrand, third one was Hugh G. Hunter. They were business men.

Now we must have an election. We must have a sheriff, and clerk of circuit court. The democrats nominated Charles Fitchell [Fitchett], for the office of sheriff and he had no opponent. Now let me tell you: General Wm. B. Ross lived two miles west of the court house. He owned about 125 negroes and he had a brother-in-law named Thomas B. Fitchpatrick [Fitzpatrick]; he gave him his chuck, raiment, lodging and $6.00 per month to look after the mules and horses. Any one that was ugly was said to be as ugly as old Tom B. Fitchpatrick. He was about forty years old, over six feet high and weighed 130 pounds and never spoke to any one unless he had business with them.

I saw that Fitchett was not going to have any opponent. I wrote the following:

NOTICE.

The friends of Thos. B. Fitchpatrick take great pleasure in announcing him as a candidate for the office of Sheriff of Columbia county at the ensuing election.

Oct. 10th, 1845. MANY VOTERS.
1776–that meant Whig.

I wrote this notice, believing it would create a big laugh, at the same time I knew if my father found out that I wrote it he would wottle me all over the back yard; but he must not know it, so I tacked it up on a country grog shop in the darkness when no one saw me.

The next day it was discovered by the whig party, they picked up and went to electioneering, but I didn't know whether he was a whig or democrat. Hugh G. Hunter was nominated for Justice of the Peace, and S[tirling] Scarborough for clerk of the circuit court.

I have told you how old Tom B. looked, now I will say something about Scarborough. He looked like he had been in bed for six weeks and never felt good one minute in his life, and so weak that he could not pull an old crow off the roost, and we didn't think he could spell Baker, but everybody both male and female loved him, because he appeared to love everybody. Hugh G. Hunter was a fine looking man, he drank whiskey and the other two didn't.

THE ELECTION IS OVER.

Old Tom B. is Sheriff, Scarborough is clerk, and Hugh G. Hunter is Justice of the Peace.[37] Now comes the tug of war. Who is to show Scarborough how to run the office?

Court convened in a short time. Now the new officers comes on deck. Old Tom was dressed the finest of any man I ever saw in my life. Hunter was very well dressed, but S. Scarborough come in with his Sunday clothes on, for he didn't have any clothes but Sunday clothes, for he bought his every day clothes, and Sunday clothes off of the same piece; don't you see the point?

Now Hunter is out side, but old Tom come to the front, and ran the court with all the dignity that S[herman] Conant ever ran the United States court for the Northern District of Fla., at Jacksonville. As to old Scarborough (as he was now called) he knew more about the duties of clerk than every man in Columbia county put together.

Suwannee, Baker and Bradford counties was all Columbia county. The Sheriff was Sheriff, Tax Assessor and collector. The perquisites of all these offices aggregated $5000.00.

Don't you see I done a mean trick by nominating Old Tom, but it was a good deed by taking him from the mule lot and putting $5000, in his grasp.

THE FIRST DUEL.

A. J. T. Wright kept a fiddle in his store house for the amusement of the boys. We were in the house talking friendly. Now I go back to John Adams; in he walked and said something to Bill Godfrey; they got to disputing; pretty soon Adams give Godfrey the lie, and Godfrey slapped his face. Adams says: "Godfrey I challenge you for a duel." Godfrey says: "I accept." Adams says: "Chose your weapons," G. says "pistols," G. says: "Set your time and place," Adams says: "Next Saturday 10 o'clock, a.m., and in front of Wright's Store house door." Adams says: "Chose your second," G. says: "Arthur Jones." Adams says: "I chose Elisha Sapp." G. Says: "Chose your dress." Adams says: "White." G. says: "I will take black," and we will leave the balance to our seconds. "All right," says Adams.

Now, we will go back for N. M. Nostrand. He is teaching the Alligator school. He goes to Squar [Squire] Hunter for warrants for A. & G. On examination they find [incorrectly that] there never has been any legislation on dueling, so its no violation to fight a duel.

Us boys wanted to see the fight, we had heard of duels being fought and wanted to see one. We did not think they could hit each other with a pistol and we thought there was lots of fun in it. The day come round. All parties interested was present.

The grounds laid off, 10 paces, they had two pistols apiece. Jones was to give the word of command and they were to fire at the word between one and three, and advance till each had fired twice, but neither was to shoot the other on the ground. All are now ready. One, two, Adams is in falling condition but fired his pistol in the air. G. ran up to shoot Adams while lying on the ground. Sapp cries out, "foul," Jones runs up hollowing hold, Godfrey, hold! Adams is lying on his back and speechless and covered with blood. Their s[e]conds picked up Adams and laid him on Wright's Stoop, and sent for the sheriff. The Doctor being away he couldn't get medical aid. He was shot in the breast. We thought it fatal. N. M. Nostrand had the warrant, leaving blank space for name wrote out.

The sheriff come but made no attempt to arrest Godfrey. He stood round chewing his tobacco like a goat not being excited one bit.

The boys had a fiddle tune that was a favorite. It was like this, "Old Jawbone can knock and tell, That everybody is a doing well." Sapp, Adam's second, walked in the house[,] picked up the fiddle and went to playing old Jaw-bone. Up jumped Adams and run into the house and commenced dancing like pouring dry peas on a cowhide for five minutes, fetched a long breath, saying, "boys that was nice," and sat down. The sheriff says well, well, and walked off. Hugh G., and N. M., sneaked off home, seeing it was all a hoax.

This sham fight was made up between Godfrey and Adams. Godfrey had a bottle of red ink in his pocket, Adams was dressed in white, and when Godfrey pretended to be trying to shoot him on the ground he was pouring the red ink on him, which looked to an excited crowd as pure blood. So ended the first duel that was ever fought in Columbia county.

One word for Dr. Bexley: He attended Wm. Simmon[s]'s wife 11 months, and charged him a peck of seed peas, and Simmons paid it.

X

Reconstruction-Era Justice

In January 1901 George G. Keen turned away from his daunting supply of antebellum Columbia County tales to author a single letter concerning the Reconstruction period. Tellingly, his series of reminiscences omits reference to the Civil War, an occurrence so complicated for Floridians, generally, and the Keen family, in particular, that George decided to leave well enough alone. He had served for a time as a private soldier in Company B, Fifth Florida Infantry (CSA), but he departed its ranks without leave in late 1863 or early 1864. As also was true for several other Keen men, the desertion may have been prompted by factors beyond personal disenchantment with the war and military service. George's cousin William Keen, an enlisted man in Company K, Third Florida Infantry, was arrested in Columbia County in early 1864 as a deserter, returned to his unit in Tennessee, and executed by firing squad. As one historian put it, "Keen's execution caused great consternation among the Florida troops." [38]

In the post–Civil War years George Keen's political inclinations led him into the Republican Party. On May 23, 1870, Gov. Harrison Reed appointed him justice of the peace, a post he held until July 1872. For six months following November 1870 he also sat on the board of county commissioners. As of May 29, 1871, Keen acted on an interim basis as Columbia County's tax assessor, and he continued to do so until March 1873, when Gov. Ossian B. Hart appointed him sheriff of the politically volatile and sometimes violent county. Hart's action set off a firestorm. Friends of former sheriff Warren Bush—a man connected with a local Ku Klux Klan–type vigilante organization—visited the homes of Keen and other new appointees "between midnight and 4 a.m., and riddle[d] them with bullets." Keen and his counterparts fled the county as the "Lake City Outrage" became public knowledge. The governor reacted firmly, ordering Lake City's streets to be patrolled for months by armed black militiamen. Still, Keen declined his commission as sheriff when he and his family returned. On March 10, 1874 (eight days before Hart's death), Hart reappointed Keen justice of the peace, a position he occupied for a good part of the remainder of his life. In 1901 Keen wrote about his experiences in that office for the entertainment of northeast Floridians.[39]

From *The Florida Index,* January 25, 1901.

MY FIRST J. P. COURT.

Ketch All, January 14th, 1901.

Brother Caldwell:—I am a Justice of the Peace, and have been acting in that capacity from the 14th day of January 1871, down to the present period.

What I want to tell you about is the first court I ever held, and you can judge from my feelings in that court what kind of a judicial officer Columbia county has had for the last twenty eight years.

At the beginning of my official career, Capt. [Charles] R. King was State Attorney and Dr. S[amuel] T. Day was County Judge. I received my commission and sat down to wait developments.

Up to this time I never had read a page of law, neither had I ever been in a magistrate's court, nor seen an affidavit, nor warrant emanating from a Justice's court.

While mediating, Mrs. Jane Joyce, a widow lady called on me for a warrant. I asked her the nature of the case and she said it was a case of bastardy. Now, imagine my feelings, for I can't express them, for I never had seen a warrant in my life.

I went for Capt. King. He wrote something and gave it to me, but I did not understand it, so I carried it to Dr. Day, asking him if it was a warrant. "Warrant, (h———l)" said he, "that's nothing but an affidavit, but I will write the warrant for you." "Do if you please," said I.

Now the papers are drawn, what must I do with them? Give them to the constable. Who is the constable? Don Tompkins. Who must he arrest? Pink Williams. Which paper [do I] give him? Both of them. Then what must I do with him? Give him a trial and bail him over to circuit court. When will he catch him? I don't know. go on. I went, and found Don Tompkins and I gave him the papers hoping he never would find Pink Williams.

In about three hours Don returned saying all parties was ready for trial. The back room of Col. A. J. T. Wright's store house was the place where magistrate's held their courts.

When I got there the room was crowded to overflowing and Col. Bob [Robert W.] Broome was among the throng. I went in smoking, and took my seat with my hat on. After remaining there about five minutes Don walked up and said in a whisper, "take off your hat and lay down your pipe." I done so and sat there like a bump on a log. Now the audience began to giggle. I looked round but could not see anything to laugh at. Don tiptoed up to me and said, "open court." I said, "what must I say!" He said, "you say Mr. constable open court.["] The crowd were laughing fit to kill themselves and not a thing could I see that was amusing.

I spoke with a loud voice, ["]Mr. constable, open court." Don stepped to the door and spoke with a ringing voice, "Hear ye, hear ye, hear ye, the honorable magistrate's court in and for Columbia county is now open, his Honor, Justice Keen presiding, those having business come forward and the same shall be heard, God save the State and this Honorable court." There I sat, and the laughing increasing, every one in the house was tickled but me, and I thought they done so in all minor courts.

Don come back to me again and said, "arraign the prisoner." I said "what prisoners?" He said, "Pink Williams." How must I arraign him? He says, say, Say Pink Williams, stand up. I said Pink Williams. stand up. Up got Williams. There I sat and there stood Pink Williams looking at each other. neither of us said a word. I didn't know what to say. About this time the laughing become uproarous.

About this time Don stepped up and spoke softly in my ear saying read the charge. I said what charge? He said the affidavit. I didn't know which was the affidavit. I took the paper with the least writing on it, and it was the affidavit. I did'nt ask him if he was guilty or not guilty, but says Pink Williams I bind you in a bond in the sum of $200, for your appearance at the next term of the circuit court to be held in and for Columbia county. Col. Broome says your Honor he is my client, and I am his attorney I want to speak in his behalf. I said. Col. Broome you can't speak in my court.

You should have heard the loud laughter at that moment. I wanted to be ten miles from there. Pink Williams standing up like a stump. Up stepped Don, saying your Honor, tell the prisoner to set down. I said which one? Williams of course. I said Pink, set down, then the laugh was renewed.

Col. Broome says, will your honor take James W. Cathey, and another man equally as responsible? The court answered in the affirmative. The court made a move to rise, hold on said constable Tompkins. You must adjourn court. How can I adjourn court? You say, Mr. constable adjourn court. I spoke at the top of my voice, Mr. constable adjourn court. Don says, hear ye, hear ye, this Honorable court is now adjourned. Col. Broome says your Honor, I wish to speak with Mr. Williams in private. No said the court, you can't take Williams out of this room. The Col. says I will be responsible for him. Go on said the court.

The court didn't give the constable any instructions in regard to the prisoner, but the court burnt the wind for home, with the full determination never to hold court in that room any more, nor he never did.

On my way home I got to thinking about the way I conducted that court and why it amused the people so much, and then and there decided that I did not have sense enough to grease a gimlet if I had a pound of lard without greasing the handles, and that I never would have got out of that house had it not been for poor old Don Tompkins, peace be to his ashes. I did love the man, but he is gone the way of all the earth.

I reasoned with myself thusly, it is injury upon insult to have such a goose as I am in office. Now, if I was as well posted in law as Don Tompkins, I would be willing to take a seat on the supreme bench as chief Justice of the supreme court of the State of Fla., but I am not. nor never can be so. I will tender my resignation in the morning.

Brother, night always brings counsel, so next morning my mind had changed and I decided that the day had been when Daniel Webster had been as ignorant in law as I was, and I would read law three months and if I gained any information I would hold on to my commission, to the contrary I would quit.

With these thoughts in mind I looked on the jail door steps, and there set the widow Joyce, saying that Pink Williams had escaped the constable and gone, and she wanted me to catch Pink and put him in jail. I was jailer. and that I had a perfect right to do anything. I said if you don't leave here I will put you in jail. She left, and so did Pink Williams, and that was the last I ever heard of the case.

A short time afterwards, Bob Mohead [Morehead], and S[ilas] Niblack, (both colored) came into my office, with a case of seduction. I didn't know no more about it than a hog. Every lawyer, sheriff and constable had gone to a picnic, but Thomas T. Long. He and I were not on very good terms, but I went to him for information, and he spoke very short and said, (D—n it,) go to the statute. I didn't know what the statute was; now I am as far to sea as ever.

I was writing in a law office, the office of Bryson and King. I was sitting there trying to diverse [devise?] a plan to put off the case till next day when the bar would be in, and I could get the desired information. I opened a little book, not looking for information, but my eye caught the caption "Seduction."

I seized into, and began writing something that I called an affidavit, but the lawyers called it a roust-about. Next I wrote a warrant and charged Mohead $1.50 when I was not entitled to only 75 cents, but he paid it. All things are ready now and I appointed S. Niblack, a darkey, to execute the papers. The parties was in Baker county, but I didn't know it. Into Baker county my constable goes. caught the gal, but the man got away. The constable and prosecuting state witness returned, made their report, requesting that the case be dismissed at the expense of the plaintiff. The court agreed to it, and now you have the facts in the case of my first experience in the two first cases that I ever disposed of, and I think I done justice to the law and honor to myself. Don't you think so too, Brother?

XI

Lafayette County and the Murders of Lige Locklier and Jim Munden

The Florida Index of April 26, 1901, carried a public notice from publisher John M. Caldwell that he had sold the newspaper, a result of health problems. "I have done the best I could for the progress and prosperity of our town and county," he asserted, "and I indulge the hope that my labors have not been entirely fruitless." George Keen reacted by praising his old friend, while offering a measure of mild chastisement. In the process he explored his own understanding of the meaning of life and personal satisfaction, expressed in his inimitable style. When subsequent events delayed transfer of control of the paper, Caldwell urged Keen to continue his historical accounts. The old pioneer obliged with a letter dated July 9, in which he related one of his most fascinating stories, the 1859 murders in Lafayette County of Elijah Locklier and James Munden.

From *The Florida Index,* May 10, 1901.

"BLACK EYE" TALKS.

Ketch All, May 4th, 1901.
This way, brother Caldwell! I just called you back to tell you good bye. Good morning, brother Black Eye. Good morning brother Caldwell, how are you? Not well. How is it with you, sick as usual? Brothers, it's much your own fault that you never feel good. Why, is it? I see in several copies of the INDEX where Berry Raulerson, Wash [George Washington] Waldron, et al had furnished the INDEX crowd with fresh hog back bones, spare ribs, Irish potatoes and buttermilk, besides many other things. You see, you eat too much. A man of your age must know that an overcharge could bust a cannon, and to eat too much good grub would make a well man sick.

The father received his works, and pronounced it good, and very good, but says be temperate in all things, follow the admonitions of the Lord.

Brother, you spent your boyhood days in Lake City, leaving many warm friends here. After passing middle life you returned to the City of Lakes, finding many old friends who received you with open arms, and making hundreds of new friends who are loath to give you up.

Was that all that you done? Echo answers no, you established one of the best papers in the world, called THE FLORIDA INDEX, a more appropriate name could not have entered the mind of man and all the happenings of any note, from the Pacific to the Atlantic, and from Maine to Texas could be found in THE INDEX. And again, you showed the people here that they were sleeping over their rights. Look at the water works, electric lights, paved streets, the red hill road, the laundry, the dairy, machine shops and ice factory. I suppose it was here when you came, but when [George W.] Kinnison knew you were coming and would have an ice factory anyhow he thought he had as well build one or enlarge and improve the one which we had.

Telephones and delivery wagons came among the rest, and had you remained here one year longer you would have had a new court house and all the hyacinths removed from Desoto lake.

When a man dies his works do follow him.

The old court house will be here for at least two decades and hyacinths will remain where they are for some time to come.

My brother, men in one sense of the word are like forward corn and late corn. Plant a piece of corn, say the first of March and a piece the first of April, and the fodder on each piece will get ripe at the same time, notwithstanding there [is] a months difference in ages. Just so it is with you and I. The fodder is ripe and pulled, and the corn almost ready for the harvest. You have started out hunting the fountain of youth, thinking when you find it you will dip yourself nine times into it, and come forth feeling like you did when you were twenty-two years old.

Stop and consider. Ponce DeLeon spent five fortunes hunting the fountain of youth and died an old man, and if you and "I" ever die, we will die old men. There is only one way that I know for us to look young and that is, to fill up the wrinkles on our faces with tallow and then tab them over with magnolia balm, then we may look young, but we will have the grunts all the same.

My brother, buy your property back, and then stay here, and let us grunt it out on that line. We have worn out our usefulness and we will do as well here as anywhere else and a great deal better.

The laws of our State make obligatory on the children to take care of the parents in their old age, so you can call on your children for assistance, but what am I to do? I've got no children. You had better go slow, if you waste your living hunting the fountain of youth you will be ashamed to call on the boys for sustenance, as you are doing well enough, you had better let well enough alone.

Now, I have said all that I can think of to keep you from going, and if you do go watch my predictions. In side of twelve months you will write to the boys to send you something to eat. Of course they will do it, and what will it be? It will be a corn sack full of Providence potatoes and a two gallon jug full of syrup, and nothing else. I will be glad of it for you might have stayed here and done well and you would'nt do it.

When you get this provision you fell happy and will say, now wife, as we have plenty to eat, let us eat hearty and grow fat. After you have eaten a square meal of roast potatoes and syrup, you will light your pipe, sit down on a three legged stool, throw yourself back on your dignity and say, take no thought of what you shall eat or drink tomorrow, let every day provide for itself.

Everything is going on as lovely as a gal and boy a courtin,' several weeks have passed and nothing said about something to eat.

When you go to supper the madam says, John, there is only three more roastings of potatoes in the sack. Is it possible, says you. It certainly is, and not more than a quart of syrup in the jug. Great Scott! I must write to the boys and will do so. They fill the sack as well as the jug and send it to you. That makes more talk but its with the boys. They agree that you can't stand your present way of living and the best thing they can do is to send teams and bring you to Lake City, and once back to the good old home, there isn't blood hounds enough in Georgia to run you away. Then, brother, I will call you the Prodigal son, forgive you, extend the right hand of fellowship and we will grunt together the balance of the time, old age and bad looks to the contrary notwithstanding.

From *The Florida Index,* July 19, 1901.

I THINK IT ENDED RIGHT.

Ketch All, July 9th, 1901.

Brother Caldwell:—as you requested me to tell you of some of the long ago happenings I will tell you what did happen.

Madison county embraced too much territory, and she divided and subdivided and formed Taylor and LaFayette counties [both in 1856].[40] Now we have a new county which is contiguous to Columbia county, only divided by Suwannee river. There is a new county coming home to us and it created quite an excitement, for us people thought the land, range and game had never been here before, and wanted to see it, but I was too little to go that far from home but some of our neighbors did go. On their return they reported it to be the finest country in the world.

Those that had seen a place that flowed with milk and honey began making arrangements to move to it. Us poor folks didn't know that the territory was there before we came here, but thought that it was fetched by some body, so the moving began in dead earnest.

Now I will give the names of a few men that moved from our settlement and which was among the first settlers of LaFayette county: James Douglass, John Sapp, Riley Wright, Steve Slade, Henry Smith and John C. C. Ponch[i]er. But that is not half that went first, and while living here they were considered belonging to the better class of people, so when they got there they settled in the same neighborhood. There was another class; these names was as follows: The Locklars [Lockliers], Corbans, Gany's Kelly's Edward[s]'s Munden's and the Hunter's. They were called the dish rag Aristocracy, so they made a settlement of their own and the two factions had nothing to do with each other. Lige [Elijah] Locklar and Jim Munden belonged to the dish-rag aristocracy; each one had a daughter about seventeen years old [Arletta Ann Locklier and Georgia Ann C. Munden], and they were good friends and neighbors.

As soon as I got big enough to make eyes at the gals I went to LaFayette county and fell into the dish-rag neighborhood, and never was more kindly treated in my life, and I liked the people well. After leaving there I went among the better class of people as they were called. There I received the kind treatment that I did in ragtown, as some people called it.

I began to inquire what was wrong with the people in ragtown. I was talking with Uncle John Sapp, (our townsman Newton Sapp's father) knowing him to be an honorable and truthful gentleman. He said they were whiskey drinkers, Saturday night dancers, Sunday hunters and profane swearers, was the principal objection they had to them.

Haven't you heard of Lige Locklar and Jim Munden swapping gals? I told him no. It come about in this way. They got on a gal swap and swapped even. Lige went and got Jim's gal and carried her home and Jim went for Lige's gal and he carried her home, notwithstanding each of them had a wife and children at home. Their wives didn't plead, answer nor demur to the trade and it was supposed to be satisfied by them. Uncle Sapp said, "now Black Eye" I will let Geo. Hunter, who is Lige Locklars step son, give you the particulars of the gal trade, he can do it better than I can for he was present when the trade was made." I said, go on George. "Well," said he, "Munden said to pa that he wanted to give his gal for Lettie who was my half-sister, and pa's daughter, and pa said I'll do it. So the trade was made in two minutes. Munden was made in two minutes. Munden carried Lettie home and pa went and fetched Munden's gal home.

Things went along nicely for about two days, at the end of that time Lettie ran away from Munden and come home. Munden come after her and she refused to go with him, and he said to pa, you make her go. Pa said I can't do it. Munden said you had better do it than always wish you had. Munden left, but returned Saturday night and fired two shots into our house; no one hurt.

The next day pa received a message from Munden saying if he did not send Lettie home during the early part of the week he would come Saturday night and kill him. Pa did not send her but expected trouble.

Saturday night pa said, George get your gun and go with me, I done so. Pa had his gun and we went to the potato patch which was near the road and lay down to wait developments; knowing that if Munden did come he would come that way.

Now we leave George Hunter for awhile and talk with Bill Cason some. Bill Cason said that Jim Munden come and got him, Noah Cason, Green Russell, and another man (I have forgotten his name) to assist him in killing Lige Locklar. They all agreed to help him, and they made something in the shape of a well curb, leaving port holes for Munden to shoot through. All four sides were walled in with timbers that a bullet couldn't penetrate, leaving each end open, and they called this thing a portable fort. They hauled it near the house; the four men was carrying it on stocks, their object was to carry it in the yard and put Munden into it, and they were to leave and Munden was to take Locklar by seige and kill him when he come out.

Just at this moment they were [with]in about fifteen steps of Locklar; they saw each other and Locklar fired. Munden was going to shoot, supporting his gun with his left hand, the next thing in order was to run. Munden grunting the others examined the wounds. He was wounded between the elbow and the hand. They regarded it as a mere scratch, and carried him ten miles to Jack Cason's the father to these Cason boys. The old man wouldn't let him go in the house, saying that a man that would trade his daughter like he would a horse or mule couldn't be carried into his house even if he was dead. So they ran the cart under a shed, loosed the horse, dro[p]ped the fills on the ground. That put Munden's head down grade. They went to the house and to bed. Next morning they went out to look after Munden and he was as dead as a crow bar.

At that time the court house was at Fayetteville, subsequently at Troy but now at Mayo. A man was sent to Fayetteville, 80 miles away, for the coroner this [was] Sunday and the coroner arrived at Jack Cason's late Monday p.m.

[The coroner examined Munden's body on July 18, 1859. It had been discovered on July 17.[41]] On examination they found that the bullet had passed through Munden's arm and entered the body in the region of the heart, so they buried him. The coroner stopped with Jack Cason for the night, and left early the next morning for home.

Now we go back to George Hunter again. He said when Munden fired, his father [Elijah Locklier] fell on his back, but he didn't know that his father was shot. Scare overtook him and he ran to the house and told his mother he thought his father was dead, and the next morning they went to the patch and there lay Lige dead. [Locklier's corpse was discovered July 17, 1859.[42]]

This is all that George Hunter told me. You must recolect that the Munden faction didn't know that Lige was dead, neither did they know that Munden was shot.

Now we go to Peter Cason and hear what he said about the killing. He lived four miles from Lige, but didn't know anything about the trouble. but he went on Tuesday a.m., to see Lige on business. After commonplace remarks he said to Mrs. Lockler, "Kissie where is Lige?" She said he was in the potato patch. He went there and there lay Lige on his back dead. The bullet entered the head just above the left eye and it drove the ball from the socket and the hot sun had drove out the other eye, and he was swollen to double his original size and he was frightful to look at. He ran to the house and said, "Kissie Lige is dead." She said "we know it, he has been dead ever since Saturday night."["]Why didn't you bury him?" ["]We were so busy with the crops, we thought it would make no difference to let him lay a few days."

Now Peter Cason pulled out for Fayetteville and a 40 mile ride. At a late hour that night he got there and found the coroner. Understand this is Wednesday a.m., in the month of July, and Lige Locklar lying dead in the potato patch ever since Saturday night. Late that p.m., the coroner with his jury was standing around the dead man. Joe Parker told me that he saw them bury Locklar. To use his own words he said they dug a hole by the side of him and put an old smutty quilt down in the bottom of it, then hitched their horse under him and rolled him in the hole, and pulled the dirt over him the best they could with their hoes, and covered him up, and not a man put his hand on him.

Now I go back to Uncle John Sapp again. He said that was one time that God Almighty raised up the rod of correction, and when he brought it down he said all things should be done well.

Brother Caldwell, this reminds me of what Old Sitting Bull said to the reporter when he was interrogating him in regard to the battle when he killed

Gen. Custer and his army. He said he didn't know at the time of the battle and for three days afterwards who he was fighting.

I don't know who I am writing to but I do know that I intend it for the INDEX.

XII

Studies in Cracker Character

The summer heat of 1901 drained George G. Keen, and his health suffered. By mid September he had revived sufficiently to pen four letters within a six-week period. Three of them offered portraits of individuals of the author's acquaintance painted in tones alternately ironic, humorous, provocative, and introspective. In them Keen introduced his readers to William Godfrey, Edward Branning, Thomas B. Holder, and the Honorable John Gideon "Gid" Slade.

From *The Florida Index,* September 20, 1901.

BLACK EYE ON OLD TIMES.

Ketch All, Sept. 14, 1901.

Brother Caldwell—I heard you inquiring for me, but I was too sick to come to the front.

It appears to me that I was confined to the house six weeks in the long month of August. Then I took two bottles of Johnson's Chill Tonic, which is the worst medicine on earth and it is the best medicine in the world for chills and fever, for it will break up the fever or kill the patient. If you don't think its bad medicine taste of it; so much for preparitory remarks.

HE GOT RICH.

In the year of 1845 two men came into our neighborhood from Emanuel county, Georgia. One was named William Godfrey and the others name was Edward Branning, both young, unmarried men and poor men. Branning was very industrious. Godfrey was so lazy that if it had been possible you could have scraped laziness off of him with a stick. He would'nt smart where the skin was off.

Branning went to work and made money, and Godfrey rode around and swapt horses. He bought the place where John A. Mole now lives, only the buildings stood on the east side of the public road. What he bought a farm for was a mystery to us for there was two men he would work for, one was himself and the other was nobody else.

In a short time after buying the land he suddenly left the country and no one knew where he went to. He was gone six or eight weeks and returned, bringing his mother and household goods with him; he had a good house and it nicely furnished for the times.

His mother was about eighty years old and he hired a woman to wait on her and do the house work; he also hired men to do the farm work, and in connection with that he put up a bottle grocery and made a decent living. I did love the man because he was so very kind to his mother.

He remained there about four years and his mother died. He then sold out and bought land on the Orange pond seven miles west of his old place, hired a house-keeper and went to farming. At the close of that year his house-keeper died, he then sold off his real and personal property and went to Troupville, Ga., and went into the grocery business.[43] At that time Troupville was a cres[c]ent city, and the capitol of Lownd[e]s county.

He was pretty successful and made some money, but yet unmarried. The widow Burnett was a rich woman, and owned the big hotel and Godfrey boarded with her for the space of two years, and everything went along nicely.

This same William Godfrey that was so lazy, was a single man, a married man, a poor man, a rich man, a father and a widower in six hours time. Do you believe it? No I don't. Why do you disbelieve it? For this reason, that was too many changes for a man to pass through in so short space of time. I don't believe one word of it. The idea of a man being a single man, a married man, a poor man, a rich man, a father and a widower in six hours. John McClelland was the biggest fool that I ever saw, he cut down a tree to catch a turkey, and has got more sense than to believe such stuff, so don't tell that tale any more for no one wont believe it. Have you investigated it? No, it needs no investigation, for this story is as thin as cheese cloth.

My Brother, that is getting to be the ways of the world; you jump at conclusions, and render judgement before you learn the evidence; you render judgement upon public sentiment, and you are wrong. Go to the law and the testimony then you will be right and not till then.

I will prove to you that this Godfrey story is the truth, and no red tape in it. Now hear me.

On a certain day at 5 o'clock p.m. the widow Burnett told William Godfrey he had got her into disgrace and if he had any regard for his varacity, honor and integrity he would take her out of it, and if he didn't do it her hidden shame would soon be brought to open light. Godfrey told her he would do it whenever it suited her. She said 6 o'clock this evening. That's the agreement, he got the license, the parson and at six o'clock sharpe, William [Godfrey] and the widow Burnett were married.

Now Brother, you will admit that one minute before William Godfrey was married he was a single man and a poor man, and one minute after he was married he was a married man. He was a married man and a rich man. I agree with you so far. All right. At 8 o'clock the same night there was a little girl baby born in the family. Now, according to the laws of our State was not William Godfrey a father? Most assuredly he was. Go on Brother, you are getting along better with it than I thought you could.

At ten o'clock the same night Mrs. Godfrey, who was originally the widow Burnett, died. Now wasn't William Godfrey a widower? Brother Black Eye, I give it up, ask your pardon for what I said. I take it all back, am sorry that I didn't say more so I could have taken it back. It is granted my brother, and I look upon you as a man of high-toned principles than I did before you apologised to me. for it is noble in a man and no signs of cowardice to acknowledge his faults and forsake them; and again, it shows that he is a wiser man today than he was yesterday. Now tell us what became of Ed Branning. Not so fast brother, wait till I get through with Bill Godfrey then I will tell you about Ed Branning. All right brother Black Eye, I will keep quiet.

After the burial of Mrs. Godfrey, Godfrey sold the hotel and the house hold and kitchen furniture. In other words he sold all the real and personal property that come into his possession in consequence of his marriage to the widow.

The widow Burnett had no heirs, unless it was some fifteenth cousins that lived in North Indiana, so the property belonged to Godfrey and city property had gone up to the zenith of its glory when he sold.

Now William Godfrey is a rich man. He went to Mill Town in Clinch county, Georgia, hired two Negroes, a man and his wife and went to housekeeping and merchandising. The darkies belonged to a Mrs. S. She was a widow and very rich; he was to pay $400 a year for the niggers, he kept them four years and had not paid anything.

He walked over to see the widow, saying, Mrs. S. I have been a little neglectful in paying for the hire of those niggers till I am due you $1600. Of course I have got the money but I don't like to take that much out of my business at one time to pay debts with. I have a project on foot and if you will assist me the debt can be satisfactory settled to all parties interested and no money paid out. Mr. Godfrey there is no one interested but you and I.

I know that Mrs. S. I am willing to do right and I would be unreasonable if
I didn't do right. What is your project? It's this, you consent to be my wife
and that would settle the debt. What do you say to that. Oh! That is so sudden, I will have to think about it before I can give you an answer. How much
time do you want? Five minutes. All right said Godfrey throwing himself back
on his dignity and went to reading the morning paper. Pretty soon he said,
Mrs. S. times up, and what is your decision. I have decided to be your wife.
Good, said Godfrey, and he took her by the hand and kissed her on her sweet
rosy lips and he got the license and they were married at candle light. Now
Godfrey says, I had money, it was my money. If I had given it to you it would
have been your money, but as it is its our money and the debt is paid. This is
so love, said Mrs. Godfrey.

Now I will tell you what Godfrey done. He put up a dry goods store, a
grocery store, and a hardware store and hired men to look after his business,
and he set down on the chair of ease, and lived from the lap of luxury till in
May 1871, then he died a rich man. After he was dead he was no better than
poor Mose Corban was when he died and I don't suppose that Corban had
a dollar in money at one time during the last thirty years of his life.

My brother, I often think of the rich and the poor; also what the poet
said, I read it when I was a boy. He said.

Why should the rich despise the poor?
Why should the poor repine?
A little time will make us one,
On equal friendship join.

Edward Branning was never married, but he put up a bar in Alligator
(now Lake City). He paid $10 State license, and $5 county license, and there
was no corporation license. He got good liquors delivered at $1 per gallon
and sold it for five cents a drink, and he made money—next to an American
mint. He could not bear prosperity, so he took to hard drink and neglected
his business and his property vanished in the air, and he died an untimely
death and filled a drunkards grave.

My brother, in the cause of truth I must say that I believe that the Lord
intended for some of us to be poor, for the Judas. You have the poor with you
always; the poor was here when I come, and I have been here nearly three
quarters of a century, and the poor is yet here. There is that much hardshellism
in me—you and I perhaps would have been rich but the Lord knew that we
could not bear prosperity. But I would like to be rich now just to see if it
would make me feel biget; how is your feelings on the subject.

Please excuse the brevity of this communication, I will write more next
time.

From *The Florida Index,* October 4, 1901.

THEY BOTH GOT RICH.

Ketch All, Sept, 28th, 1901.

EDITOR INDEX—Why will some men strive so hard to get rich? If it is God's will for them to be rich, they will be rich, whether they strive for riches or not. When I began in the world my whole aim was to get rich. In 1860 I paid taxes on $9,554 worth of property, and had $3,000 at interest, and money enough to keep the devil out of the house. I was making enough in one year to last me three years, and I knew I would soon be a rich man.

In 1865 I found myself a very poor man. I had hundreds of acres of land. I was land poor on the 11th day of May, 1871. I moved to Lake City in December, I was summoned as grand juror in the U.S. Court at Jacksonville, remained there eight weeks and two days, receiving from $3 to $14 per day for my services. I next got the contract to survey the public school lots and to take deeds. I bought a bay roan mare from Ed. [James Edward] Henry for $110 to do the riding. It took 36 days to do the work, for which I received $7 per day, amounting in the aggregate to $252, and then sold the mare to Frank Raulerson for $160, making $50 in the trade; add that to the work and we have $302. Then John P. Mahon[e]y was killed. He was tax assessor and I got the office and three months to do the work in. The job was worth $1200 and I did the work in the prescribed [time], gained four days and got the $1200—that was $400 per month, and I wish the job would have lasted till now; and I have made some money all the way ever since I was 16 years old, and I am yet a poor man, and the Lord intended me to be poor; but the poor will have the gospel preached to them.

Now I am going to tell you about Thomas Holder and Gideon Slade. I will tell you about Tom Holder first, as he was the best, and as the sister told the brother to take the best first was good manners.

Joseph Holder was the father of Tom Holder. He was raised on the place where T. P. Bethea lives. We children and the Holder children played together on Sundays. I never saw Tom Holder with a pair of shoes on till he was grown and married. His dress was a pair of pants, the cloth made at home, and the clothes made of the cloth by his mother; and he wore what was called a hunting shirt, and his hat was made of the buds o'saw palmetto; he went barefooted till he was twenty-one years old; he could not spell baker.

Now, please hold on till I take hold of the other end of the story. Tom's father owned a nigger named Czar. They disagreed and Czar struck Holder on the head with a stick and came near killing him. Holder was afraid of

Czar, so he carried him across the Georgia line and sold him to old Tommy Ellis. By that means Holder and the Ellis family became acquainted.

Now we go back to barefooted Tom. He is now 21 years old. So his father said: "Now, Tom, you must get married."

He said: "Pa, I never talked to a girl in my life, and I don't know any girls.["]

The old man said: "You go to Tommy Ellis's; he has two pretty gals."

"Pa, what must I say to a gal?"

"Tell her you want a wife and if she says 'yes,' that is sufficient."

"But suppose she says 'no?'"

"Then try the other one, But, hold on; you must have a suit of clothes a hat and a pair of shoes."

"All right," said Tom, "I'll do it."

"Now, Tom you must ride Ball," which is a red roan horse with a white face.

Tom had to ride about 80 miles to see his girl. There were two of them. One had dark hair, blue eyes and a creamy complexion. He[r] name was Lydia. Betsy had red hair, a red face and blues eyes.

Tom got there in good time, told whose son he was and met with a warm reception. He remained till next morning without saying anything to the girls. He selected Betsy. Then he said:

"Betsy, will you have me?"

She said: "Yes; ask the old folks for me."

He went to the old folks and said; "Will both of you give me Betsy? I want her for my wife."

"Yes," was the reply of both. This was on Friday. So the next Thursday was fixed for the wedding day. Tom went home and told his father of his success. The following Thursday Tom and his father went to Ellis's and Tom and Betsy were united in holy matrimony.

The next day the Holders went home. After a few weeks the old man said "Tom, you must have a place you can call home and Ansel Walker wants to sell out."

So Tom bought Walker's improvement. It was in about a mile of where the Suwannee Valley now stands. Tom moved to it. There was a little house on it and three acres of cleared land; but it was a home for Tom. His father fitted him up for housekeeping and gave him a horse and some cattle. Tom hired Edmond Revels to split him 5,000 rails.

Now Tom and his wife went to work. A few months passed and Mr. Ellis sent for Tom and Betsy to come and see him. They did so. When they got ready to go back home Ellis told Betsy he wanted to give her something. She told him all right. He called up this same Czar and Tom, another negro, and he said: "Betsy, I make you a present of them niggers." So Tom and Betsy went home well pleased with their short-haired people, and all hands went to work and made the fur fly.

Cotton in those days brought from 38 to 40c a pound. In a short time Tom bought another nigger, named Arch, from Capt. J. T. Goodbread. Tom now decided that there was more money in cattle than in farming. He sold out up here and moved eight miles below Newnan[s]ville, on a little stream called Mounteoark (an Indian name.) Then he went into the stock business, and it was a success. He ran quite a farm in connection with his cattle ranch.

After being there a few years his wife died, and he was rich and only 31 or 32 years old. Then he married the widow Doggett; she was worth $200,000. He g[o]t all of her property. She lived about two years and she died. Then he m[a]rried the widow Stanly; she was said to be worth half a million. Now he is so rich that he don't know what to do with his money. So he remained there for quite a number of years. The big head never struck him. He was kind and friendly. I never knew him to have but one fight. He fought P. K. Walker and whipped him; but he had it to do or run.

About this time the Lone Star State came into notice. It was called the finest stock range in North America. It was also called the land of promise for all rogues, liars and discontented people. A great many went from Florida to Texas. Tom Holder had all the money and property that any reasonable man could have wanted. So he got the Texas fever, or it got him.

Now comes the question, was it the money he had on hand that he wanted, or the dollar that he did not have. Echo says that it was the dollar that he did not have and was going to Texas after it. Why should the rich strive after gain? It is a mystery to me. But he sold off all his land, horses, cattle and mules but 36. Lewis Daughtry told me that he saw Holder take the boat at Tampa on his way to Texas. He said that he counted 60 young negro men standing in line. He had them divided, all the young men in one line, and all the old men and boys, women and children in another. It took six-mule teams to haul their luggage. He put everything on the boat and pulled for Texas [in 1860]. That was the last time that I heard from Tom Holder. No doubt he got there and made more money.

Let us look at old A[lexander]. T. Stewart of New York. He was the first millionaire that ever died in the United States. He came to New York, a wild Irish boy, without money and without friends, and in due course of time he accumulated between seventy and eighty millions of dollars. He and his wife could not agree. He offered her ten millions of dollars to give him a divorce. She told him she would wait till he died, and then she would get it all; and she did so. A. T. Stewart lived in a marble mansion—but he died.

Now Stewart was dead. The next thing was a division of his estate. As we are not directly interested in the assets of the estate, we see what part of his vast estate A. T. Stewart got for his share. Just his burial outfit. How hardly shall a rich man enter the kingdom of heaven!

Now we will go back to the Holder family. Tom Holder had a younger brother named Joe, after his father. Now the old man loved Joe and tried to help him along in a way of making a living. Joe was a good worker, very industrious, and to all appearances had as much sense as Tom had. But everything that Joe undertook was a failure. He neither drank nor gambled, but he remained poor, and very poor.

Brother, my argument is, if we are satisfied with our lot and there is love at home, there is as much happiness in a cottage as there is in a mansion. But if there is no love at home there is no happiness for us anywhere.

I hold and contend that we make our troubles, and three-fourths of our troubles are made up out of imaginary evils. It is what I call meeting trouble half way. If we would take equal parts of common sense, reason and good judgment, mix them together, shake them up well and take one teaspoonful every morning when we first get up, we all would get along better than what we do.

If anything should happen that is contrary to the common course of things, stop right there and consider for a moment, and see if the wrong can be righted. When your wife asks you what are you going to do about it, say in a pleasant voice, "Oh it don't amount to much; I will fix it up." But if it is something that can not be remedied, say, "Wife, this is bad; I am very sorry about it, but it could have been a good deal worse. We have got to submit to it. As it has got to go let us try to dismiss it from our minds.["]

Don't jump up and curse and try to find some one to lay the blame on, and try to make the place hideous with your howls that stir up bad blood. Home is just what we make it. You can make it a little paradise or a howling wilderness.

From *The Florida Index*, November 8, 1901.

"BLACK EYE'S LETTER."

He Writes the Biography of Hon. Gid. Slade.

KETCH ALL. October 29, 1901.

Editor of the Index:

As my last communication has come to the front, I will tell you more about Gideon Slade, better known as Gid. Slade. Miss Nancy Slade was the mother of Gid. Slade. Col. [Thomas] Bell was the reputed father of Gid.

Slade. Col. Bell was among the richest men in the territory of Florida, but he didn't do anything for Gid. When Gid was about 10 years old he left his mother and started in the wide world to make his fortune.

Col. Bell left Florida [around 1836 or1837] and went to Texas. We will leave him there for the present and hunt up Gid. Gid. was a poor little ragged orphan boy, without kindred, home or money. In his deplorable condition, Capt. Henry Harrington (the father of Cap. [Henry Monroe] and Lib[erty] Harrington), picked him up and kept an eye on him.

In justice to Gid., I must say he was the worst boy I ever saw. He was raised at Blount's Ferry, at Lake City and on the road between the two places, and fought some one every time he got a good chance; but he never went to school a day in his life. He would do as Capt. Harrington told him to—only when he got too much whiskey on board; then he would not be controlled by anybody, and Harrington would take him down and wear him out. He continued in this way till he was nearly 20 years old. Notwithstanding his mean ways, he was honest, industrious, truthful and had a great many friends. When he was 26 he married [actually Slade was aged 19 when he married Penelope Green in Hamilton County on October 13, 1837], and married a girl as rich as he was, and he was as poor as a man ever gets.

When his mother was 50 years old she married James Douglas[s] (the grandfather of our townsman, Newton Sapp, and my step-grandfather), of Lafayette county, Fla. But Gid. remained at Blounts Ferry, Columbia county. After Gid. married he got him a little home and went to work—made a living, but remained very poor. In them days we had to pay 25 cents postage on a letter, if it was carried over 500 hundred miles. When Gid. was 25 [35] years old his wife had two babies, and he toned down and got to conducting himself like a gentleman, and had a great many friends. About this time he received a letter—the first one he had ever received in his life. He could not read it, so he got Capt. John Bryan to read it for him. The letter was from Col. Bell, of Texas, and it was in substance as follows:

"Mr. Gideon Slade:

"Dear Sir—If you are yet alive and receive this letter—also, if Nancy Slade, your mother, is still living—if you will get her and a magistrate and go before the Clerk of the Circuit Court of Columbia county, Fla. and Nancy Slade will swear before said magistrate that you are her son, and I, James [actually, Thomas] Bell, the real father of you, and that you are the identical Gideon Slade that she is the mother of, and the clerk of the circuit court of said county will give a certificate that this magistrate is a lawful officer of the State of Florida and all his official acts are entitled to credit, and then you come to me, bringing said papers, I will give you $10,000 in cash."

Now, you can imagine Gid.'s feelings better than I can describe them. He got up and got there, Eli. His first move was to go for his mother. She and her husband came back with Gid. Gen. William B. Ross was next brought into requisition. They all appeared before the clerk of the court, who was S[tirling] Scarborough, the father of our present clerk, Mat. Scarborough. The papers were all properly fixed up and given to Gid., and he made his arrangements and left for Texas; and went the whole way on a horse and saddle. No railroads in them days; and we didn't want any better transport than a good horse and saddle. After riding many hundred miles in a land of strangers, Gid. Slade found Col. Bell, his father. His father examined his papers and found them O. K. and gave Gid. a warm reception. Gid. remained with his father several weeks, looking at the country.

Now, the time has come for Gid. to come back to Florida. His father counted out $10,000 in cash and gave it to Gid. Mrs. Col. [Abigail] Bell, Gid.'s stepmother, said: "Now, Gid., your father has no relatives on earth but you; neither have I, and we are both old and must soon die, and we have a great deal of property, both real and personal, and no one to inherit it but you. Now, as your father has given you $10,000, I will give you $10,000, conditionally if you will take of this money enough to defray your expenses to Florida and back, and will leave the balance as a guarantee that you will come back." Gid. says: "I will do it." She counted out $10,000 and gave it to Gid.

Now, Col. Bell comes to the front, saying: "Gid, we want you to move in the house with us, and at our demise you will be in possession and hold possession. No need of any administrations, for there is no debts nor heirs—everything that we die seized and possessed of is yours, as our last will and testament will better explain.

They bid each other good bye. Gid., after taking as much money as he wanted, leaving the balance with the old folks, turned his face homewards.

I knew that Gid. had gone to Texas, but had not heard that he had returned. I walked into Zemri Lamb's blacksmith shop. There stood Gid. He had on an old wool hat, brogan shoes, yellow homespun shirt, no vest, round coat and pants made of what used to be called negro cloth. I said: "Hello! Gid,: I expected to see you dressed as fine as split silk." He said: "You know I never had anything till now, and I am trying to keep off the big head." A good idea. The first thing that Gid. does is to sell off little belongings and go round and see his mother and best friends and bid them a long fare you well and leave for Texas.

Did he do right? I say yes, in part; but in my judgment he failed to do the part that a dutiful son would have done. If he had been right from the ground up he, after selling the little property he had here, would have took that money, together with $1,000 more, and given it to his mother. He could have done that, which would have made her last days pass off softly, and he yet would have had $600,000 left "to buy friendships and an in-title with," as the darkey said. He wasn't built that way.

Now, Col. Gideon Slade has gone to Texas to take charge of his vast estate. He once was as poor as any of us and could not spell his name.

Now, we lose sight of Gid. Slade for sixteen long years. Then he wrote to Capt. Harrington; he had been under a teacher and could write a little. He said Col. Bell and wife had been dead near ten years and left him about $600,000, and he was now independent to the world. He was one of the ones that the Lord intended to be rich.

We don't hear anything more of Col. Gideon Slade for three years. What do we hear then? That this same Gid. Slade is representing the State of Texas in Congress [rather, Slade, as John Gideon Bell, sat in the Texas state senate as of 1870]. Stop and think for a moment. Did we ever hear of Gid. sending his poor old mother $100? No; never one cent. Oh! how ungrateful some people are. I very much doubt his ever thinking of his mother.

It don't take education, development of the brain and popularity nor beauty to make a fortune. If it did Absalom of old would have been the richest man in the civilized world. It's the will of a higher power than that of man to make a rich man.

XIII

Passing

During the fall and early winter of 1901 George G. Keen's constitution deteriorated. In addition to his letters of September 14 and 28 and October 29 printed above, his last efforts included a communication of October 3 (published October 11) that argued with *The Florida Index*'s new owners about a proposal to build a rock road from Lake City to White Springs. He also wrote two letters entitled "Why I Am A Mormon," which consisted primarily of quoted Bible verses and were published November 20, 1901, and January 3, 1902. The final one was written from "Ketch All" on December 30, 1901.

From the *Lake City Citizen-Reporter,* February 14, 1902.

DEATH OF GEO. G. KEEN.

Mr. George G. Keen, an old and universally respected citizen and one of the pioneer settlers of the county, died at his home at "Ketchall," Wednesday, January 29th.

The deceased was among the first settlers in this county and knew all the events connected with the pioneers, the Indians wars, etc.

His was a life useful to others. He had the confidence of many and had few enemies. He was a frequent contributor to the local papers under the nom de plume of "Black Eye," and his writings were read with interest.

Like those who knew him best, we can say, "Peace to his ashes."

His religious hope was that he would have a part in the first resurrection. Few of our people have given the same thought to the Bible that he did, and while his life, like many others, was bound by circumstances, he looked beyond human agency.

PART TWO

Sarah Pamela Williams

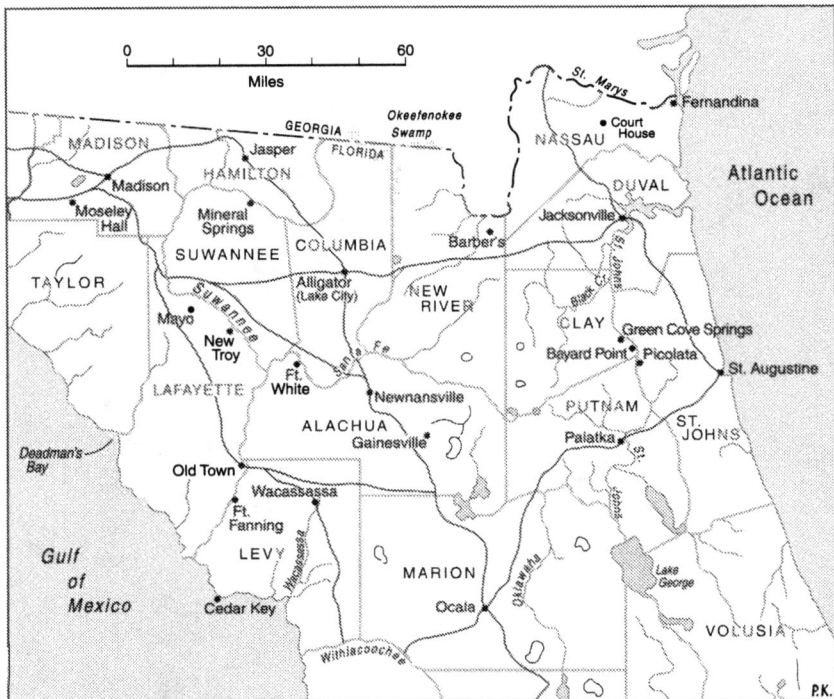

Northeastern Florida, circa 1858

I

Childhood at
Picolata

A few years after George Gillett Keen's 1902 death in Columbia County, Florida, another aging survivor of that region's pioneer days set her recollections down for posterity. Writing from Atlanta, where she had moved with her second husband in the 1870s, Sarah Pamela Williams Niblack Kelly rendered a portrait far different from the Cracker world painted by Keen. In place of his masculine perspective and hardy Cracker tales, she viewed her times and life through the eyes of a young planter's wife and widow. Further, she lived in or near the village and, later, town that represented the area's closest attempt at urbanity, whereas Keen's rural experiences comprised the gristmill for his frontier-life tales.

Relatively speaking, Sarah Pamela Williams's life had been one of privilege, at least within the context of developing East Florida during the territorial and early statehood period. Her father, John Lee Williams, had graduated from Hamilton College before practicing law in New York and Virginia. When his first wife passed away about 1820, he relocated to Florida at a time when the transfer of possession of Spanish Florida to the United States still awaited final action. Settling in Pensacola, he received appointment in 1823 from Gov. William Pope DuVal to serve with St. Augustine's William Hayne Simmons to select the site for Florida's capital.

The capital-selection duties led Williams to other activities, residences, and responsibilities. He investigated the territory's natural resources and surveyed one of its early and major roads. Eventually he settled in St. Augustine, where in 1829 he married a widow, Mrs. Martha Mackey Ives, who already had two sons. With his new bride Williams had three children. The first, Maria

Mackey Williams, was born in 1830 in St. Augustine; then a son named Rudolph, born in 1833, died in infancy. In 1834 Williams removed the family to a site opposite Picolata, the old Spanish settlement that served as St. Augustine's port on the St. Johns River. There, in 1837, John and Martha Williams celebrated the birth of a second daughter, whom they called Sarah Pamela.

Though the world into which she was born appeared to her as a rustic, remote, and tropical paradise, Sarah Pamela Williams's early family life sparkled with intellectual vigor. Her father's friends included historian Charles Goodrich, writer Washington Irving, and botanist John J. Audubon, and a parade of those and other acquaintances passed through the Williams home. For his part, Sarah's father penned two of the territory's first histories and surveys of resources: *Views of West Florida* and *Williams's History of Florida.* As to educational opportunities, John Lee Williams assumed responsibility for tutoring his children. From him Sarah Pamela learned botany, literature, and all manner of other subjects that constituted his passions. Although to the young Sarah Pamela her father loomed as a wonder of the world, to John Lee Williams's wife his eccentricities posed irreconcilable problems. But let us permit Sarah Pamela to tell her own story.[1]

FROM "SARAH PAMELA WILLIAMS (HER AUTOBIOGRAPHY)."

I, Sarah Pamela Williams, was born December 23, 1837, [during] the Seminole War, in the United States Barracks at Picolata, St Johns County, on the east bank of the St Johns river, in Florida. My family had taken refuge there at the beginning of the war [in December 1835], from their home on the west bank of the river. The house there was burned down during the war and my father purchased some land near the barracks at Picolata from a Mr. [Chauncey L.?] Hatch, and here he built a new house. When I was three weeks old he moved his family into this new home.

The house was a large two-storied wooden building with long upper and lower piazzas and fronted on the St Johns river. There was a large grove of live oaks in front of the house and large vegetable and flower gardens in the back. On the north side was a grove of fruit trees—orange, peach, lemon and plum. Three sides of the grounds were surrounded by a ditch with a bridge and gate at each. There were hedges of Spanish bayonet on the east and south sides and next to the gardens was a row of mulberry trees.

The barracks, where I was born, were kept up near us for several years for I can remember the soldiers drilling on the common opposite our front gate. I remember the flag flying and the fife and drum sounding. I used to hear Taps at night and the bugle blowing in the morning. The barracks was a large three-storied house which Judge Law of Savannah, Georgia, had built to be used as a hotel for the accommodation of the numbers of northern invalids, especially consumptives, who used to visit Florida in the winter months because of the mildness of the climate.

My family was living at Bayard on the west side of the St Johns river when the Seminole war broke out but were obliged to cross the river and seek refuge in the barracks at Picolata on the east side, for they were too exposed to the Indians on the other side. The home at Bayard was destroyed during the war by United States troops who camped nearby. The soldiers accidently set fire to the house and all the lumber, which my father had cut and cured to build another home. The troops had also butchered his cattle and hogs for the use of the army. Although the officers gave my father certificates stating the number of animals and price so that he could get indemnity from the United States for his losses, the papers were lost in the course of time and he never received a penny. When we moved from Picolata in 1847, my Mother left the papers on the floor of the garret thinking that they were of no use. Some years afterwards, if she had held onto them she could have proved her claims and the Government would have paid for all her losses. She was sorry that she did not preserve the papers.

I had an older sister, Maria, and two half brothers[;] however the two boys, Washington [Ives] and Edward [Ives], married and left home when I was quite young. Brother Washie's wife died when their little boy, Sam was a baby and brother brought him to mother to care for. We three children, Sister, Sam and I lived a quiet happy life at Picolata.

Sister had gone to school in St Augustine where she boarded with an old friend of my mother's (a Mrs. Loring) [Hannah Kenan Loring], but when my sister's teacher married and quit teaching, sister returned home. After that, father taught her, Sam and me and some neighbor's children. When some new neighbors, named Smith, came, he taught two of their children—they were free scholars, the same as we were. The Smiths occupied the barracks after the U.S. troops left, and when the large house burned down one windy March morning, the Smiths moved into a small two-roomed house that Father had used as a school house. They eventually moved to their own home at a plantation seven miles up the river from us, and named it Sampatricia. As children, we enjoyed many simple pleasures, such as fishing, fruit harvests, excursions into the woods, boating and swimming. I was my father's chosen companion in the long rambles through the woods, searching for rare plants and flowers. Or sheltered on a seat next to him in his boat we would sail upon the bosom of the shiny river, often seeking a snug cove where the lillypads floated their broad leaves and yellow blossoms upon the tide and the frogwort sent up its clusters of white flowers above the water. We would sit and he would fish for hours, drawing the pretty brown trout or catfish until he felt it was time to return home. Brother Ned and Mr John, our hired hand, used often to fish with cast nets. Brother used to net them himself, for mother had taught him the art of netting when he was a small boy.

We used often to go in one of the large flat boats to visit the wild orange groves. My brother Ned, mother, father, sister, Mr John and I would take our dinner with us and make a regular picnic, returning home in the evening with bushels of sour oranges and lemons which my mother used for various purposes. The oranges were used for preserves and marmalade. There were groves of plums too, on deserted plantations where the Indians had destroyed the houses and killed the families during the Seminole war.

We used to gather quantities of plums and they were made into preserves and jelly or dried for winter use. We used to dry okra, tomatoes, peaches, plums and bushels of huckleberries. We children enjoyed the berry picking and we helped about most of the preparation for drying things. We could peel peaches and cut them up and the plums were cut without peeling. Many hands were required to help and we children were always ready to assist. Also we delighted in the haying season. I used to admire my father with his scythe, cutting the swaths of long grass and the whetting of the scythe was sweet music to my ears. I used to enjoy the scent of the drying grass, raked in great billows by the men and tossed, when dry, with pitch forks onto the ox wagon where the two large oxen, Diamond and Jolly, stood patiently chewing their cuds until the hay could be piled no higher. Then I was tossed on top and went laughing and rolling to the place for stacking the hay. There were long poles driven into the ground just back at the end of the barn and the hay was piled and piled with the forks until it arose in a great "cone" quite to the upper door of the barn. The hay stacks were built so that they shed water so that the inside hay was kept sweet and clean.

We used to have mattresses made of moss for beds; and Maum Kitty, Bet and the other negroes used to go out and gather it. The black moss was the best for it was dry and like fine wire or horsehair. We young ones used to go moss hunting with the negroes. They all had long poles which they twisted around in the long drooping bunches of moss and pulled it down and piled it in heaps on the ground where it was gathered up and placed in wagons or carts and hauled to the house. There it was placed on scaffolds in the back yard, beaten with sticks and pulled apart by our fingers; all sticks, twigs and fungi being removed. Later it was put in the ticks and sewed in. Father hired an old German, Frederick Zolindi, to make these mattresses up, or rather he was the presiding genius. He also had him teach sister music. One day, having imbibed too much his breath was unpleasant and sister objected to it, and to the music lesson. He cursed, so sister promptly threw the large music book in his face and walked out of the room and would never take another lesson from him.

Father purchased an Indian pony from some horse traders and turned it over to us children to use in learning to ride, and we soon became so accomplished in the art that we often rode him without saddle or bridle. When the pony got tired of us he would trot rapidly for awhile and then suddenly stop and pitch his rider over his head. We fell on the soft white sand and so we were never hurt by the fall.

At certain seasons of the year the turtles used to come out to lay their eggs on land. They would dig a large hole in the soft sand, deposit their eggs in the hole, which was dug above high water mark, pat the ground down smoothly and leave them for the sun to hatch. Our men often met the turtles coming out to lay and would catch several, put them in a pen, feed them on parsley and butcher them as needed for soups or steaks. (Sometimes the sun proved too hot and baked the little turtles after they came out. Oftener, the crows, of which there were numerous flocks about the river banks, would watch the turtles digging their nests and as soon as the turtle went back in the water, the crows would fly down by the hundreds and rifle the nests, devouring every egg they could find.

My father knew a sick old man named [Zephaniah] Kingsley who lived on a plantation near St Augustine. He had travelled a great deal for those days and in visiting Haiti and Jamaica had brought back casava and arrowroot and met with great success in raising crops of both. He gave Father some of each and we used to raise cassava very successfully.

In the St Johns river were many alligators, large and small. They were hideous creatures and looked like enormous brown or black lizards. They built their nests of bullrushes, sticks and water-grass and mud, on some low tongue of land, projecting into the water or among the rushes near the river's banks.

We used to go in bathing sometimes at night when the moon was very bright and it was almost like day. Sister and I went once when the tide was low and all about among the long sand banks were deep pools of water where we could swim and have a good time. We plunged into a pool and were swimming about when all at once an alligator struck Sister with his tail. She caught me up in her arms and fled across the sand banks for the wharf. As Sister ran she trod on the bottom of an old glass bottle and cut her foot dreadfully. It bled so much she nearly fainted before we reached the house. We were never allowed to go swimming by moonlight again. Parties of ladies and gentlemen used often to come out from St. Augustine and spend several days at our house. They used to go on picnics up the river and to the sulphur springs twelve miles from us on the western side of the river, (now Green Cove Springs).

There were also fishing parties, riding parties and dances on the broad back piazza, which used to be enclosed in canvas and decorated with vines and flowers and lighted by wax candles in scon[c]es and hand-made chandiliers. Sometimes there were boating parties as many of our neighbors had plantations up the river toward Jacksonville—the [Lewis] Flemings of Fleming Island, a family of Halidays [S. F. Haliday], and General Finnegan [Joseph J. Finegan], celebrated as a Confederate General, was about twelve miles from us.

My father was a magistrate and the first marriage I ever saw was one [in which] my father performed the ceremony. The contracting parties were a soldier and a soldier's daughter and the ceremony took place in a large room over my father's store. Our whole family, white and black[,] attended.

Christmas used to be a great time with the darkies in my young days. The negroes belonging to our near neighbors used to assemble in our kitchen on Christmas night and dance. They brought fiddles and tambourines and all had a great time. Maum Kitty, our cook, was a large fat woman, but she was a fine dancer. Many of the negroes danced the Spanish dances and some of them were very graceful. Some of the more old-fashioned bucks used to do the "double shuffle" and cut the "pigeon wing." We would stand in the door and watch the dancers.

On Christmas morning, the negroes of a household always greeted the master and mistress with "Merry Christmas, Masters," "Merry Christmas, Mistis." Each got a present and both male and female, a dram of liquor. Before breakfast, egg-nogg was beaten up and served with cake.

I liked the Spring and Summer on the river for then the flowers, trees and shrubs were in bloom. We were all, from my father down, passionately fond of flowers. In the month of May, Father used to dig up all plants that flowered that he could find and set them out in his garden where they improved by cultivation.

Some distance below our stable lot there was a long tongue of land that stretched out into the water and was quite covered by it at high tide. It bore a lot of bullrushes, grass and a few shrubs called cottonwood. The place held a weird history for us children. A soldier had drowned himself in the river while the barracks was occupied by the Army and his swollen corpse had lodged on that spot and was found there, high and dry,—a gruesome spectacle.

There had been a military graveyard near where our stables were built and the river had by degrees so encroached upon it that most of the bodies had been removed to a new graveyard on the south side of the St Augustine Road, a half mile perhaps from our house; but the river never ceased to undermine the old ones. During the Spring equinox we had heavy storms of winder [winds?] and the river rose and battled with the land. Frequently we found skulls and leg bones and sometimes partly rotted coffins with skeletons inside, which had evidently been overlooked in the removal of the others. The waves tossed them about for awhile and then left them on the beach to be removed to a quieter place among their comrades on drier land.

Just in front of our house in the oak grove were the remains of the breastworks (a fort, we called it) that the Spaniards had used as a defense against the Indians during the time that the Spaniards owned that part of the country. On the opposite side of the river where Brother Ned lived, there were similar breastworks just below his house. They had been built on a bank that overlooked the river and I suppose that the garrisons watched for the Indian canoes day and night. The forts were not opposite each other; the one built at Bayard was to the north and the one on our side toward the south. I remember the deep hollow with the high ridge running partly around the two sides. This hollow was used as a deposit for all the broken glass and china from our household. There we got our bits of colored china to set our tables under the oaks—we used to find lots of queer articles there.

We used whale oil in our lamps or alligator oil, and wax candles. Our lamps had astral shades; some of our candles were made from the berries of the wax myrtle. This sweet-scented bush grew in abundance all over the woods and yielded a pale green wax when the berries were boiled. The candles were moulded in tin moulds. We also used to buy sperm and white wax candles.

Brother Ned was hunting wild turkeys one day all alone; he did not even take a dog with him for a hunter had to keep very quiet when in pursuit of turkeys. He had a turkey call (a small instrument made from a joint of cane); when he blew on the cane it made a noise like a female turkey and the gobblers would approach near enough for him to shoot them. He had a double-barreled gun; one barrel was loaded with turkey shot and the other was empty, as he had killed two turkeys and had them tied together and slung over one shoulder.

He went further and further into the depths of the hammock until he came across a large tree which a storm had uprooted and the dirt, still sticking to the great roots made a fine shelter for him to crouch behind and watch for his game. He had scarcely secured a good position before he was attracted by the sound of a stealthy movement behind him. He turned to see what it could be and there he beheld an immense panther (or catamount) crouched ready to spring upon him. He sprang to one side and fired the loaded barrel of the gun as the great beast hurtled himself through the air. It caught his shoulder with one of its paws and tore his clothes clear through to the skin. It had been shot between the eyes and the blood partially blinded it, but it was so enraged with pain from the small shot that it tried to get hold of Brother Ned to tear him to pieces. He had no time to reload his gun and knew that he could not kill the panther with turkey shot as they were too small, so he clubbed his gun and beat on the beast's head with it until he killed it. He was a mile and a half from home and he did not know but what the panther's mate was nearby so he took a short cut out of the hammock with his couple of dead turkeys and got to Bayard safely.

As Mr John happened to be staying over there for a few days, he got John and returned to the hammock, tied the panther's feet together with strong ropes, cut down a pine sapling and thrust it through the legs. It was a great tawny cat with large yellow eyes; its claws were frightful, so large and strong and made to rend flesh. Brother Ned's shoulder was scratched, but not very deep and soon got well. As he walked through the hammock, the blood from the turkeys had dripped on the ground and the panther had trailed him by it.

The years passed happily for me at Picolata until I was about ten years old. For several years the relationship between my parents had not been a happy one. So, in 1847 my brother Eddie came for us and took Mother, Sister and me to live with him in Lake City. We never returned to Picolata again, but I will always have happy memories of my childhood there.

II

Moving to Alligator

In 1847 Columbia County's seat of Alligator, later known as Lake City for reasons explained in George G. Keen's reminiscences, was still recovering from the effects of the Second Seminole War. One of the conflict's outcomes had been the congressional passage in 1842 of the Armed Occupation Act, which guaranteed 160 acres of land to claimants agreeable to moving deeper within the peninsula in return for their willingness to live on and defend the property for five years while cultivating a portion of it. Scores of Columbia County residents, impoverished by the war, jumped at the chance and departed for the newer frontiers.

Moving into the vacated areas were numerous more affluent families who intended to establish cotton plantations where their predecessors had survived through subsistence farming and cattle grazing. By the late 1840s they had begun to remake Alligator into something resembling a real town, with social and commercial amenities previously unknown to the area.[2] As her parents' marriage dissolved, Sarah Pamela Williams at the age of ten was introduced to that town and region in transformation.

FROM "SARAH PAMELA WILLIAMS (HER AUTOBIOGRAPHY)."

My two half brothers, Washington [Ives] and Ned [Ives], married when I was quite young. After Brother Washie's second marriage he lived in St Augustine, later moving to a place called Alligator (now Lake City) in Columbia County, Florida. It was only a small village at that time, of about fifteen or twenty families, but was the show town of the county and a growing place.

Washington found a good law practice here and wrote to Brother Ned to come, as there was work enough to be obtained. So Brother Ned soon followed his brother, built himself a house and hiring some carpenters to help him, set up as a building contractor. He bought books on architecture and studied them so that he could carry on his business systematically.

Alligator (now Lake City) was originally named Lancaster after a noted Judge [Joseph B. Lancaster] who was what was called a Locofer in those days (he would be known as a Democrat now) ["Loco Foco" was a nickname bestowed upon their opponents by Whigs in the 1840s].³ The Loco[fo]coes had a rooster as their emblem and after the Locofocoes were beaten in some political contest by the Whigs (I think Judge Lancaster was the defeated candidate) there was an immense placard nailed upon a prominent building in the town and it represented an alligator swallowing a rooster. It pleased the Whigs so much that they, being in power, changed the name of the town to Alligator; and so it remained until it grew to such a size that it had a mayor, town council, etc.⁴ Brother Washington was elected first mayor and he insisted on the name of the town being changed to Lake City, a very appropriate name as there are fine lakes in and around the town. Lakes DeSoto and Dalgreen are in the town (they used to be Steam Mill Pond and Petis Pond); a large beautiful lake is at the northeast, named for the Indian Chief Alligator, and two other lakes, one called Lake Louise.

Brother Ned and his wife, Eliza had a little boy, Norman, who Eliza brought to visit us. He was six months old at the time and was a good baby with beautiful brown eyes like Eliza and black hair like Brother Ned. We hated for them to leave and we never saw Eliza again for she died three weeks after the birth of her second son, Frederick. Norman was about two years old then. Soon after Brother Ned came to take us to Lake City to live with him and his two babies.

It was in the month of September 1847 that Brother returned home and Mother, Sister and I accompanied him. Mother had planned to leave Father before this. We took passage on a steamboat, the Sarah Spaulding, one of the regular mail and passenger steamboats which came twice a week from Jacksonville or Savannah and stopped at Picolata to leave mail and passengers. It went down as far as Enterprise, stopping at Palatka enroute.

We left the boat at Jacksonville and remained there ten days. Then Brother hired a four-mule wagon and driver for transportation. Some furniture, beds and bedding, with provisions were placed in the wagon, for the journey of 60 miles to Lake City took us ten days. Such a journey—the rain poured down nearly every day and the roads were gullied and washed out. Bridges over large streams were either washed away or impassable. In some places we had to wait until the water fell sufficiently to ford the stream. Some nights we stopped at farm houses and spent the night, others we camped out. Mother, Sister and I slept in the wagon—Brother Ned and Bill, the driver, would cut down saplings and make a tent, covered with branches, under which they rested for the night. We had plenty of baker's bread, ham and rice and we purchased sweet potatoes, chickens and eggs from the country people—often cooking our meals in the woods.

Soon after reaching Lake City, we were everyone taken sick with chills and fever. Some days we were all in bed at the same time, for we had contracted maleria [malaria], camping in those wet woods. We all finally recovered and the two babies were brought home; but little Freddie only lived three months after we took him. Norman was a lovely child, his hair curled in pretty black ringlets all around his head and he was very fair. He was Sister's especial care and the first word he ever said was "Nina," Sister's pet name.

There was a rich old man named Summerlin [Jacob Summerlin Sr.], living near us who wanted a teacher for his two daughters, so Sister took the position. I went to school to her too. For a school room we had a large room upstairs in Capt Summerlin's house, and for a short time we had a pleasant time at school. But when Capt Summerlin died [on January 15, 1848] the family dispersed and the two [Summerlin] girls, Rebecca and Louise, were sent to Bowman's Academy at Quincy, near Tallahassee, Florida.[5]

My Mother and Brother rented the Summerlin home and kept boarders. Brother had started a wheelright shop on a street opposite us and here he also made all the coffins supplied to the town and surrounding country. Every wealthy planter kept a carriage in those days and many of these were sent to Brother's shop to be repaired.

While Capt Summerlin was living, I used to go with Lou and a lot of little darkie girls back of their field in the pine woods near a graveyard; there we used to ride on a "Flying Jenny,"—a tree stump, on which a wide thick puncheon was attached. A hole had been bored in the puncheon and a peg of hardwood, driven through it so that when an equal number of children got on each end of the puncheon and one of them gave the board a push we'd go whirling around. The old grave-yard near which we had our sport is now the fine cemetery of Lake City [Oak Lawn]. Brother Ned and Norman both lie there.

When Norman was four years old, Brother married again to Mary Jane Hogan, a half sister of his first wife. After his marriage Brother bought land away on the other side of town and built himself a two-storied house near Lake DeSoto and there he took his family to live a short time after Mary Jane[']s first child, Albert, was born.

Mother kept the hotel for another year and while we were still there Sister and I went to dancing school. Our teacher was an Alabamian who possessed the romantic name of "Marquise de Lafietty Rose." He was slender but not very tall, played the violin beautifully but was really a man of very little intellect. I was always fond of dancing and when I was a very small child Father used to play his violin for us and Mother and Sister used to teach us how to dance. So the dancing school was a delight to me and I learned steps and figures very quickly. Every Wednesday evening Mr Rose would let any of the relatives and friends of his scholars come and dance with us. I enjoyed these evenings and grown gentlemen used to seek me for a partner because I danced so well.

The young gentlemen of the town very often got up what we called "Cold Water Parties." They commenced at early candle-light and lasted until about eleven o'clock. I was always included in the invitations, along with Mother and Sister, and we used the large upper floor of the court house as a ballroom. The room was decorated the morning before the ball with great branches of magnolia leaves, vines and flowers. All the young ladies and gentlemen used to assist. After we moved to Lake City Mother and Sister used to prepare the refreshments for these balls for years. When I was about seventeen [c. 1854], I went to an [af]fair at a farmhouse in the country, about four miles from Lake City, for a young couple who had married the night before. We danced from seven o'clock and had supper about eleven. As soon as supper was over we danced until two o'clock in the morning and then sat around until about four, when it was light enough to start home.

Many a night we danced in the courthouse when court was in session. We [also] used the Crystal Palace as a ballroom. Capt [William B.] Ross had built a large drygoods and grocery store just opposite the public square and the upper floor extended the whole length of the store below. This room made a fine ballroom and many a night we held a dance there.

One day Sister went to Capt Asa Stewart's to spend the day, in company with a friend, Mrs. [Harriet Scarborough] Wright. They both rode horseback. Sister was a fine rider and perfectly fearless, but Dolphin, the horse she rode was not very gentle. They spent a very pleasant day, but when they started homeward they had to pass through a long lane at the entrance to town. Just as they were nearing the lane a lot of hogs came running, grunting and squealing out of the woods. Dolphin took fright and away he went, running full speed through the lane. Sister's girth became disarranged, the saddle turned, and she was thrown face downward across a stump in the middle of the road, her chest striking the stump, injuring her internally. Mrs Wright's horse carried her into town as far as the Hancock Hotel and threw her over the pailings into the yard, the sharp point of a pailing tearing off a piece of her scalp.

It was nearly suppertime when Dolphin and Mrs Wright's horse passed our gate, still running. Dolphin belonged to Dr [James S.] Jones, who boarded at Mr [John Wesley] Lowe's and he never stopped his mad flight until he reached the Lowe's house. Mother was frantic, the servants all frightened and we were all sure that Sister was killed. We saw some men carrying Mrs Wright's unconscious body home, so several neighbors went up the road where they met Sister walking home by herself for she had never lost consciousness. She did not appear ill until that night when she started hemorrhaging. For several months she was very ill and had to be kept quiet. The doctor would not even allow her to wear the tight dresses that were the fashion of the day, so she was confined to the house in her wrapper. She continued to have hemorrhages every now and then for about three years. The doctor said that one of her lungs was injured by the fall and she was always delicate after that and tired easily.

The Summerlin place where we were living was on the outer edge of the town proper; so when Mother decided to discontinue taking boarders, we moved into town. Here we lived a very quiet life in a small cottage belonging to Brother Eddie which he let us have—rent-free.

III

Sojourn in Charleston

Florida in the 1850s possessed no town with a population greater than 3,000. Key West with 2,800 led the list, while Jacksonville's 2,100 residents merited it only fourth place. Lake City, half of whose population consisted of black slaves, by 1860 contained only 659 souls. Yet the town stood as Florida's tenth largest urban center.[6] Many Floridians, accordingly, lived and died without experiencing the wonder of a real city, but in 1852 Sarah Pamela Williams received what was denied to most of her fellow Lake City inhabitants: She was permitted a voyage to the Southeast's grandest city.

FROM "SARAH PAMELA WILLIAMS (HER AUTOBIOGRAPHY)."

When I was thirteen years of age my mother's youngest (and only living[)] brother came to visit us. He was Albert Gallatin Mackey, a celebrated Mason who had come to visit the Lodge of Ancient Free and Accepted Masons in Lake City, as well as Mother and her family. I had not seen him in ten years but Sister had visited Charleston when she was about sixteen. Uncle had been a practicing physician in Charleston, S.C. when he was quite a young man, but had given up his practice and devoted his life to the Masonic cause. He begged Mother to let me visit his family for at least six months so I could study with his eldest daughter and get acquainted with my kin. I had never been away from home longer than three weeks in my life and I was not very anxious to leave Mother and Sister. But I did wish to see Aunt (I had been named for her) and my mother was very fond of her.

So,—in April, Brother Ned [Ives] went with me as he was on his way to New York to purchase goods for his store. On the 11th of April 1852, we got into the big old jostling mail coach for Jacksonville. We left Alligator about 10:00 AM and travelled all night long, changing horses every fifteen or twenty miles along the route. We had breakfast at Moses Barber's [present-day

Macclenny], where we stopped that night out of the rain in '47, on our way to Lake City to live. The women wore sunbonnets still and waited on the table.

We reached Jacksonville late in the afternoon on the 12th of April. Here I stayed with the Bisbees [merchant Cyrus Bisbee and his wife Virginia J. Robion Bisbee] who were friends of my mother's. The next afternoon we boarded the steamboat "Florida" and proceeded on our journey to Charleston where we arrived on Saturday at 11:00 pm.

Soon after the gangplank was put out, Uncle came aboard, and we all got into an omnibus (I had never seen such a vehicle before). It was very comfortable and commodious and rolled along very smoothly on the paved streets. Street lights blazed from every corner and I felt like I had reached Fairyland. The handsome stores on King Street were all lit up and the drug stores with their great fancy bottles filled with colored water seemed charming; besides the moving throng of gayly dressed people were a continual feast to my "country" eyes.

Uncle lived on East Calhoun Street near the corner of Washington Street and it was quite a long ride from the Southern Wharf. When we reached Uncle's house, Aunt and the older children, Charlotte, Franklin and Harriet came running to meet us. Edmund and Arthur had gone to bed long before we arrived. My dear Aunt hugged and kissed me and made me welcome to her heart and home, and all the remaining years of her life I loved her fondly. She had such lovely hazel eyes and the sweetest smile imaginable. Brother Ned remained with us a few days, then continued his journey North; he returned after a few weeks on his way home and spent a few more days with us, and after he left I suffered all the tortures of homesickness. I would have given ten years of my life just for one look at my mother's face. But this passed after awhile.

Every afternoon Lottie and I dressed and either received callers (young girls about our age) or returned their visits; or we went for long walks with Nurse Mary (an Irishwoman) and the little boys.

Uncle had planned to send Lottie and me to Madame DuPre's school for young ladies but when a yellow fever epedemic broke out (though I had it when I was three years old, I was not yet acclimated), Madame DuPre moved her school up to Akin [Aiken] for the term. Then the smallpox came and after that, in the winter months, the cholera; so we were kept at home.

Uncle had written to Mother before the six months of my visit had elapsed and begged her to let me stay for the rest of the year and he would return home with me himself, so I was permitted to remain. Oh how different this city life [was] from all I had ever known before! I felt like a wild bird of the forest whose wings had been clipped and who was held bound by the bars of a cage. All were kind, especially Aunt and Uncle, but things were so different,—my dress, my pronunciation and my very individuality were changed! I never went with a skip and a jump anywhere, not even in the backyard. My skirts were lengthened a little and when I went on the street I wore a thick blue veil over my face [and] a bonnet and my hands were encased in kid gloves. My hair was no longer in "pigtails" but braided smoothly and pinned up in the back. When there was company for tea, or we went to a friend's for that social occasion, we had tea handed to us, which we placed on one knee and a tiny plate of refreshments on the other. We sat very quietly and listened to the talk of our elders and replied very meekly and modestly if we were addressed.

We never called boys by their first names, as Charlie, Tom or Harry. It was always Mr Cotchet, Mr Wightman, etc. Two of the boys I liked were Charles Wightman and Charley Cotchet. They were nice, gentlemanly boys and used to try to make me feel at ease, but although I was passionately fond of dancing I would not have danced with one of those half-grown boys for anything. Charlie used to send me books to read and bo[u]quets of the most beautiful flowers and lovely fruit but I learned to hate the sight of him because even Uncle used to tease me about him. In later years he married a third cousin of mine, [Mary] Victoria Miller.

Uncle and Aunt used to teach Lottie and me French, history, reading, writing, grammar, geography, arithmetic etc. I learned fairly well but I learned more of people and things.

I was very fond of my cousin Frank who was eleven years old.

When the War broke out Frank went into the Army at sixteen and made a brave Confederate soldier.

Charleston, South Carolina was a beautiful old city when I visited it. There were so many aristocratic dwellings, surrounded by high stone walls— usually surmounted by broken glass bottles, with little iron gates let in the walls and large folding gates for the carriages to pass through. I could some- times get a glimpse of oleanders and fruit trees through an open gate and often I saw trees laden with bright scarlet fruit like large haws—I think they must have been Siberian crab-apples. I have often thought of those trees when handling crab-apples.

When my year's visit was up Uncle took me home and stayed with us for ten days. Then Sister went back to Charleston with him and remained there for a year.

When I returned to Alligator after my year in Charleston I was fifteen years of age and in our village was considered a young lady. Mother and I lived in a small cottage at the corner of two streets (they had no names then).

I soon got a school of small children to teach and Mother taught piano in several families.

Mother and I bought a town lot together and were having a house built at the time of my marriage in 1857. After my marriage, I gave my share of the property to her and she and Sister continued to live there and teach until Sister married in 1859. After that, Mother divided her time between Brother Eddie, Sister and myself. When my husband died in 1861 she moved into my home and continued to live with me until her death.

IV

Planter's Wife and Widow

A gay and polished Sarah Pamela Williams returned from Charleston, South Carolina, to remote Lake City, Florida, and she soon became one of the small community's true belles. While her immediate family suffered some financial discomforts (her father died in 1856), she attracted the attentions of many of the county's leading young blades, sons and heirs of area planter families.

FROM "SARAH PAMELA WILLIAMS (HER AUTOBIOGRAPHY)."

In 1854 I returned to my home in Alligator, Florida from Charleston, South Carolina, where I had spent a year with my aunt and uncle,—Sarah Pamela and Albert Gallatin Mackey.

One afternoon, Sister and I went to a store owned by Mr Silas [L.] Niblack and Mr Alexander Young. Here we met Mr Niblack's nephew, William Niblack, who was clerking in the store. We had known Mr Niblack and his wife from our earliest residence in Alligator, and had visited in their home. Willie, who was an orphan, had come to live with them. He was a handsome boy with large brown eyes and beautiful hair. Soon after our meeting he began to visit our home.

Willie and I became engaged, with Mother's approval, when he was eighteen and I was sixteen. We were married on the 24th day of May, 1857, after having been engaged for three years. Willie was twenty-one on the 16th of April and I was nineteen, the December before our marriage.

After our marriage, we boarded for four months and then went to housekeeping in our own home, five miles south of Lake City. Willie purchased a plantation of 360 acres, with a small log house on it and in which we set up our lares and penates until our dwelling house was completed. It was already framed, but lumber was very scarce as there were no mills nearer than Lake City, and they could not supply the increasing demands. But Willie found a man who had bought enough to build a house (and never had built it as he and his wife parted company before the foundation was laid.)

Our house was of the commonest style of that part of the country. It was what they called a double penned log house. These houses were never known to be blown down in storms nor to fall down from old age. The roof might fall in and decay but the sturdy pine logs gradually sank, from age and as I heard a country man remark: "They never fell down, they squatted."

We had boarded in town for one month; the rest of the time we boarded with Willie's Uncle Silas and Aunt Atty Niblack [Atalie Scarborough Niblack], in the country.

On the 1st of November 1857 we moved to Chicora (the name I gave our home; the Seminole name for the mocking bird). We had no mocking birds around us at first, but after we got our shade trees to growing we had plenty of them. One sang every summer for years in an oak tree near the house and on moonlight nights he sang all night long.

We had oaks planted in front, a Pride of India at each end of the house, with dogwood and redbud (Judas) trees, at the north end where the parlors were. There was a broad walk from our front steps to the gate and it used to be swept nearly every day. On each side of it were two immense cape jasamin bushes (fully 6 ft. in diameter) which bore bushels of flowers. By the front gate were oleanders and several date palms. In the course of time we had sweet and bitter-sweet orange trees as well as lemon. We also had peach and plum orchards, quince and pomegranite bushes just as everyone else did.

Willie owned several negro slaves who had been hired out during his minority. He brought them home when we moved to Chicora. Willie had given me a nice pony that I named Roland. I also had a fine saddle. Willie bought himself a grey horse and we used to ride all over the woods together. Sometimes we rode to Rose Creek to fish in the deep ponds; sometimes just to enjoy the ride. We had good neighbors. Our nearest were the [Clark D. and Minerva J.] Parks family, three quarters of a mile south. The two families of Hunters [Green H. and Mary B. Hunter and John C. and Rosannah Young Hunter?] lived east of us one and a half miles and Uncle John Niblack lived two miles southwest; the Bryants [Langley and Mary Ann Worthington Bryant] east of us and the [Stephen] Sparkmans northeast.

In the Fall of 1857, my husband was elected Tax Assessor and Collector for the County of Columbia (since divided into four counties, Suwanee, Bradford, New River and Columbia). His duties kept him from home three weeks out of every month but two. He went once or twice a year to Tallahassee to turn over all monies collected. Many a time when he was away from home I had thousands of dollars in the house but I was never molested in any way. If I went out to spend the day, I carried the money in a covered basket, with work or some article of clothing over it and none suspected that I had it.

In June 1859, my husband had a dreadful fall. He drove a very wild horse attached to his buggy. The horse had been trained by a former owner to start the instant his master stepped into the buggy. Unfortunately William was talking to a man and never thought about what the horse would do. He stepped up to take his seat in the buggy, but before he got well up the horse started off and Willie was thrown out face downward with so much force that he ruptured a blood vessel in the pit of his stomach and he had a dreadful hemorrhage. Everyone was very kind to him. They caught and restored his horse, and would have detained him if they could but he was determined to get home. He ate a little salt, then drove the six miles home by himself. Soon after he had eaten supper the hemorrhage commenced again and we sent for Dr. [James Hamilton] Hill. He gave him something that stopped the hemorrhage for that night, but the doctor said he had lost a gallon and a half of arterial blood, which no medical skill could restore, and he could not live over twelve months. He was never well again.

Our little boy [Albert Leslie Niblack] was born the 23rd of August 1859, the joy of my life. He had the dark brown eyes of his father but his hair was like spun gold and grew in such soft pretty rings about his head, when he was an infant but turned a dark red when he grew older. He was very fair and fat and weighed 25 pounds when he was two months and a half. All of his dresses had to be enlarged in the sleeves when he was three weeks old.

In 1861, on the 10th day of March, William died; had he lived to the 16th of April he would have been 25 years of age. He took consumption and for three months before his death was confined to his bed and lost his voice. His death was very peaceful.

The baby was my comfort all the troublous times that followed William's death. What would I have done without him?

Norman [Ives], my nephew had come to live with us, with his father's consent. He was a good child, about fourteen years of age when William died.

My mother came to live with me too, as Sister had married [William Daly Burtchaell] the 17th of February 1859. Mother stayed with Brother Eddy and also with Sister and her husband and also at my house. At the time William and I married she had a home of her own.

V

Civil War and
Its Aftermath

While family experiences, regional divisions, and political changes in place by the turn of the century proffered complications that discouraged George G. Keen from reminiscing about Civil War and Reconstruction, Sarah Pamela Williams felt no such constraints. A planter's widow, she had struggled mightily to maintain her husband's legacy, and she took great pride in her accomplishments. Her relation of them completed her memoir of Florida life.

FROM "SARAH PAMELA WILLIAMS (HER AUTOBIOGRAPHY)."

On the 8th of April 1861 the first gun was fired from Fort Sumter on the Star of the West, a northern vessel entering Charleston Harbour; and the Civil War began between the North and South. My husband held a commission as Captain of a militia company, which he was too sick to ever drill.

We, in our quiet country neighborhood, never felt the horrors of invasion as so many places did; but we never knew but what our turn would come next. The [February 20, 1864,] battle of the Ocean Pond (or by some called the battle of Olustee) was the nearest to us. It was thirteen miles [eastward] from us and there were skirmishes within three miles of Lake City, at the Sand Pond; but the Northern forces were driven back and never reached Lake City. We could hear the cannon distinctly and the rifle rallies. My brother-in-law [William Daly Burtchaell] had joined the Confederate forces and was away in Virginia at that time with General Lee's army; and my sister and her two children were living with us. I shall never forget the day of that battle. From early morning, vehicles of all sorts and descriptions filled with people, traversed the public road in front of my house, fleeing from the town and seeking safety in the settlements south of us. I was having sugar cane planted back of the kitchen, and Henry, my oldest negro man[,] advised me to bu[r]y some provisions in case the Yankees did come. I told him to go ahead and so he and Jiggins, the other negro man, dug a hole and buried in boxes,—meat, salt, sugar and other necessities. I had them all dug up again when the excitement had passed away.

We all learned to spin and to weave. We wore dresses for common everyday use of homespun, coarse and heavy and trimmed with rows of buttons. The foundations of these buttons were pieces of gourds cut round about the size of a fifty cent piece and covered with scraps of the dress material. Some girls made buttons of persimmon seeds.

We did not raise wheat in our neighborhood before the war, so wheat flour became a scarce article. We did raise rye and made bread and battercakes of it. But after awhile sugar got scarce in Georgia and men began to bring loads of wheat flour in sacks and trade it to us for sugar. For the last two years of the war we bought wheat seed, sowed it and made our own flour. It was coarse because we had no mills with bolting cloths so it had to be ground as our corn was, in the same mills, but it was wholesome and tasted all right. Coffee was another need and the women tried all sorts of substitutes; parched rye, peas, beans and okra, even cornmeal and sweet potatoes. The potatoes were cut in thin squares, dried in the sun, parched and ground, and it did taste something like coffee. If we mixed in a portion of real coffee (java, for instance) with a substitute, it made it more palatable. We even tried peanuts (Floridans called them "pindars") for coffee. Sister and I tried all kinds of dishes made of cornmeal. Confederate Cake was one of them. We used butter, eggs and dried peaches, and it was something like a pudding or more on the order of a fruit cake. It did not taste bad, but the cornmeal foundation was against its popularity.

We gave tithes of all our crops (except cotton) to the Confederate States Government for the support of our soldiers. Poor Norman and all of our neighbor's boys had to go into the army or navy at sixteen years of age. Norman went to Charleston and enlisted in the Navy, becoming one of the crew of the "Indian Chief," a ship employed as one of the guard ships in Charleston harbour.

It was near the close of the war when the boys were forced to enlist or be conscripted and all of the boys volunteered. I think they were anxious to go. Young Hunter and William Hunter (cousins) John Parker and Norman were what the women of our immediate neighborhood called "our boys." They all returned home after a few month's hardships and I don't think any of them ever saw a battle.

We heard the news of General Lee's surrender at Appomatox with anguish—to us it was as though the heavens had fallen. My brother-in-law had been taken prisoner at Gettysburg and my sister didn't hear anything of him for three months. Several men, on their return home, reported him dead. Sister never believed these tales and said she knew he was alive. At last she got a letter from him; he was a prisoner on Johnston's Island [Johnson's Island Prison, Ohio—located in Lake Erie] and there he remained for nearly two years, where he was subjected to every kind of hardship.[7] When he was at last released and returned to us, he was quite broken down; so weak that he used to faint.

We all saw hard times for several years after the war closed. The negroes were declared free in May 1865 in our part of the country. Jiggins left me immediately, though he attended to the crops on the land I let him use before he was declared free. Henry [Niblack], Bet and their children remained for eight months until the crops were gathered in. I gave Henry a fourth of all we made. As I furnished the seed, land, horses and mules, that was a lawful division. Norman had returned to me and helped about the farm in various ways. He took charge of everything after Henry left and we hired laborers for the next year's work.

Sister and her husband started a school soon after he came back. The neighbors built a schoolhouse on a piece of my land that was in the central part of the community, about a half mile from my house; and many of the boys who had been in the war went there. I hired a negro woman who cooked part of the time and who worked in the field when an extra hand was needed. We got along some how and had plenty to eat, if not of the best.

Sister and her family moved to Lake City and her husband started a steam saw mill below the town on the road to Jacksonville. Then he ran a farm on his land beyond Lake City. Finally they moved to Newark, New Jersey and Mr Burtchaell went to railroading in Duchess County, New York. After living in the North for three years, Sister and the four children returned to us and Mr Burtchaell went railroading in Alabama.

On the 15th of January 1870, Brother Eddie [Ives] died of [the grippe; i.e., the flu] and on the 28th of October of the same year, my son, Leslie died of a general congestion. In 1871 Sister removed with her children to join her husband in Cuthbert, Georgia where he was Chief Engineer on the Brunswick and Albany Railroad.

Norman went to work for that Railroad too but did not remain long. Only Mother and I were left so we moved to Lake City on January 8, 1872 and rented rooms from Brother Eddie's widow; and I rented out my place in the country. Two months later, on the 8th of March 1872 my mother died of catarrhal fever. Norman went into the Express Company and I was left alone.

Sister and her husband wrote for me to visit them which I did in May 1872. I went to stay six months and I was there with them from 1872 to

September 1877, having married [William Spence Kelly] at their house on the 3rd of June 1874.

My son, Charles was born November 18, 1875 and in 1877 my husband myself and son moved in September to Atlanta, Georgia where we have lived ever since. Charles was eight years old before I ever visited Lake City again. (My visit of six months was extended to eleven years).

APPENDIX
THE CAST OF CHARACTERS

The reminiscences of George Gillett Keen and Sarah Pamela Williams contain references to hundreds of individuals whose lives affected the authors' personal stories, as well as the evolution of nineteenth-century Florida history. The following list offers basic information, where available, concerning these persons and their interrelationships with the authors and other principal characters of the reminiscences. Unfortunately, courthouse fires in Columbia and Lafayette Counties destroyed many pertinent records, creating an information void that was compounded by the unavailability of most area newspapers of the period. Adding to the paucity of available information, the Civil War ravaged Levy and Lafayette Counties and surrounding vicinities. Doubtlessly some individuals died unrecorded deaths during the conflict, while many Unionist refugees departed Florida soon after the coming of peace in 1865.

Adams, John. Born about 1826 in South Carolina, Adams in 1850 clerked for Lake City merchant Thomas D. Dexter. He apparently departed Columbia County by 1851, and his whereabouts thereafter are not known.[1]

Alexander, Rebecca B. Summerlin Steele. A daughter of Jacob Summerlin Sr. and his first wife, Mary Ann Hagan, Rebecca Summerlin was born in September 1835, probably in Columbia County, Florida. Raised at Lake City and educated at Quincy, she was married about 1859 to Dr. Holmes Steele of Jacksonville, who served as state senator for Duval County in 1865–1866 and as his city's mayor. Steele died May 6, 1867, and Rebecca was remarried in early 1872, to James H. Alexander of Liberty County, Georgia. She died in Reidsville, Tattnall County, Georgia, on July 26, 1900.[2]

Alligator. The Seminole leader Alligator (or Halpatter Tustenuggee) likely was born in Florida about 1795. Prior to 1813 he kept his camp near the site of present-day Lake City, but thereafter he lived in the Hernando County area and on the Peace and Alafia Rivers. Believed to be a brother or half brother of the chief Billy Bowlegs, Alligator emerged as an important figure during the Second Seminole War. Ultimately removed from Florida, he remained alive in Indian Territory at least as late as January 1857.[3]

Autrey, Fennell. See Fennell Otray.

Baker, James McNair. Born July 20, 1821, in Robeson County, North Carolina, Baker arrived in Columbia County, Florida, as a young lawyer about 1849. He served during 1861–1865 as a Confederate States senator and sat as an associate justice of the Supreme Court of Florida in 1866–1868. Baker died at Jacksonville on June 20, 1892. Baker County, Florida, was named in his honor.[4]

Barber, Moses. Barber was born about 1808 near Augusta, Georgia. He settled near present-day Macclenny in Baker County, Florida, during the 1830s. He died there, likely in connection with the Battle of Olustee, in February 1864.[5]

Barnes, James A. A native of Darlington County, South Carolina, James A. Barnes was born about 1832. A carpenter by trade, he arrived at Lake City, Florida, during the 1850s. Likely following the Civil War he married Laura K. Barnes there. About the turn of the century the couple relocated to Osceola County. James A. Barnes died at Kissimmee on March 11, 1903.[6]

Bell, Abigail. Born in Tennessee about 1810, Abigail Grimes married Thomas Bell on September 9, 1837, in Austin County, Texas. She apparently died there about 1858–1860.[7]

Bell, John Gideon. Born during 1818 in Nassau County, Florida, John Gideon Slade Bell was the son of Nancy Slade and Thomas Bell. He married Penelope Green in Hamilton County, Florida, on October 13, 1837. On January 4, 1854, Slade, as he then was known, was adopted by Thomas Bell in Austin County, Texas, following the death of Bell's legitimate son. John Gideon Bell and his wife relocated in February 1855 from Hamilton County to Bellville, Austin County, Texas. In 1870 he was elected state senator for the Thirteenth District, which encompassed Austin, Wharton, and Fort Bend Counties. Bell died at Bellville on September 17, 1895.[8]

Bell, Thomas. A North Carolina native, Bell was born about 1792. Departing Florida soon after the outbreak of the Second Seminole War, he settled in present-day Austin County, Texas. There on September 9, 1837, he married Abigail Bell. They are credited as founders of Bellville, Texas. Thomas's son John died on January 4, 1854, precipitating the legal adoption by Thomas of his illegitimate son, John Gideon Slade. Thomas died at his Bellville residence on January 10, 1858.[9]

Bexley, Augustus R. Born in Georgia about 1820, Bexley began to practice medicine at Lake City, Florida, during the 1840s. His first wife, Clarissa, died on June 21, 1855, and he was soon remarried to Sarah Scarborough, daughter of Stirling and Susan Scarborough. Dr. Bexley died at Lake City in 1864.[10]

Bisbee, Cyrus. Merchant Cyrus Bisbee was born in New Hampshire on November 20, 1817. He settled in Jacksonville in 1837, later marrying Virginia J. Robion. Bisbee died in Jacksonville on June 18, 1889.[11]

Bisbee, Virginia J. Born Virginia J. Robion in St. Augustine on March 27, 1829, Mrs. Bisbee met Cyrus Bisbee in Jacksonville, where the couple lived for the remainder of their lives. She died on April 25, 1888.[12]

Blount, John (Chief Blount). A Creek chieftain also known as Laufauka, Blount served with Andrew Jackson's forces during the Creek War of 1813–1814 and the War of 1812. He settled after 1816 on the Apalachicola River at modern Blountstown before emigrating to Texas in 1833. He died about 1834–1835, but some of his warriors who remained behind in Florida assisted in operations against hostile Indians during the Second Seminole War.[13]

Blount, Riley Readding. Born February 14, 1824, in Beaufort District, South Carolina, Blount moved with his parents, John Churchill Golding Readding Blount and Elizabeth Varn Blount, to Columbia County, Florida, in 1835. He married Jane Varn Knight on October 24, 1844, and moved with her to the area of modern Bartow, Polk County, in 1851. Jane died November 15, 1878, and Blount married Emma L. Whidden on March 10, 1879. He died in Hillsborough County, Florida, on October 9, 1887.[14]

Bonnell, John, Jr. Bonnell was born about 1814 in Georgia. He married Carolina Beal in Columbia County, Florida, in April 1837. He was remarried by 1861 to Elizabeth Mole. Bonnell died, likely in Columbia County, in late 1892 or early 1893.[15]

Bonnell, John, Sr. Bonnell was born in South Carolina about 1778. He remained alive in Columbia County, Florida, in 1850 but apparently died before 1860.[16]

Boozer, Rufus T. Lake City attorney Rufus T. Boozer was born August 28, 1866, in Prosperity, Newberry County, South Carolina, the son of Henry S. and Mary Elizabeth Young Boozer. He moved in 1885 to Lake City, Florida, where for several years he clerked for J. E. Young. In 1894 Boozer achieved admission to the local bar. At Lake City he served on the city commission and for two terms as mayor. He also sat for a time on the county commission. On June 20, 1889, Boozer married Fannie Honorine Ross, daughter of Adolphus A. and Emma A. Francis Ross. Rufus T. Boozer died in West Palm Beach on November 14, 1948.[17]

Bowman, S. B. (Mrs.). During 1848 and 1849 Mrs. Bowman conducted the "Female Department" of the Quincy Male & Female Institute in Quincy, Florida. According to one advertisement of January 1849: "Her former patrons, and those who know her best, all agree in recommending her as a highly accomplished and successful teacher. She is competent to instruct in Music, French, Drawing, Embroidery and the English Branches."[18]

Bradley, Robert Duke. Born in South Carolina about 1803, Bradley arrived in Florida during December 1827. An Armed Occupation Act settler in present-day Hernando County, he served as state senator for the Eighteenth District in 1846 and as Hernando (then Benton) County state representative in 1850. Bradley's family, including his wife Nancy Wiggens Bradley, suffered an 1856 Indian attack during the Third Seminole, or Billy Bowlegs, War that resulted in the deaths of two of his children. Bradley died in Hernando County on December 14, 1857.[19]

Brannen, John Milledge. A native Georgian, Brannen was born to John Brannen Sr. and Eleanor Baggs Brannen on January 8, 1809. Present in Alachua (now Columbia) County by 1831, he married Eliza Bonnell there the following year. They remained alive in Columbia County in 1880.[20]

Branning, Edward. A man named B. E. Branning is listed on the 1845 Columbia County tax list. No other information concerning him is available.[21]

Brewer, Burriss. Brewer was born about 1790, likely in North or South Carolina. He married Lydia Mobley on November 25, 1819, in Effingham County, Georgia. Brewer had arrived in northeastern Florida by 1830 but relocated to Camden County before 1840. There he married Mary Nettles in December 1847. He was living in Camden County in 1853.[22]

Brewer, James W., Sr. The son of Burriss Brewer, James W. Brewer was born about 1815 in Georgia. With his wife Elizabeth Whidden Brewer he was living in Columbia County by the mid 1830s. After relocating in subsequent years to Madison and Hamilton Counties, they had returned to Columbia by 1860. Discharged from the Confederate army for disability in 1862, he apparently died in Columbia County during 1864–1865. His widow was living in Polk County in 1870.[23]

Broome, Robert W. Attorney Robert W. Broome was born in Florida during 1840. Living in Nassau County in 1860, he had opened up a legal practice at Lake City by 1866, where he remained until 1873. His whereabouts thereafter are not known.[24]

Brown, Epaminondas. The son of Robert Brown and Eliza Ann Clementine Pendergast, Epaminondas Brown was born April 29, 1841, in Columbia County, Florida. He married Mary J. King there on July 3, 1862. Except for service in the Confederate army, he worked in the county for the remainder of his life as a retail merchant, holding numerous local offices. He died on November 19, 1905.[25]

Brown, Esther Howell. Born in Camden County, Georgia, in 1801, Esther Howell was the sister of Joseph Howell. About 1820 she married Rigdon Brown in that county, moving to Florida with him in 1830. During the 1840s they relocated from Columbia to that portion of Hillsborough County that would become Polk County. Esther died in Hillsborough County on October 26, 1878.[26]

Brown, Loram P. Brown was born in Tattnall County, Georgia, in 1816, but he and his wife Eleanor were living in Columbia County, Florida, by the 1830s. Suffering from pneumonia, Brown was discharged from the Confederate army in Virginia on February 5, 1862. Presumably he died soon thereafter.[27]

Brown, Rigdon. Born about 1789 in Franklin County, Georgia, Rigdon Brown was the son of Meredith Brown. Rigdon was married to Esther Williams, daughter of Wilson Williams of Camden County. About 1820, in the same county, he was married to Esther Howell, daughter of Thomas Howell and sister of Joseph Howell. The Browns moved to Florida in 1830. He represented Columbia County in the legislative council's 1836 session before relocating to Hillsborough County in the early 1840s as an Armed Occupation Act settler. Rigdon and Esther are credited as being among the earliest pioneers of Polk County. Rigdon died in Hillsborough County on February 12, 1871.[28]

Brown, Robert. Robert Brown was born December 14, 1804, in Camden County, Georgia, to John and Sarah Brown. There he married Eliza Ann Clementine Pendergast on November 11, 1829, but within months they had moved to Florida, settling at Suwannee Shoals. Robert represented Columbia County on the legislative council in 1835, 1837, and 1838. In 1846 he became speaker of the Florida House of Representatives, afterward serving as senator for the Thirteenth District in 1850 and 1852. Brown died in Columbia County on February 28, 1860.[29]

Bryan, John. Born in Wayne County, Georgia, in 1810, John Bryan was the son of Philemon Bryan and Nancy Hawthorne. Before 1831 he moved to Hamilton County, Florida, where he and his wife Susan Singletary made their home near Blount's Ferry. John represented Hamilton County on the legislative council in 1837, in the territorial house of representatives in 1844, and in the state house of representatives in 1847. He died in Columbia County, Florida, in 1875.[30]

Bryant, Julia A. See Julia A. Bryant Niblack.

Bryant, Langley. The son of James and Sarah Bryant, Langley Bryant was born in Camden County, Georgia, on December 19, 1812. He married Mary Ann Worthington in Columbia County, Florida, on January 8, 1845. A substantial planter prior to the Civil War, Bryant died in Columbia County on November 2, 1878.[31]

Bryant, Mary Ann Worthington. Born November 13, 1825, in Georgia as the daughter of Samuel Worthington, Mary Ann married Langley Bryant in

Columbia County, Florida, on January 8, 1845. After his 1878 death she remained in the county until her own death at Lake City on June 2, 1907.[32]

Bryson, William, Sr. A North Carolina native, William Bryson was born September 20, 1811. He moved to Florida in 1858 to assist the construction of the Florida, Atlantic, and Gulf Central Railroad from Jacksonville to Lake City. Beginning in 1865 he practiced law at Lake City before moving to Live Oak in 1871 upon his appointment as circuit judge. Bryson died in Live Oak on August 29, 1881.[33]

Burtchaell, Maria Mackey Williams. A daughter of John Lee and Martha Mackey Ives Williams, Maria Mackey Williams was born in St. Augustine, Florida, on January 11, 1830. In the late 1840s she moved to Alligator (Lake City) with her mother and sister, Sarah Pamela Williams. There on February 17, 1859, she married William Daly Burtchaell. Maria Burtchaell died in Norcross, Georgia, on February 24, 1879.[34]

Burtchaell, William Daly. A native of Ireland and a civil engineer, William Daly Burtchaell was born about 1834. After moving to Lake City, Florida, in the 1850s he married Maria Mackey Williams, daughter of John Lee and Martha Mackey Ives Williams, on February 17, 1859. Following Civil War service in the Confederate States army and a postwar career discussed in Sarah Pamela Williams's reminiscences, Burtchaell died in Norcross, Georgia, on August 20, 1919.[35]

Caldwell, John M. Eventually becoming one of Florida's leading newspapermen, Caldwell was born November 21, 1846, in Madison, Florida, to William H. Caldwell and Lamanda Tarpley Strickland. Following Civil War service John married Jennie Goolsby in Hamilton County on August 25, 1867. Also a Baptist minister, he edited at various times the *Lake City Florida Index,* the *Jasper News,* and other organs. Caldwell died in Jasper on February 26, 1923.[36]

Call, Rhydon Mays. Born January 13, 1858, in Fernandina, Florida, R. M. Call was the son of George William Call and Sarah Stark Call. He married Ida C. Holmes in Jacksonville on April 11, 1877. Following two decades of service as a circuit judge, Call died in Jacksonville on December 15, 1927.[37]

Cannon, Peter. A pioneer of Columbia and, later, Lafayette Counties, Peter Cannon was born about 1812 in Georgia. He first married Elvy Cannon, born in Georgia, about 1817 and, seemingly, later married Betsy Cannon, born about 1823 in Florida. Apparently Peter remained alive in Lafayette County in 1885.[38]

Cannon, Samuel. Early biographical information on Samuel Cannon is not available. According to one report, he died at Lake City, Florida, on April 6, 1862.[39]

Caraway [Carroway], Archibald. Caraway was born about 1814 in South Carolina. He arrived in Columbia County during the 1830s, settling eventually in that portion that became Suwannee County. He married Susannah, who was born in North Carolina during 1818, and later married Charity (?), a Georgia native born in 1826. Caraway died in Suwannee County on November 25, 1871.[40]

Carruth, Cotesworth Logan. The son of Robert Carruth, C. L. Carruth was born in Cumberland, North Carolina, on October 14, 1802. He moved to Madison County, Florida, about 1830, and on March 26, 1833, he married Caroline White Livingston there. In subsequent years Carruth served in several local offices, including clerk of the circuit court. Caroline died in December 1847, and during 1851 C. L. married Rhoda A. Hinson Dean. He died, possibly in Suwannee County, Florida, in January 1865.[41]

Carruth, Rhoda A. Hinson Dean. Born in South Carolina about 1803, Rhoda A. Hinson married Micajah Dean before March 1820. The couple established a plantation in Columbia County, Florida, long before his death circa 1849–1850. In 1851 Rhoda married Cotesworth L. Carruth of Madison County. They lived in that portion of Columbia that became Suwannee County, and Rhoda continued to reside there at least until February 1863.[42]

Cason, John ("Jack"). Jack Cason was born in Georgia about 1785, the son of Ransom Cason and Phoebe Munden. He married Sarah Gillett, daughter of William and Elizabeth Gillett, in Wayne County, Georgia, in 1822. According to George G. Keen, Cason remained alive in Lafayette County, Florida, in July 1859, but he apparently soon thereafter died or moved from Florida.[43]

Cason, Noah. The son of John (Jack) and Sarah Gillett Cason, Noah Cason was born in Florida during 1836. He died as a Confederate soldier at Chattanooga, Tennessee, on July 3, 1862, leaving a widow, Jemima.[44]

Cason, Peter. See Peter Cannon.

Cason, William. Born about 1810 in Georgia, William Cason was the son of John (Jack) and Sarah Gillett Cason. He married Patience Cason, who was born in Georgia about 1830. Until the Civil War they lived in Lafayette County, Florida.[45]

Cathey, James Wiley. J. W. Cathey was born May 15, 1816, in North Carolina. A merchant at Lake City, Florida, he married Louisa, daughter of Sterling and Susan B. Scarborough, on September 5, 1847. James died November 22, 1879, in Columbia County.[46]

Cheshire, Handen. Cheshire was born in North Carolina on January 31, 1816. He and his wife Nancy became pioneer settlers of Hamilton County, Florida.

A minister and farmer, Cheshire was still living in Hamilton County at the time of his death on May 27, 1902.[47]

Collier, Joe. A Henry J. Collier, then residing in Statenville, Echols County, Georgia, sold land in Columbia County, Florida, on June 17, 1878. Collier, according to census records, was born in Georgia during 1845. He was still living in Echols County in late 1886.[48]

Conant, Sherman. Born about 1840 in Boston, Massachusetts, Conant came to Florida during the Civil War as a Union army officer. He emerged during the Reconstruction era as a leader of the state Republican Party and served as attorney general during 1870–1871. Conant also represented Duval County in the Florida House of Representatives in 1881. At various times he held other offices, including Leon County judge, United States marshal, and clerk of the United States District Court. He died in Palatka, Florida, on November 21, 1890.[49]

Cone, Kesiah. See Kesiah Cone Sheffield Hagan.

Cone, William (Billy). William Cone looms large as a pioneer settler and leader of southern Georgia and northeastern Florida. He was born December 24, 1777, in North Carolina to Maj. William Cone and Keziah Barber Cone. He married Jane Cason about 1800 in Screven County, Georgia, and in 1812 married Sarah Haddock in Glynn County, Georgia. Cone represented Glynn County in the Georgia House of Representatives in 1804 and Camden County at various times from 1807 to 1839. Soon thereafter he moved to Columbia County, Florida, which he represented in the territorial house of representatives in 1841–1842 and as a state senator in 1854 and 1856. Cone died in Columbia County on August 24, 1857.[50]

Corban, Arletta Ann Locklier. A daughter of Elijah and Keziah Locklier, Arletta Ann was born in Columbia County, Florida, about 1838–1841. In Lafayette County on January 8, 1860, she married William Corban, the son of Moses Corban. The couple refugeed during the Civil War in Cedar Keys, where William died on September 23, 1864. Arletta Ann's whereabouts thereafter are not known.[51]

Corban, Moses. Corban was born circa 1813–1815 in South Carolina. He and his wife Harriet settled in Columbia County, Florida, during the 1830s. After 1850 they relocated to Lafayette County, where he remained in 1873.[52]

Cotchet, Charley. Information not available.

Curry, Georgia Ann C. Munden. A daughter of James Munden, Georgia Ann was born in Florida about 1845. She married Leonard L. Curry in Lafayette County on August 31, 1859. They were living in Levy County in 1885, but her whereabouts thereafter are not known.[53]

Curry, Martha Harris Hooker Hagler. A daughter of William B. Hooker and Mary Amanda Hair Hooker, Martha Harris Hooker was born in Hamilton County, Florida, on February 21, 1835. On May 27, 1851, she married Benjamin Hagler in Tampa. They were divorced in 1866, and Martha married Zorrie J. Curry in Manatee County on October 30, 1869. Martha died in Tampa, Florida, on April 28, 1911.[54]

Curry, William A. William A. Curry's name appears on the 1847 Columbia County tax rolls, but other information about him is unavailable.[55]

Curtis, Virginia C. Smith. The daughter of Matthew Whit Smith and Martha Jane Smith, Jennie Smith was born in Georgia about 1844. She moved with her family to Columbia County, Florida, in the early 1850s. Likely soon after the Civil War she married Samuel Curtis. Seemingly, she died in Columbia County prior to 1880.[56]

Dancy, Francis Littlebury. Born in Tarboro, North Carolina, in 1806–1807, Dancy graduated from the United States Military Academy in 1826. He moved to Florida in 1833, where he married Florida Forsyth Reid in October. Dancy represented St. Johns County in the territorial house of representatives in 1842 and served during the Civil War as quartermaster general of Florida. He died in Orange Mills in 1890.[57]

Daniels, Aaron E. Aaron Daniels was born February 16, 1823, in Georgia. Likely he lived in Columbia County, Florida, by the 1830s, settling in the portion that became Suwannee County. His wife Adaline E. Daniels was born in Florida on January 15, 1841. Aaron died in Suwannee County on February 14, 1908.[58]

Daniels, Elam J. Born about 1821 in Georgia, Elam Daniels was a son of Isaac Daniels, according to George G. Keen. Elam fought in the Second Seminole War under Capt. Arthur Roberts. Subsequently he married Jensie M. Sullivan on February 22, 1856, in present-day Clay County, Florida. He died on December 31, 1864, in Highland, Clay County.[59]

Daniels, Isaac. Isaac Daniels was born in Georgia about 1795. On July 5, 1817, he married Celia Parker in Tattnall County, Georgia. By the 1830s they were living in Columbia County, Florida, where on February 12, 1837, Isaac received appointment as a justice of the peace. Isaac lived on his farm in Columbia County until 1862 when, apparently, he died.[60]

Daniels, J. W. (Berry). The son of Isaac and Celia Daniels, Berry Daniels was born in Columbia County, Florida, in 1843. During his relatively brief life Berry earned a reputation as a desperado. Eventually he was shot and killed in Fort Meade, Florida, in July 1876, leaving a widow, Mary E. Daniels, in Columbia County.[61]

Daniels, Jeff. Information not available.

Daughtrey, Arthur. Born July 15, 1812, Arthur Daughtrey was a North Carolina native. He immigrated to Columbia County in the 1830s, likely with his first wife, Eliza, who died in the county on May 20, 1863. Arthur was remarried there on January 5, 1865, to Lanetta A. Bridges. He died in Columbia County on October 30 or 31, 1883.[62]

Daughtrey, Lewis. Originally a Tennessean, Lewis Daughtrey was born about 1821. By 1850 he was living in Columbia County, Florida, but before 1870 he and his wife Lydia moved to Levy County. Apparently he died there circa 1878–1879.[63]

Day, Samuel T. A Columbia County, Florida, physician and planter prior to 1860, Samuel T. Day was born in Hanover County, Virginia, about 1838. Day remained a Loyalist during the Civil War and later helped to organize Florida's Republican Party. In 1871–1872 he held office as lieutenant governor, serving for several months in early 1872 as acting governor. In 1874 Day moved his family to Caldwell County, Texas, where he died on December 26, 1877.[64]

Dean, Rhoda Hinson. See Rhoda A. Hinson Dean Carruth.

Dees, James, Jr. The son of James and Nancy Dees, James Dees Jr. was born in Georgia (probably Pulaski County) about 1810. He may have moved to present-day Columbia County, Florida, with his parents prior to 1830. He remained there with his wife Sarah until 1856 and likely died sometime that year or soon afterward.[65]

Dees, James, Sr. Born during the 1770s, James Dees lived by 1810 in Pulaski County, Georgia. There he married Nancy Mason, the daughter of Mark Mason. They relocated to Alachua (now Columbia) County, Florida, by 1830. Available records suggest that he died in Columbia County about 1846.[66]

Dees, Mlton (or Melton Deese). Born March 6, 1852, in Hamilton County, Florida, Milton Dees was the son of Leonard and Malinda Towler Dees. He married Mary M. Sistrunk. Dees died in Columbia County, Florida, on September 20, 1899.[67]

DeLoach, Edmond J. A native of Bullock County, Georgia, DeLoach was born about 1830. During the 1850s he married Mary Ann Summerall, likely in Columbia County, Florida. DeLoach died in that county on March 3, 1883.[68]

DeShong, Caroline C. Born in Orange County, North Carolina, on July 16, 1834, Caroline was the daughter of Jesse Franklin and Manerva Boyles DeShong.

Jesse Franklin DeShong and Dr. Lewis DeShong were brothers, and Caroline was a cousin to Edna DeShong. Caroline lived in Tampa for a time during the 1850s. There on December 3, 1858, she married William C. Buchanan, a blacksmith from South Carolina. The date and place of Caroline's death are not known.[69]

DeShong, Edna. The daughter of Dr. Lewis DeShong and Rebecca Ann Pitman DeShong, Edna was born on August 7, 1845, near Tallahassee, Florida. During 1861 she married Seabren G. Hayman in Hillsborough County. Edna lived until January 1936, when she died in Tampa.[70]

Didwell, Josiah. Information not available.

Douglas, Tasset. Information not available.

Douglass, James. South Carolina native James Douglass was born about 1780. Apparently he married George G. Keen's grandmother Elizabeth Gillett, the widow of William Gillett. After her death he was remarried circa 1847 in Columbia County, Florida, to Nancy Slade. Having lived in Columbia County since 1830 or before, Douglass relocated in the late 1840s to Alachua County and then settled in present-day Lafayette County. He likely died there about 1876.[71]

Douglass, Nancy Slade. Born in Georgia about 1797, Nancy Slade married James Douglass in Columbia County, Florida, about 1847. Her date and place of death are not known.[72]

DuVal, William Pope. Florida's first territorial governor and the son of William and Ann Pope DuVal, William Pope DuVal was born at Mount Comfort near Richmond, Virginia, in 1784. On October 3, 1804, in Bardstown, Kentucky, he married Nancy Hynes, the daughter of Andrew and Elizabeth Wardford Hynes. A lawyer by profession, DuVal during 1813–1815 represented a Kentucky district in the United States Congress. President James Monroe in 1821 designated DuVal as a federal district judge for Florida and the following year appointed him governor. DuVal served as governor until 1834. Five years afterward he represented Calhoun County in the 1838–1839 constitutional convention, and in 1839–1841 he sat in the territorial senate (as president in 1841). DuVal moved to Texas in 1848, although he died in Washington, D.C., on March 18, 1854.[73]

Dyall, Joseph. The son of John Dyall, Joseph Dyall was born in Darlington District, South Carolina, in 1790. His first wife was named Jane, but he later married Martha Elizabeth Newsom in Suwannee County, Florida, on August 14, 1866. Although George G. Keen asserted to the contrary, Dyall did not serve in Florida's territorial council or state legislature. However, on February 11, 1835, he was appointed judge of the county court of Columbia County for a term of four years. He died in Suwannee County in March 1867.[74]

Edwards, William. Information not available.

Ellinger, Abraham. Born about 1830 in Germany, Ellinger worked during the 1850s as a clerk at Lake City, Florida. He was unmarried in 1860, and the following year he enlisted in the Second Florida Infantry (CSA). Ellinger was killed in Williamsburg, Virginia, on May 5, 1862.[75]

Ellis, Elizabeth. See Elizabeth Ellis Holder.

Ellis, Giles Underhill. The son of Giles and Elizabeth Hagan Ellis, Giles U. Ellis was born in Bulloch County, Georgia, on March 22, 1809. On April 22, 1830, he married Mary Branning, and following her death he married Nancy L. Jones Townsend during the 1850s. During the 1845 and 1848 legislative sessions Ellis represented Columbia County in the Florida House of Representatives. He died in the county on March 20, 1886.[76]

Ellis, Lydia. Information not available.

Ellis, Lydia Gillett. Born in Florida about 1830, Lydia was the daughter of George A. and Tempy Hull Gillett. On December 30, 1855, she was married in Alachua County to William Henry Ellis. After his death about 1866 her whereabouts are not known.[77]

Ellis, Thomas. The father of Lydia Ellis and Elizabeth Ellis Holder, Thomas was born during the 1770s in North Carolina. His parents were William and Mary Ellis, and his brothers included William and Giles Ellis. Thomas and his wife Elizabeth had at least one son, Herman, born in Pulaski County, Georgia, in 1810. By 1830 Thomas was living in Alachua (now Columbia) County, Florida, although during the decade he likely returned for a time to Georgia. By 1840 Thomas again called Florida his home, and he died in Columbia County about 1846.[78]

Ellis, William Henry. Born in South Carolina about 1820, William Henry Ellis lived in Alachua County, Florida, by the 1850s. There on December 30, 1855, he married Lydia Gillett. Following brief service in the Confederate army, he died in Alachua County about 1866.[79]

Emery, Nancy. See Nancy Emery Stewart.

Finegan, Joseph J. Born in Cloonis, Ireland, on November 17, 1814, Joseph J. Finegan settled in St. Augustine, Florida, prior to the 1835 outbreak of the Second Seminole War. After soldiering in that conflict he located at a plantation on Black Creek and engaged in numerous business enterprises, closely associating at times with David Levy Yulee. In 1861 Finegan represented Nassau County in

Florida's secession convention. During the Civil War he attained the rank of brigadier general in the Confederate States army. In 1865–1866 he sat in the state senate. Finegan died at Rutledge, near Fort Read, Orange County, Florida, on October 29, 1885.[80]

Fitchett, Charles H. A native of Georgia, Fitchett was born about 1807. During the 1830s he moved to Columbia County, Florida. There he was elected sheriff for a two-year term in November 1843, having already, according to George G. Keen, served in that capacity in the mid 1830s. Charles was defeated in a reelection attempt, and he and his wife Martha W. Fitchett relocated to Alachua County where he worked as a tailor. He died in Tampa on October 11, 1856.[81]

Fitzpatrick, Thomas B. According to George G. Keen, Fitzpatrick was about forty years of age in 1845, never married, and was the brother-in-law of William B. Ross. A Floridian by 1841, he was elected Columbia County sheriff over Charles H. Fitchett and William H. Rousseau on October 6, 1845. He retained the office until resigning on March 22, 1849. Fitzpatrick died in Columbia County, circa April 1849.[82]

Fleming, Lewis (Louis). A native of Spanish Florida, Lewis Fleming was born in 1798 to George and Susan Fatio Fleming. He was first married in Cuba to Augustina Cortez, a descendant of Hernando Cortez, but after her death he married Margaret Seton, daughter of Charles Seton. One of their sons, Francis P. Fleming, served as governor of Florida during 1889–1893. Lewis and Margaret Fleming lived primarily at their St. Johns River plantation on Fleming's Island, called by them Hibernia. Lewis died August 3, 1862.[83]

Floyd, Charles Rinaldo. The son of Congressman John Floyd and Isabella Mira Hazzard Floyd, Charles Rinaldo Floyd was born in Camden County, Georgia, on October 14, 1797. During a lifetime filled with public service he married twice: first to Catherine S. Powell on May 22, 1823; and then to Julia Ross Boog on September 9, 1831. Following service during the Second Seminole War he died at Fairfield Plantation, Camden County, on March 22, 1845.[84]

French, George W. George French was born about 1826 in Georgia. He and Mary Ann French were living in Columbia County, Florida, in 1850 and in Clay County ten years later. A farmer, George was released from the Tenth Florida Infantry (CSA) in February 1862 due to illness and may have died soon thereafter. His widow remained in Clay County in 1870.[85]

Futch, John. Georgia native John Futch was born April 28, 1807. He was present in Columbia County, Florida, in the 1830s and married Nancy Raulerson, likely Nickabod Raulerson's daughter, about 1836–1837. Within a year or two after the 1842 conclusion of the Second Seminole War, the couple joined in-laws already living on the new frontier in Hillsborough County. John died in Polk County on March 20, 1871.[86]

Gandy, Ned. Information not available.

Garrison, Sebourn D. (Sebe). Born about 1825 in Georgia, Garrison likely was a relation of Hernando County pioneer Isaac Garrison. Sebourn was residing in Hillsborough County by 1850 and working as a blacksmith. He remained there with his wife Martha a decade later, where he served in a Tampa home guard unit during the summer and early fall of 1861. Garrison's whereabouts thereafter are not known.[87]

Gillett, Adaline. According to George G. Keen, Adaline was the daughter of George and Tempy Gillett. Born in 1835 in Columbia County, Florida, she was killed by Indians during a March 16, 1838, attack on her family.[88]

Gillett, Anderson. Born 1802 in Georgia, Anderson was a son of William and Elizabeth Gillett. He married Sarah Morgan on May 13, 1824, and they moved to Alachua (now Columbia) County, Florida, in 1829. Gillett was living in Alachua County in 1860.[89]

Gillett, Daniel. Anderson Gillett's brother Daniel was born January 14, 1810, in Wayne County, Georgia, and he also resided in Alachua County, Florida, prior to 1830. Daniel's first wife, Myantha Raulerson, died in 1834, and he married Molcy Mariah Hair on December 22, 1836, in Columbia County. In the 1840s they relocated to Hillsborough County. Daniel died at Parrish, Manatee County, on September 6, 1890.[90]

Gillett, David. Another son of William and Elizabeth Gillett, David Gillett was born circa 1800 in Wayne County, Georgia. About 1826 he married Mary Collins, and they accompanied the family to Florida three years later. David died in Alachua County on January 8, 1859.[91]

Gillett, George A. George A. Gillett, fourth son of William and Elizabeth Gillett, was born in Wayne County, Georgia, but his date of birth is unknown. He married Tempy Hull on December 14, 1825. The couple spent just over twelve years together before they were killed by Indians in Columbia County on March 16, 1838.[92]

Gillett, Jackson J. Born in Columbia County, Florida, in February 1832, Jack Gillett was the son of Anderson and Sarah Gillett. On June 19, 1852, he married Malinda Morgan, the daughter of Ephraim and Mary Parker Morgan. After Civil War service Jack and Malinda moved further down the peninsula. He died in Pasco County on August 8, 1900.[93]

Gillett, Lydia. See Lydia Gillett Ellis.

Gillett, Molcy Mariah Hair. A daughter of William Hair, Molcy Mariah was born April 23, 1813, in Wayne County, Georgia. She married Daniel Gillett in Columbia County, Florida, on December 22, 1836, and died in Manatee County on February 26, 1895.[94]

Gillett, Tempy Hull. Personal information on Tempy Hull Gillett is scarce. She married George A. Gillett on December 15, 1825, and was killed with him by Indians in Columbia County, Florida, on March 16, 1838.[95]

Gillett, William. Fanny Raulerson's son William was born in Georgia about 1822. Having survived the Columbia County Indian attack of March 16, 1838, he married Queen Esther Revels in Madison County, Florida, on December 14, 1848. In July 1855 the Gilletts sold their Madison County holdings. Their where-abouts thereafter are not known.[96]

Gipson, John. Information not available.

Godfrey, Mrs. Other than that she was William Godfrey's mother, personal information is not available.

Godfrey, William. William Godfrey's name does not appear on Florida or Georgia census records, and personal data concerning him is not available from other sources. His presence was noted at Troupville, Lowndes County, Georgia, in November 1854 (organization of a Masonic lodge) and again in the county four years later (problems with debts). His reasons for leaving Columbia County, Florida, in early 1850 seem plain. A business dispute occurring between William Godfrey, Jacob E. Goodbread, and George W. S. Waldron at Suwannee Shoals during the fall of 1849 resulted in charges being filed against Godfrey for larceny. When the county grand jury refused to indict him, Godfrey chose to leave for better opportunities in Georgia.[97]

Goodbread, Adam Sowder. Born September 22, 1807, in Camden County, Georgia, Adam Sowder Goodbread was the son of Phillip and Catherine Sowder Goodbread. He married Elizabeth VanZandt, daughter of William and Maria B. VanZandt, in Nassau County, Florida, during 1837. She died in 1864, and on October 12, 1870, he married Julia V. McClellan Densler. Goodbread represented Florida's Fourteenth District in the state senate in 1845 and the Sixteenth in 1846. He died in Hamilton County, Florida, on October 25, 1887.[98]

Goodbread, Jacob Tapley. A brother of Adam Sowder Goodbread, Jacob Tapley Goodbread was born in Camden County, Georgia, on March 28, 1811. Along with his wife Jane D. Goodbread, daughter of Hugh and Elizabeth Dean Brown, he moved to Columbia County, Florida, in the 1840s. He died there on November 12, 1869.[99]

Goodbread, John McPherson Berrien. Born in Camden County, Georgia, in 1819, John M. B. Goodbread was the son of John S. Goodbread and Charity Crews Goodbread. In April 1845 he married Julia A. Hardee. Goodbread died at Wellborn, Suwannee County, on August 27, 1861.[100]

Goolsby, Thomas H. A native of Georgia, Goolsby was born about 1813. He was a resident of Columbia County, Florida, by the 1830s, and he and his wife Rebecca remained there at least until 1855. The date and place of his death are not known.[101]

Green, Penelope. Other than the fact that she married John Gideon Bell, personal information is not available.

Green[e], Thomas Jefferson. Green was born in South Carolina on September 30, 1838, and married Evaline E. Harvey. During 1868, 1869, and 1870 he represented Baker County in the Florida House of Representatives. He died in Columbia County on October 17, 1898.[102]

Greene, Burwell K. Born August 12, 1839, in Sumter County, Georgia, Burwell K. Greene resided in the Suwannee/Lafayette County, Florida, area by 1859. He married America Kirkpatrick in Madison County on January 7, 1866. Greene died in Hillsborough County, Florida, on June 7, 1913.[103]

Grime, George. Information not available.

Gunby, John H. Personal information concerning Gunby is not available. By May 1840 he lived at Jacksonville, and he appears on the 1846 Duval County tax rolls as John H. Gunby & Co., merchant. Jacksonville newspapers carried advertisements for him as a Savannah merchant in November 1851 and January 1853.[104]

Hagan, Kesiah Cone Sheffield. William A. Sheffield's mother, Kesiah Cone Sheffield, was born June 4, 1806, at Ivanhoe plantation, Bulloch County, Georgia. She was the daughter of Aaron Cone and Susan Marlow Cone. In 1828 she married Simon Sheffield in Bulloch County. He died in February 1837, and she later married James Hagan. Kesiah died in Bulloch County on October 10, 1897.[105]

Hagler, Benjamin J. Born in 1810 in Tennessee, Hagler lived in Hillsborough County by the 1840s. During 1849–1853 he served as sheriff. His first wife, Nancy, died in Tampa in 1850, and he subsequently married Martha Harris Hooker on May 27, 1851. They later divorced, and Hagler married Mrs. Viney Gage on July 26, 1866. He was living in Hillsborough County in 1885. The date and place of his death are not known.[106]

Hagler, Martha Harris Hooker. See Martha Harris Hooker Hagler Curry.

Hair, Martin. A brother of William Hair and uncle to Molcy Mariah Hair, Martin Hair was born in North Carolina about 1767. He died in Columbia County, Florida, circa May 1853.[107]

Hair, Mary Amanda. See Mary Amanda Hair Hooker.

Hair, Molcy Mariah. See Molcy Mariah Hair Gillett.

Haliday, S. F. The Reverend S. F. Haliday was born in New York about 1805. By 1840 he resided in Duval County, but ten years later he lived in Gainesville. During the Reconstruction era he served Alachua County as superintendent of schools, county treasurer, and justice of the peace. Haliday remained alive in Alachua County in 1878 but likely died soon thereafter.[108]

Hall, Charles B. Merchant and saloon keeper Charlie Hall was born in Maine about 1817. With his wife Rebecca he apparently moved to Lake City, Florida, in the mid 1850s. Seemingly the Halls departed Florida with the outbreak of the Civil War.[109]

Hancock, Minerva J. Parks. Georgia native Minerva Parks Hancock was born in May 1830. Her first husband, Clark D. Parks, died in Columbia County, Florida, in 1864. Minerva was married on August 5, 1866, to George W. Hancock (born February 12, 1829; died, Columbia County, October 13, 1882). Minerva lived at Lake City until 1907, when she relocated to Jacksonville. The date and place of her death are not known.[110]

Hanson, John M. Born in Maine during 1800, Hanson moved to Florida as a United States army officer. He married Elizabeth B. Cook in St. Augustine on November 14, 1826. Hanson died in St. Augustine on May 10, 1871.[111]

Harrington, Henry Monroe. Georgia native Henry M. Harrington was born June 2, 1819. After immigrating to Columbia County, Florida, in the 1830s, he married Pelester Raulerson there in 1840. He died in the county on October 18, 1889.[112]

Harrington, Henry Monroe, Jr. ("Cap"). A son of Henry M. and Pelester Harrington, Henry M. Harrington Jr. was born in Columbia County, Florida, on November 27, 1851. He married Martha[sometimes spelled Matha] A. Roberts on January 15, 1884, and died in the county on April 10, 1930.[113]

Harrington, Liberty Franklin. A brother to Henry M. Harrington Jr., Liberty Franklin Harrington was born on January 17, 1853, in Columbia County, Florida. He never married, and he died in Columbia County on June 22, 1930.[114]

Harrington, Pelester Raulerson. Born September 2, 1818, in Wayne County, Georgia, Pelester was the daughter of Frances Raulerson. She married Henry Monroe Harrington in Columbia County, Florida, in 1840. She died there on April 12, 1907.[115]

Hart, Isaiah David. Georgia native Isaiah David Hart was born the son of William and Elizabeth Streetman Hart on November 6, 1792. He moved with his family to Spanish Florida in 1801, after which they settled near Trout and Moncrief Creeks on the St. Johns River. Hart married Nancy Nelson in 1818. Among their children was Florida governor Ossian Bingley Hart. In 1821–1822 Isaiah helped to found the town of Jacksonville. He represented Duval County in the legislative council's 1837 and 1838 sessions and the eastern senatorial district in the territorial council during 1839–1840 and 1843–1845. He died in Duval County on September 4, 1861.[116]

Hart, Ossian Bingley. The son of Isaiah David and Nancy Nelson Hart, Ossian Bingley Hart was born near the St. Marys River in Spanish Florida on January 17, 1821. He studied law with his father at Jacksonville, achieving admission to the Duval County bar in October 1842. On October 2 of the following year he married Catharine Smith Campbell in Newark, New Jersey. In 1845 Hart represented St. Lucie County in the last territorial house of representatives. A Unionist during the Civil War, he helped to found Florida's Republican Party in 1867. Hart served in the constitutional convention of 1868 and sat as an associate justice of the Supreme Court of Florida during 1868–1873. In 1872 he won an election for governor, and he took the oath of office in January 1873. He died at his Jacksonville home on March 18, 1874.[117]

Hart, William Bartola. Isaiah David Hart's nephew William B. Hart was born November 10, 1811, in Spanish East Florida to William and Catalina Francesca Maestre Hart. He married Mary Ann Higginbotham in Duval County on February 22, 1834. Hart died in Seville, Volusia County, on April 3, 1864.[118]

Hartsuff, George L. Born in Tyne, Seneca County, New York, on May 28, 1830, George L. Hartsuff graduated from the United States Military Academy in 1852. He served in Florida during the 1850s, and the attack upon a surveying party led by him sparked the Third Seminole, or Billy Bowlegs, War in December 1855. During the Civil War he rose to the rank of major general of volunteers in the United States Army. He died in New York City on May 16, 1874.[119]

Hatch, Chauncey L. Farmer and confectioner Chauncey L. Hatch was born in Vermont about 1799. A resident of Duval County, Florida, by 1840, he had relocated to Key West by decade's end. He died in that island city about December 1872.[120]

Henry, Abigail G. Hunter. The daughter of Columbia County's John C. Hunter and sister of William M. Hunter, Abigail G. Hunter was born March 11, 1843. On June 5, 1866, she married James Edward Henry at Lake City. She died there, five years after her husband passed away, on August 30, 1912.[121]

Henry, James Edward. Originally from Summerville, Georgia, James Edward Henry was born November 4, 1841, the son of W. J. Henry. He moved to Lake City, Florida, in 1866. That year he married Abigail G. Hunter. Henry was a merchant at Lake City in subsequent decades and died in Jacksonville on November 6, 1907.[122]

Hickman, Jake. Information not available.

Hickman, William. William Hickman was born about 1799 in Maryland and arrived in Jacksonville, Florida, during the 1830s. As executor of the estate of Joshua Hickman, he was involved heavily in the town's commercial life during the 1840s. William died in Jacksonville on October 10, 1851.[123]

Hill, James Hamilton. A Columbia County, Florida, physician and planter, James Hamilton Hill was born in Georgia about 1812. On March 28, 1844, he married Martha Elizabeth Thomas. During or just after the Civil War the couple relocated to Madison County, where James Hill died on August 6, 1865.[124]

Hogan[s], Lewis Zachariah. Lewis Z. Hogans, one of the Jacksonville area's early settlers, was born in Florida the son of Reuben Hogans of Virginia about 1795. Lewis married Marie Raphaela Suarez. He died in northeastern Florida, apparently while in volunteer service during the Second Seminole War, in the spring of 1837.[125]

Holder, Elizabeth Ellis. A daughter of Thomas Ellis, Elizabeth Ellis was born in Georgia about 1824. Before 1840 she married Thomas Holder Jr., afterward settling in Alachua County, Florida. According to George G. Keen, she died there circa 1854.[126]

Holder, Joseph, Sr. A South Carolina native, Joseph Holder was born between 1780 and 1790. In 1800 he resided in the Pendleton District. He married his wife Hannah before 1821, when they were living in Camden County, Georgia. By 1834 the couple had relocated to Columbia County, Florida, where they remained until resettling in Alachua County during the early 1840s. Joseph died in the latter county about 1847.[127]

Holder, Joseph J. B. Born in 1826 in Camden County, Georgia, Joseph J. B. Holder (or Joseph Holder Jr.) was the son of Joseph Holder Sr. and Hannah Holder. He moved with the family to Florida in the early 1830s and married

Elizabeth in Alachua County on February 15, 1853. He died in the county on February 10, 1906. [128]

Holder, Thomas B. The brother of Joseph J. B. Holder and a son of Joseph and Hannah Holder, Thomas B. Holder was born in Camden County, Georgia, about 1823. He married Thomas Ellis's daughter Elizabeth in Georgia in the late 1830s. After her death about 1854, he married again—first, according to George G. Keen, the "Widow Doggett" and then Mary A. Standley. A resident of Columbia County, Florida, in the 1830s and early 1840s, Thomas relocated to Alachua County circa 1846. He and his third wife, Mary, sold their holdings in that county in late 1859 and early 1860 before moving to Harris County, Texas. Thomas remained alive there in 1870. [129]

Hooker, Eliza Jane. See Eliza Jane Hooker Stallings.

Hooker, Martha Harris. See Martha Harris Hooker Hagler Curry.

Hooker, Mary Amanda Hair. Born in North Carolina on April 3, 1810, Mary Amanda Hair was the daughter of William Hair. She married William Brinton Hooker in Hamilton County, Florida, on August 1, 1830. Mary Amanda died near Brooksville, Hernando County, Florida, on January 2, 1863. [130]

Hooker, William Brinton. The son of Stephen Hooker and Elizabeth Brinton Hooker, William Brinton Hooker was born in Montgomery County, Georgia, on May 3, 1800. He moved to Hamilton County, Florida, with his parents in early 1830 and married Mary Amanda Hair there on August 1. A volunteer captain during the Second Seminole War, Hooker represented Hamilton County in Florida's 1838–1839 constitutional convention. In 1843 Hooker relocated his family to Hillsborough County, becoming one of southwestern Florida's leading cattlemen. He died in Tampa on June 11, 1871. [131]

Hope, John ("Jack"). Born in Georgia about 1800, Jack Hope was the son of William Hope Sr. and Celia Hope. He was the brother of early Florida settlers William and David Hope. On November 30, 1819, Jack married Jerusha Gordon in Liberty County, Georgia. The couple moved to Florida in 1833, settling in Alachua County. As the Second Seminole War persisted in 1840, Hope left the territory for Colorado County, Texas. There he divorced Jerusha and subsequently married Hannah Minerva Alexander, Nancy Cummins, Julia Bateman, and Milly Ann Newsom. Hope died prior to 1870 in Kerrville, Kerr County, Texas. [132]

Howell, Joseph. Howell was born on January 8, 1803, in South Carolina. The identities of his parents are not known. The name of his first wife is uncertain, although she may have been Martha or Sarah Handcock, daughter of William M. Handcock. She was killed in Columbia County, Florida, on August 14, 1840, during an Indian attack described by George G. Keen. A similar tragedy struck Howell in 1856. On that occasion, near Fort Meade, Indians killed his son George, who had escaped death in the 1840 attack. Howell married Sarah Turner Sistrunk in 1844 after he settled an Armed Occupation Act claim in Hillsborough County. In 1860 and 1861 he represented Hillsborough in the Florida House of Representatives. Howell died in that county on January 9 (some authorities say June 9), 1862.[133]

Hull, Tempy. See Tempy Hull Gillett.

Hunter, Elijah. Elijah Hunter was born in Georgia about 1834. His wife Sarah was a native of the same state, born at roughly the same time. Hunter deserted from the Ninth Florida Infantry (CSA) in December 1862, and his whereabouts thereafter are not known.[134]

Hunter, George. Born about 1837 in Florida, Georgia Hunter was living in 1860 in the Lafayette County household of Keziah Locklier. He deserted from the Ninth Florida Infantry (CSA) in December 1862 and later joined the Second Florida Cavalry (USA). Hunter's whereabouts following his discharge at Tallahassee in late November 1865 are not known.[135]

Hunter, Green H. A well-regarded merchant at Lake City, Green Hunter was born in Georgia in 1824. With his wife Mary B. Hunter he remained in the county until his death at Lake City on September 22, 1888. Hunter served as a Columbia County delegate to the Florida secession convention of 1861 and represented Columbia and Suwannee Counties in the 1864 session of the Florida House of Representatives.[136]

Hunter, Hugh G. Born in North Carolina about 1826, Hugh Hunter worked as a carpenter at Lake City, Florida, during the mid to late 1840s. From July 26, 1845, he served the county as a justice of the peace. Hunter died there on February 12, 1850.[137]

Hunter, John C. Columbia County planter John C. Hunter was born in South Carolina on August 8, 1815. He married Rosannah Young there, and they moved from Newberry District in that state to Columbia County, Florida, in the 1850s. John died in Columbia County on June 2, 1864.[138]

Hunter, Mary B. The wife of Green H. Hunter, Mary was born in Georgia about 1831. She died at Lake City, Florida, on August 10, 1888, a few weeks before her husband passed away.[139]

Hunter, Rosannah Young. Rosannah Young, who married John C. Hunter, was born in Newberry District, South Carolina, on January 4, 1822. She died in Columbia County, Florida, on October 8, 1898.[140]

Hunter, Thompson Young. Born November 9, 1841, in South Carolina, Thompson Young Hunter was the son of John C. and Rosannah Young Hunter. He died at Lake City, Florida, on April 15, 1865.[141]

Hunter, William Marcus. A brother to Thompson Young Hunter, William Marcus Hunter was born in Newberry District, South Carolina, on October 13, 1847. He married Rebecca Jane Bryant in Columbia County, Florida, on December 4, 1867. William M. Hunter died in that county on October 2, 1912. [142]

Hunter, William Miles, Sr. A native of Effingham County, Georgia, William Miles Hunter was born the son of Miles and Mary Knight Hunter on October 21, 1793. On September 23, 1812, he married Catherine Roberts. During 1814–1815 Hunter served as sheriff of Wayne County, Georgia, and in 1824–1825 he acted as a justice of the peace. About 1825 he and Catherine relocated to present-day Hamilton County, Florida. Hunter served as the county's delegate to the territorial council in 1835–1836. He died in Hamilton County in 1855. [143]

Hunter, William Young. William Young Hunter was born in South Carolina on December 28, 1845. He died in Columbia County, Florida, on September 3, 1874, leaving behind a wife, Aristha F. Hunter.[144]

Hyatt, Mahaly. Information not available.

Ives, Edward Rutledge ("Ned"). Born July 31, 1818, in Charleston, South Carolina, Ned Ives was a son of Washington M. Ives and Eliza Boyd Ives. In 1824 the family relocated to the area of New Smyrna, Florida. On May 21, 1845, Ned Ives married Eliza Ann Hogans in Mandarin. Following her death in Alligator on July 23, 1847, he married Eliza Ann's sister, Mary Jane Hogans. Ned Ives died at Lake City on January 15, 1870.[145]

Ives, Martha Lockhart Mackey. See Martha Lockhart Mackey Ives Williams.

Ives, Norman Mackey. The son of Edward R. and Eliza Ann Hogans Ives, Norman Ives was born in Alligator, Florida, on February 21, 1846. On September 3, 1872, he married Eugenia Carter at Lake City. Apparently the Iveses departed Lake City prior to 1880. The date and place of Norman's death are not known.[146]

Ives, Washington Mackey. A son of Washington M. Ives and Eliza Boyd Ives, Washington Mackey Ives was born in St. Augustine, Florida, on September 29, 1843. He married Arabella E. Parshley on November 1, 1870. Ives served as Lake City's mayor by 1875 and became judge of the Columbia County court in 1877. Eight years later he represented the county in Florida's 1885 constitutional convention. One of Lake City's leading citizens for over half a century, he died there on February 16, 1925.[147]

Jerkins, James. Information not available.

Johnson, David Bartow. Born in Lowndes County, Georgia, on April 17, 1833, David B. Johnson was the son of John J. and Elizabeth Staten Johnson. He was married first to Cynthia Haney, then to Maggie P. Morgan, and finally to Florence T. Moore. During 1892–1900 he served as judge of the Hamilton County, Florida, county court, and in 1896–1897 and 1900–1902 he presided as mayor of Jasper. He died in Jasper on October 13, 1921.[148]

Johnson, James H. James H. Johnson was born on the island of New Providence in the British Bahamas about 1800. Though he was a farmer, he also kept a tavern at Lake City during the early 1840s. With his wife Mary he remained at Lake City as late as May 1855. His whereabouts thereafter are not known.[149]

Jones, James S. Columbia County physician James S. Jones was born in Virginia about 1817. Apparently he was married three times, to Mary A., Elizabeth, and Mahaly Jones. He served in the late 1840s as Columbia County probate judge and represented the county in the Florida House of Representatives in 1850. In November 1854 he moved to Tampa to publish the *Tampa Herald* (later *Florida Peninsular*) newspaper. Finding that the journal "did not pay sufficient to support my family," he relocated after August 1855 to Pensacola, where he edited the *Pensacola Observer*. During or just after the Civil War, Jones sought a new life in Savannah. He retired in 1868 as editor of the *Savannah News and Herald*. As of 1880 he remained alive in Webster, Florida.[150]

Jones, John Arthur. Columbia County farmer John Arthur Jones was born in Florida about 1824. He married Mary M. Jones, a native Georgian born circa 1838. Jones died as a soldier in the Confederate army in Cold Harbor, Virginia, on June 4, 1864.[151]

Jones, John W. Columbia County planter John W. Jones was born in Georgia on April 23, 1810. He was married twice: first to Sarah Ann Moore, daughter of Arthur T. and Priscilla Goodbread Moore; then to Elizabeth H. Jones. He sat in the Florida House of Representatives for Columbia County in 1850 and represented the county in the Florida secession convention of 1861. Jones died in Columbia County on April 10, 1894.[152]

Joyce, Jane. Information not available.

Keen, Andrew Jackson ("Jack"). Jack Keen was born in 1843 in Columbia County, Florida, the son of Joseph Bryant and Martha Elizabeth Griffin Keen. In May 1862 he enlisted in the Seventh Florida Infantry (CSA). Keen died while serving in Atlanta, Georgia, on January 11, 1864.[153]

Keen, Arkina Lane. A native of Appling County, Georgia, Arkina Lane was born on May 11, 1839. On January 14, 1856, she married George Gillett Keen in Columbia County, Florida. She lived there until her death at Lake City on October 20, 1921.[154]

Keen, George Gillett. Arkina Lane Keen's husband, George Gillett Keen, was born in Appling County, Georgia, on March (or May) 4, 1827, the child of William Henry Keen and Lydia Gillett Keen. He died in Columbia County, Florida, on January 29, 1902.[155]

Keen, John. The son of David and Elizabeth Fitzgerald Keen, John Keen was born in Tattnall County, Georgia, likely in December 1822. He married Candacia Morgan in Columbia County, Florida, on March 11, 1847. Following the Civil War, Keen relocated to Manatee (now DeSoto) County, Florida. He died in Arcadia on June 11, 1889.[156]

Keen, Joseph Bryant. Joseph B. Keen was born in Oglethorpe County, Georgia, in November 1810 to David and Nancy Brown Keen. He relocated to Columbia County, Florida, circa 1830–1833 with his wife Martha Elizabeth Griffin. He died in Columbia County, seemingly between 1847 and 1850.[157]

Keen, Lydia Gillett. George Gillett Keen's mother, Lydia Gillett Keen, was born circa 1792, possibly in Florida but more likely in Georgia, to William and Elizabeth Gillett. She was the sister of Anderson Gillett, George Gillett, and Sarah (Mrs. John) Cason. Lydia married William Henry Keen. After moving with her family to Florida in 1830, Lydia lived in Columbia County until her death during an influenza epidemic, probably in 1856.[158]

Keen, Moses H. Born in Georgia on May 4, 1823, Moses H. Keen was the son of Theophilus and Elizabeth Raulerson Keen. He moved to Columbia County, Florida, with his family in the early 1830s. At Lake City in March 1862 he enlisted in the Fifth Florida Infantry (CSA). Keen was captured in Spotsylvania, Virginia, in May 1864 and died at Elmira Prison, Elmira, New York, on August 18, 1864.[159]

Keen, Sherod S. Brother of George Gillett Keen and son of William H. and Lydia G. Keen, Sherod Keen was born in Georgia about 1820. According to family sources, he died during the Civil War while serving in the Confederate army.[160]

Keen, Wiley. Born in Tattnall County, Georgia, about 1824–1825, Wiley Keen was a son of David Keen and brother to Jack Keen. Wiley married Elizabeth Harrington, who likely was a sister of Henry Harrington. Wiley died circa 1870–1871 in Columbia County, Florida.[161]

Keen, William Henry. George Gillett Keen's father, William Henry Keen, was born about 1782 in North Carolina. He married Lydia Gillett in Georgia before moving his family to Alachua (now Columbia) County, Florida, in 1830. Keen lived in the county until his death, which apparently occurred in 1852. In addition to George G. Keen, his children included Sherod S. Keen and William R. Keen.[162]

Keen, William R. A brother to George Gillett Keen, William R. Keen was born in Georgia about 1824. He came to Florida with the family in 1830, making his permanent home in Columbia County. Keen married Eliza A. Keen. He was murdered at his home near Suwannee Shoals on February 21, 1889.[163] According to Columbia County Sheriff J. A. Bethea, Keen's killing was "a most atrocious assassination." He urged Governor Francis P. Fleming to do everything possible to bring the perpetrator to justice. Suspicion fell on a man named Will Adams, a man whom Keen had charged with hog stealing. Adams was subsequently arrested and swore vengeance on him several times. As one local attorney explained to Gov. Fleming, the evidence against Adams was "circumstantial in the main . . . it is strong." Whether or not Adams was ever prosecuted is not known. Court records have been lost.

Kelly, Charles John. The son of William Spence Kelly and Sarah Pamela Williams Niblack Kelly, Charles John Kelly was born in Holyoke, Georgia, on November 18, 1875. On September 14, 1899, in Atlanta he married Ester Elizabeth LaRose, who was born November 21, 1876, in Upton, Quebec, Canada. Charles John Kelly died in Atlanta on March 19, 1935.[164]

Kelly, Sarah Pamela Williams Niblack. Born December 2, 1837, in Picolata, Florida, Sarah Pamela Williams was the daughter of John Lee Williams and Martha Lockhart Mackey Ives. In 1847 she moved with her mother to Alligator (Lake City). There, on May 24, 1857, she married William Henry Niblack. Following his death Sarah Pamela married William Spence Kelly in Cuthbert, Georgia, on June 3, 1874. She died March 17, 1929, in Atlanta.[165]

Kelly, William Spence. Second husband to Sarah Pamela Williams, William Spence Kelly was born in Ireland in 1837. There he was a boyhood friend to William Daly Burtchaell, who became Sarah Pamela's brother-in-law. Kelly and Sarah Pamela Williams Niblack married at the Burtchaell home in Cuthbert, Georgia, on June 3, 1874. He died in Atlanta on March 19, 1935.[166]

Kendrick, James. Although the date and place of his birth and parentage are unknown, James Kendrick reportedly served as an officer in the British army during the War of 1812. On October 20, 1814, he married Elizabeth Mickler, the daughter of William and Temperance Matthews Mickler, in St. Marys, Georgia. They moved to present-day Hamilton County, Florida, in the 1820s, settling on the Suwannee River. James served as quartermaster to several volunteer and militia companies during the Second Seminole War. He died in Hamilton County, seemingly in early 1838.[167]

Kendrick, William Harney. Born in Hamilton County, Florida, in 1823, William Harney Kendrick was the son of James and Elizabeth Mickler Kendrick. Kendrick first married Mrs. Mary Townsend Gibbons, who died in 1845. Then on August 10, 1858, he married Martha E. Johnson, daughter of Abner Johnson. A well-known military, political, and social figure in Florida, Kendrick served as state senator for the Twenty-third District from 1868 to 1872. He died in Jacksonville on November 26, 1901.[168]

King, Charles R. The son of James King, Charles R. King was born in Gates County, North Carolina, on May 1, 1834. In that state he married Sallie R. Harden, daughter of Peter R. Harden of Graham. King moved to Florida in 1867 due to health problems. He settled at Lake City where he opened a law practice. He served as secretary of the Florida Senate in 1873 and for three years afterward occupied the office of state attorney. King died at Lake City on December 24, 1895.[169]

Kingsley, Zephaniah. Born in Scotland on December 4, 1765, Zephaniah Kingsley was the son of Zephaniah and Isabella Johnstone Kingsley. A merchant and slave trader in Spanish East Florida, Kingsley in 1806 purchased in Havana the slave Anta Majigeen Ndiaye, who would become his wife. Kingsley owned numerous properties in East Florida, especially Fort George Island near the mouth of the St. Johns River and his upriver estate at Laurel Grove. In 1823 he served as a member of the territorial council. Kingsley died in New York City on September 13, 1843.[170]

Kinnison, George W. Indiana native George W. Kinnison was born in June 1849. With his wife Sarah he moved in the late 1880s or early 1890s to Lake City, Florida, where he engaged in a number of business enterprises including, according to George G. Keen, operation of an ice plant. Apparently he moved from Florida prior to 1910.[171]

Lamb, Zemri. A blacksmith by trade, Zemri Lamb was born in North Carolina about 1818. With his wife Mary he resided at Lake City, Florida, by the 1850s. He remained at that town until 1863. His whereabouts thereafter are not known.[172]

Lancaster, Joseph Bradford. One of East Florida's leading political figures during the antebellum era, Joseph B. Lancaster was born in Kentucky about 1790. His parents were John and Catherine Miles Lancaster. He married Annie Blair, daughter of a Presbyterian minister, in Lebanon, Kentucky, in 1815. Lancaster moved to Florida in the early 1820s, soon finding a home in Jacksonville. Over three decades he occupied numerous positions of trust. He helped to found Florida's Whig Party and held office as mayor of Jacksonville and Tampa, member and chief clerk of the territorial council, Speaker of the territorial house and of the Florida House of Representatives, circuit judge, and member of the Supreme Court of Florida. He died in Tampa on November 25, 1856.[173]

Lockhart, Joel L. Lockhart was born circa 1804–1810 in Georgia and resided in Florida by the 1840s, living principally in Hernando and Hillsborough Counties. He was a veteran of the First Florida Cow Cavalry (CSA). Lockhart married Harriet Oneil on May 24, 1865. He died in Hillsborough County on April 7, 1885.[174]

Locklier [or Locklear], Arletta Ann. See Arletta Ann Locklier Corban.

Locklier [or Locklear], Elijah ("Lige"). Elijah Locklier was born in Georgia between 1815 and 1821. His first wife apparently was named Sarah (born in Georgia in 1819 and alive in 1850), and his second wife was named Keziah. Locklier moved into present-day Lafayette County prior to 1850. He was murdered there by Jim Munden about July 17, 1859.[175]

Locklier [or Locklear], Keziah ("Kissie"). Elijah Locklier's wife Keziah was born in Florida about 1820. Following his death in Lafayette County in 1859, she may have remarried, as county records note a marriage of "Miss Kiziah Locklier" with Archibald Hurst on February 4, 1861. Hurst enlisted in the Confederate army in Madison, Florida, on May 8, 1862. Keziah's whereabouts thereafter are not known.[176]

Locklier [or Locklear], William. A William A. Locklier, born in Georgia about 1813, was living with his wife Mary in Lafayette County in the 1850s. His whereabouts after 1860 are not known. Elijah Locklier also had a son named William, born circa 1843 in Florida. William was living with Keziah Locklier in Lafayette County in 1860, but his whereabouts thereafter are not known. Additionally, Elijah Locklier's brother Joseph Locklier had a son named William Henry Locklier, born in Columbia County, Florida, on November 26, 1845. William H. married Clara Ann Alice Edwards, daughter of William Edwards, on March 5, 1866. William H. died in Sarasota, Florida, on March 15, 1923.[177]

Long, Jesse. Born in Georgia on April 29, 1790, farmer Jesse Long moved to Columbia County, Florida, in the 1840s, having previously resided in Nassau County. With his wife Elizabeth, Long continued to live in Columbia County until his death on May 12, 1856.[178]

Long, Thomas Telfair. Attorney Thomas Telfair Long was born in Georgia on May 14, 1824. He married Theodosia Susan Scarlett, daughter of Francis M.

Scarlett of Glynn County, on May 14, 1845. Following her death on February 10, 1850, he married Anna Long. Thomas T. Long held the position of secretary to Florida's territorial senate in 1843 and represented Columbia County in the 1865 constitutional convention. He served during the Civil War as a colonel in Florida's Ordnance Department. He relocated after the conflict to Lake City and served for several years as a circuit judge. By 1874 Long had moved to Brunswick, Georgia, and six years afterward he was living in Starke, Bradford County. He died there on May 14, 1884. [179]

Loring, Hannah Kenan. St. Augustine schoolteacher Hannah Kenan Loring was born in Wilmington, North Carolina, about 1787. There, on May 19, 1811, she married Reuben Loring, who was born at Higham, North Carolina, on November 30, 1787. The couple moved to St. Augustine, Florida, in 1823. Their son William Wing Loring became a major general in the Confederate States army. Hannah died in St. Augustine in 1852. [180]

Lowe, John Wesley. Columbia County farmer John Wesley Lowe was born in South Carolina about 1802. He arrived in Florida with his wife Anne prior to 1840, and from February to October 1843 he served as Columbia County sheriff. He remained in the county until at least 1855. His whereabouts thereafter are not known. [181]

Mahoney, John Percy. A North Carolina native, John P. Mahoney was born about 1839. He moved to Florida following the Civil War and settled at Lake City. A Republican and an attorney, he held office as Columbia County tax assessor during 1870–1871 and also sat in the Florida House of Representatives in 1871. Following a disagreement resulting from a perceived insult to his wife Carrie, Mahoney was shot to death at Lake City on April 26, 1871. [182]

Marcum [or Markham], William W. The son of William and Mary Gorman Marcum, William Marcum was born in Camden County, Georgia, in 1810. He married Rithey Roberts in Alligator (Lake City), Florida, on March 15, 1831. Markham remained in Columbia County until his death on September 2, 1866. [183]

McAuley, Angus. Born about 1808 in Georgia (likely in Morvin), Angus McAuley, with his wife Margaret, moved to Florida about 1849 and helped pioneer settlement in present-day Suwannee County. He served as county clerk from 1868 to 1870 and thereafter represented the Eleventh District in the Florida Senate during 1873–1875. He died in Suwannee County on November 20, 1883. [184]

McClellan, George Edmond. A native of Barnwell District, South Carolina, George E. McClellan was born on July 11, 1807. His parents were the Reverend

Charles McClellan and Elizabeth McClellan, who moved to Jefferson County, Florida, by 1827. George married Isabelle Sidney Tison, daughter of Job and Sidney Sheffield Tison, in 1830. Following her death thirty years later he married Celesta Relief Holman on January 16, 1861. McClellan represented Columbia County in the Florida constitutional convention of 1838–1839, the lower house of the territorial council in 1844–1845, and the Florida House of Representatives in 1845 and 1848. He died in Suwannee County on October 18, 1866.[185]

McClelland, John L. The son of Silas and Penelope Anderson McClelland, John L. McClelland was born in Tattnall County, Georgia, circa 1820. About 1836 John's family relocated to Hamilton County, Florida. He married Winnie Vickers Tanner, widow of Simon B. Tanner, in Blount's Ferry, Columbia County, on April 20, 1845. The McClellands moved circa 1846 to Hillsborough (now Polk) County. John died there on June 24, 1872.[186]

McClelland, Silas. Silas McClelland was born about 1795, likely in South Carolina. He was a resident of Georgia by the time of the War of 1812 and married Penelope Anderson, the daughter of Joseph and Sarah Anderson, on October 29, 1818, in Bulloch County. The couple had removed their family to either Columbia or Hamilton County, Florida, by 1836. Ten years afterward they moved again, to that portion of Hillsborough County that would become Polk County. Silas died there on August 1, 1875.[187]

McCullough, William. Born October 1, 1821, in Kentucky and raised in Ohio, William McCullough arrived in Florida as a Second Seminole War soldier. He remained in the territory to marry Nancy Ann Whidden, daughter of James W. and Mary Altman Whidden, in Hillsborough County on November 14, 1844. McCullough received wounds during engagements with Indians in 1849 and 1856 in modern Hardee and Polk Counties. During the Civil War he served as a lieutenant in the Second Florida Cavalry (USA). After the conflict McCullough and his family moved to Illinois and then Missouri. He died in Kahoka, Clark County, Missouri, on April 2, 1890.[188]

McNeill, Archibald D. A native of Scotland, Archibald D. McNeill was born in the mid 1810s. By the 1830s he was living in Madison County, Florida, which he represented on the territorial council during 1835–1837. In 1839 he sat in the new territorial house of representatives for Alachua County. Following the Second Seminole War's end in 1842 McNeill moved to Tampa and, later, present-day Manatee County. On May 26, 1853, he married Ellen Farley Clarke, widow of Henry S. Clarke, in Tampa. In 1858–1859 he returned to the state capital to represent Manatee in the house of representatives. McNeill apparently died in Manatee County in the early 1880s.[189]

Miller, Mary Victoria. See Mary Victoria Miller Wightman.

Mizell, David, Jr. Born in Georgia on February 23, 1808, David Mizell Jr. was the brother of Joseph and Enoch E. Mizell. He married Mary Pearce on December 24, 1829. David Mizell served Orange County in the Florida House of Representatives during 1860–1863 and represented Volusia, Orange, Brevard, and Dade Counties in the Florida constitutional convention of 1868. He died in Orange County on January 16, 1884.[190]

Mizell, Enoch Everett. A son of David Mizell Sr. and his wife Sarah, Enoch E. Mizell was born April 6, 1806, in Camden County, Georgia. Likely a resident of Columbia County, Florida, by 1830, he eventually headed his own volunteer company as captain during the Second Seminole War. Mizell married Minerva Ann Parrish in Alachua County on November 4, 1846. Minerva died in Hernando (then Benton) County in 1855, and two years later he married Annie Jackson. Mizell moved the family to Manatee (now DeSoto) County during the Civil War. He served as judge of the Manatee County criminal court beginning in 1866. Mizell died in Pine Level on September 22, 1887.[191]

Mizell, Joseph. Brother to David and Enoch E. Mizell, Joseph Mizell was born in Camden County, Georgia, on April 17, 1804. He married Martha Pearce Skipper, and they resided in Columbia County, Florida, by the 1830s. When Polk County was created in 1861, Mizell served as one of its first commissioners. He died there or in neighboring Hillsborough County about 1862.[192]

Mobley, Edward. Mobley was born in Georgia about 1818. He married Judia Scott in Camden County on April 25, 1839, and after 1870 married Mary M. Mobley [maiden name unavailable]. Finally, on February 9, 1893, in Baker County, Florida, he married for a third time, to Mary Ann Raulerson. Mobley died in Baker County circa 1894.[193]

Mole, John A. A native of Beaufort County, South Carolina, Mole was born on December 27, 1841. After serving in the Confederate army from Columbia County, Florida, he married Ellen Hunt on December 16, 1874. Mole died in Columbia County on February 8, 1931.[194]

Moody, Benjamin. Born in Telfair County, Georgia, on April 15, 1811, Benjamin Moody was the son of Sarah Lee Moody. Raised in the household of his uncle John Lee, Moody lived in Hamilton County, Florida, from 1830. There, on February 7, 1833, he married Nancy Hooker, sister of William B. Hooker. Following her death in 1845 Moody married Mary E. Knight on March 24, 1849. He was married for a third time, to Lydia Carlton Hendry, on November 5, 1854. Briefly a resident of Hernando County, Moody eventually settled during the 1840s in Hillsborough and, later, Polk Counties. He died in Polk County on October 13, 1896.[195]

Moore, Luke. A farmer and ferry keeper, Luke Moore apparently was born in England about 1811. He helped to pioneer Hernando and Hillsborough Counties, and he was murdered in the latter county on September 8, 1859.[196]

Moore, Walter Raleigh. The son of Joseph and Elpenice Stanford Moore, Walter Raleigh Moore was born in Leon County, Florida, in 1835. The family moved to Tampa in the 1840s, but in 1856 Walter relocated to Lake City where he operated a mercantile establishment. At Lake City after 1860 he married Elizabeth A. Peeples, daughter of John and Jemina Peeples. During the Civil War, Moore rose to the rank of colonel of the Second Florida Infantry (CSA). From 1881 to 1883 he represented Columbia County in the Florida House of Representatives. Walter R. Moore died in Wellborn, Suwannee County, on October 10, 1898. [197]

Morehead, Robert. A onetime Columbia County, Florida, slave, Robert Morehead was born about 1825 in either South Carolina or Virginia. His first wife, Mary, was born circa 1834 in South Carolina, and a second wife, Mahalia, was born circa 1835 in Virginia. Morehead remained alive in Columbia County in 1880. His whereabouts thereafter are not known. [198]

Morgan, Adeline Raulerson. A daughter of Fanny Raulerson, Adeline was born in 1823 in Georgia. She married Daniel A. Morgan of Levy County, Florida. Adeline died in that county about 1858.[199]

Morgan, Ephraim. A South Carolina native, Ephraim Morgan was born about 1810. He married Mary Parker, the daughter of Luke Parker and sister of John Parker, in Columbia County, Florida, on March 21, 1833. The Morgans later moved to Levy County, where Ephraim died on September 30, 1859.[200]

Morgan, Sookie. Identity unclear, but see Joseph Wilkerson.

Munden, Georgia Ann C. See Georgia Ann C. Munden Curry.

Munden, James. The son of William and Sarah Howell Munden, James Munden was born in Wayne County, Georgia, between 1810 and 1820. He was living in Florida by the 1840s and settled in Lafayette County with his wife Eleanor Strickland Munden. As discussed by George G. Keen, he died in Lafayette County about July 19, 1859, as a result of gunshot wounds at the hands of Elijah Locklier.[201]

Newmans, Bill. Information not available.

Niblack, Albert Leslie. The son of William Henry and Sarah Pamela Williams Niblack, Albert Leslie Niblack was born near Lake City, Florida, on August 23, 1859. He died in Columbia County on October 28, 1870.[202]

Niblack, Atalie Scarborough. Decatur County, Georgia, native Atalie Scarborough was born about 1830, the daughter of Stirling and Susan Brooks Scarborough. She moved with her family to Columbia County, Florida, in the 1840s. There before 1850 she married Silas Leslie Niblack. Atalie died at Lake City on November 18, 1892.[203]

Niblack, Henry. According to the account of Sarah Pamela Williams, whom Niblack at one time served as a bondsman, Henry Niblack was born about 1810. He was owned by William H. Niblack in 1860 and remained in Columbia County in 1866. His whereabouts thereafter are not known, although a Henry Niblack born in Florida circa 1829 lived by 1868 with his wife Frances in Manatee County. By 1880 they had relocated to Hillsborough County, where Henry remained alive in 1890.[204]

Niblack, John. Columbia County planter John Niblack was born in Camden County, Georgia, on December 26, 1816. His father was William Niblack. John married Julia A. Bryant about 1847 in Columbia County, Florida. He lived in that county until his death on October 18, 1885.[205]

Niblack, Julia A. Bryant. John Niblack's wife Julia A. Bryant was born in Camden County, Georgia, on June 20, 1828 [or 1829], the daughter of James Bryant. Following her 1847 Columbia County, Florida, marriage to Niblack, she remained a resident of Columbia County until her death there on September 5, 1876.[206]

Niblack, Sarah Pamela Williams. See Sarah Pamela Williams Niblack Kelly.

Niblack, Silas. A slave of the Niblack family prior to emancipation, Silas Niblack was born about 1849 in Florida. With his wife Martha he continued to live in Columbia County, where he remained in 1910. The date and place of his death are not known.[207]

Niblack, Silas Leslie. A leading figure in Florida's post–Civil War Democratic politics, Silas Leslie Niblack was born in Camden County, Georgia, on March 17, 1825. Before 1850 he married Atalie Scarborough in Columbia County, Florida. A lawyer, planter, and businessman, Niblack served as a Columbia County delegate to the Florida constitutional convention of 1865, sat in the Florida Senate during 1879–1881, and represented his state in the United States Congress in 1873. He died at Lake City on February 15, 1883.[208]

Niblack, William Henry. Born at Alligator, Florida, on April 16, 1836, William Henry Niblack was orphaned at an early age. The names of his parents are not available. He married in Columbia County on May 24, 1857, to Sarah Pamela Williams. Niblack died at his home in Columbia County on March 10, 1861.[209]

North, William B. Second Seminole War captain William B. North was born during the 1790s, likely in Colleton District, South Carolina. He was a son of John North and a brother to John J. North, who commanded Georgia volunteers during the Second Seminole War. William B. North and his wife were living in Ware County, Georgia, in 1830 but relocated to Columbia County, Florida, during the decade. According to family tradition, within a few years after William B. North's last official volunteer company was mustered out of service on January 12, 1839, he moved to Texas. The date and place of his death are not known.[210]

Nostrand, N. M. Information not available.

Osceola. Florida's premier Indian leader of the nineteenth century, Osceola was born about 1804 in the Creek Nation (present-day Alabama). His father likely was a trader, William Powell, and his mother a Creek woman with connections to the powerful McQueen family. Pushed out of Alabama after the 1814 Battle of Horseshoe Bend, Osceola found sanctuary in Spanish Florida along with his uncle Peter McQueen. Following the First Seminole War of 1817–1818, uncle and nephew retreated to the headwaters of Peace River, near modern Fort Meade in Polk County. By the 1830s Osceola was representing his chief and McQueen's successor, Holata Micco, at councils with white officials. At that time he was living within an easy distance of the Indian agency at Fort King (Ocala). Osceola played a central role in organizing for the Second Seminole War, which began in 1835, and personally led Indian and black followers in numerous engagements. He was captured by American troops in the fall of 1837 and sent, ailing, to Fort Moultrie, Charleston Harbor, South Carolina. He died there on January 30, 1838.[211]

Osteen, James. The son of Shadrach and Winnifred Osteen, James Osteen was born in Georgia on April 23, 1815. Present in Alachua (now Columbia) County, Florida, by 1830, Osteen was married there to Mary Ann "Polly" Marcum before 1842. He died in Gilchrist County, Florida, on February 5, 1877.[212]

Otray, Fennell. Apparently born in Georgia, Fennell Otray was old enough to vote in Columbia County, Florida, by February 1834. He served in several volunteer companies during the Second Seminole War but was listed as "sick at Mineral Springs" on November 28, 1840. He may have died soon thereafter or else moved outside Florida.[213]

Overstreet, Silas, Jr. A native of Barnwell District, South Carolina, Silas Overstreet Jr. was born about 1812. His parents were Silas Overstreet Sr. and Rebecca Smith Overstreet. He married Nicy English in Madison County, Florida, on January 23, 1833. They lived in Columbia County until 1858. Silas possibly remained alive in Madison County until 1866.[214]

Palmer, Bascom Headen. Bascom H. Palmer was born in Randolph County, North Carolina, in February 1846 or 1852. He graduated from Trinity College before achieving admission to the North Carolina bar in 1879. The next year he moved to Lake City, Florida, to practice law. He represented Columbia County in the Florida House of Representatives in 1885 and in the Florida Senate during 1895–1901. In 1901 he secured appointment as circuit judge. He died at Lake City on April 2, 1916.[215]

Parker, John Stafford. South Carolina native John S. Parker was born April 16, 1832. By 1860 he and his wife Mariah were living on a Suwannee County, Florida, farm. Mariah seemingly died soon thereafter, and John remarried about 1863, to Celia Stafford. After the Civil War they moved to Levy County, where John served as sheriff during 1881–1883. He died there on September 8, 1901.[216]

Parker, Joseph. Joseph Parker was born in Columbia County, Florida, about 1843. He was a resident of Lafayette County in 1860, living in the household of Joseph Locklier. He served in the Second Florida Cavalry (USA) and was discharged at Tallahassee on November 29, 1865. In October 1866 he and Polly Gipson married in Lafayette County. They resided there in 1880.[217]

Parks, Clark D. Georgia native Clark D. Parks, who prospered during the 1850s as a Columbia County, Florida, planter, was born August 12, 1806. He died in Columbia County on November 11, 1864, leaving a widow, Minerva J. Parks.[218]

Parks, Minerva J. See Minerva J. Parks Hancock.

Parrish, Ransom. Likely the son of Josiah Parrish, Ransom Parrish was born in Camden County, Georgia, about 1798. He relocated with his family to Florida during the 1820s and was living in present-day Columbia County by 1830. He married Mary Bernell in Georgia on January 25, 1821. On June 29, 1858, he married Mary Johnston. Parrish was living in Columbia County in 1850. He died after 1860, although the exact date and place of his death are not known.[219]

Payne, Robert S. Georgian Robert S. Payne, born about 1803, moved to Alachua (now Columbia) County, Florida, during the 1820s. Before 1840 he married Lovie Cason, daughter of Eli and Cassandra Osteen Cason. Payne died at Lake City on November 13, 1863.[220]

Pearce, James C. Methodist minister James C. Pearce was born in North Carolina about 1798, the son of John and Ann Cain Pearce. James was brother to Florida pioneers John J. and Levy Pearce. He relocated to Columbia County, Florida, in the 1830s, likely already married to his wife Fanny. An Armed Occupation Act settler in Hillsborough County during the 1840s, Pearce returned to Columbia County where he died in November 1875.[221]

Peeples [Peoples], John H. ("Jack"). Georgia native John H. Peeples was born about 1812. On December 31, 1836, he married Jemina Barber. In 1840 the couple were living in Nassau County, Florida, and during the decade they relocated to Columbia County, where Peeples established a plantation. Peeples died in Hamilton County on December 10, 1880.[222]

Pennington, Jesse. The son of Stephen and Elizabeth Pennington, Jesse Pennington was born in Georgia about 1777. The name of his wife is not known. Pennington moved to present-day Columbia County, Florida, during the 1820s, settling on the upper Suwannee River. Following the 1842 conclusion of the Second Seminole War, he moved down the peninsula to Hillsborough County with his son-in-law, Willoughby Whidden. He died in Manatee (now Hardee) County in 1863.[223]

Ponchier, John C. C. John C. C. Ponchier was born in Georgia during the first decade of the 1800s. He moved to Columbia County, Florida, in the 1830s with his wife Mary E. Ponchier but the following decade helped to pioneer settlement in present-day Lafayette County. From 1868 to 1871 he served as that county's clerk of court. Ponchier, who lived in New Troy, brought notoriety to himself in 1871 when he assassinated Republican state senator John Newton Krimminger. Ponchier was gunned down on July 5, 1873, at Deadman's Bay. It was said at the time, "He has long been noted as a desperate character."[224]

Price, Joseph. Georgian Joseph Price was born in 1819 but settled in Columbia County, Florida, with his wife Mary well prior to the Civil War. From 1860 to 1863 he represented Columbia and Suwannee Counties in the Florida House of Representatives. Price died in Columbia County on October 8, 1882.[225]

Purviance, Louisa Summerlin Frink. Louisa Summerlin was born in Hamilton County, Florida, on June 10, 1839, the daughter of Jacob Summerlin Sr. and his second wife. After schooling in Quincy and residence in Pensacola with Dr. and Mrs. James S. Jones, Louisa married John Frink of Hamilton County on December 23, 1860. He had represented his county in the state house of representatives during 1856–1859 but was killed in the Confederate army at Gettysburg, Pennsylvania, on July 2, 1863. She was married on January 19, 1868, in Columbia County to John S. Purviance, who briefly held office as secretary of the state senate. After their marriage they lived in Hamilton County. Louisa died in Jasper on May 5, 1918.[226]

Putnam, Benjamin Alexander. One of Florida's most distinguished political and judicial leaders of the nineteenth century, Benjamin A. Putnam was born December 16, 1801, on the family plantation near Savannah, Georgia. His parents were Benjamin and Anne Sophia Putnam. In 1821 Putnam located in Florida, where he studied law and achieved admission to the bar in 1824. On March 26, 1830, he married Helen Kirby, daughter of Ephraim Kirby, in St. Augustine. While also distinguishing himself as a volunteer and militia officer during the Second Seminole War, Putnam sat in the legislative council in 1835, in the territorial house in 1840, and in the territorial senate in 1845. In 1848 he served as speaker of the Florida House of Representatives. In the 1850s he accepted appointment as circuit judge. Putnam died in Palatka, Florida, on January 25, 1869. Putnam County is named in his honor.[227]

Raulerson, Adeline. See Adeline Raulerson Morgan.

Raulerson, Berry E. A native of present-day Baker County, Florida, Berry E. Raulerson was born August 8, 1846, the son of Elias Raulerson and Melvina Williams Beasley. In January 1866 he married Mary E. Wildston (or Waldstrom) in Columbia County. During the Reconstruction era Berry served at various times in Hamilton County as chairman of the board of county commissioners, clerk of the circuit court, justice of the peace, and Jasper postmaster. During 1898–1906 and 1910–1912 he presided as Lake City's postmaster. Raulerson died at Lake City on April 13, 1912.[228]

Raulerson, David. A son of Fanny Raulerson, David was born in Georgia in 1824. He moved to Florida with his mother in the late 1820s and later married Candace Catherine Wright. Raulerson died in Hillsborough County on January 28, 1853.[229]

Raulerson, Fanny. The daughter of John Raulerson, Fanny was born in Effingham County, Georgia, about 1796. Her brothers included Florida pioneers William, Noel, Jacob, and Nimrod Raulerson. Apparently Fanny did not marry. Present in the area of modern Columbia County from the late 1820s, Fanny died there early in the 1840s.[230]

Raulerson, Independence. Fanny Raulerson's son Independence Raulerson was born in Camden County, Georgia, on July 4, 1814. He moved to Florida with his mother in the late 1820s, and on June 20, 1853, he married Rachel Newman in Columbia County. He died on October 1, 1875, in Dry Prairie, Manatee County.[231]

Raulerson, Jackson Tharp. Born in Georgia about 1829 or in Florida about 1831, Jackson Tharp Raulerson was another son of Fanny Raulerson. After 1850 he married Rebecca Raulerson, likely in Columbia County, Florida. He died as a Confederate soldier on December 12, 1862, in Chattanooga, Tennessee.[232]

Raulerson, Liberty Franklin. Yet another son of Fanny Raulerson, Liberty Franklin Raulerson was born in Georgia about 1822. He was married to Soporonia Wright and then to Sarah Naomi Wylly. Raulerson died in Polk County, Florida, on May 30, 1904.[233]

Raulerson, Pelester. See Pelester Raulerson Harrington.

Raulerson, William ("Old Billie"). South Carolina native William Raulerson was born about 1780, the son of John Raulerson. He was brother to Fanny, Jacob, Noel, and Nimrod Raulerson. He moved from Ware County, Georgia, to modern-day Columbia County, Florida, in 1826. He previously had married Elizabeth Moore, the daughter of Caleb Moore. Raulerson died in Baker County, Florida, in 1858.[234]

Raulerson, William. A son of Fanny Raulerson, William Raulerson was born about 1824 in Georgia. He died in Columbia County, Florida, on March 16, 1838, in the Indian attack on the Gillett family, as described by George G. Keen.[235]

Raulerson, William. A son of Noel and Elizabeth Raulerson and nephew to Fanny Raulerson, William was born in Georgia during the 1820s. In the 1830s and 1840s he worked for George G. Keen's father, William R. Keen, and later witnessed George G. Keen's marriage to Arkina Lane. Raulerson died in Columbia County, Florida, on October 29, 1907.[236]

Reed, Harrison. Born in Littleton, Middlesex County, Massachusetts, on August 26, 1813, Harrison Reed was the son of Seth Harrison and Rhoda Finney Reed. A Wisconsin businessman and editor prior to the Civil War, Reed moved to Florida in 1863 as a United States tax commissioner. He was elected the state's first Republican governor five years later. On August 10, 1869, in Syracuse, New York, Reed married Chloe Merrick. Frustrated in 1872 by attempts to secure reelection, Reed moved to Jacksonville, and in 1879 he represented Duval County in the Florida House of Representatives. During 1889–1893 he acted as Tallahassee's postmaster. Reed died in Jacksonville on May 25, 1899.[237]

Revels, Edmond. Information not available.

Rid, Wop. Information not available; likely a literary character.

Roberts, Asa. Born in South Carolina in 1799, Asa Roberts was the son of Zachariah and Mary Weeks Roberts. He married Belinda Burnett in Camden County, Georgia, on September 20, 1827. He later married an unknown woman with whom he had a son. His third wife was Argent Cason O'Steen, the daughter of Eli Cason and widow of Capt. James O'Steen. By 1830 Roberts was living in Alachua (now Columbia) County, Florida. He died at Lake City in July 1879.[238]

Rogers, Robert Furman. A leader in Florida's farmers' revolt of the late 1880s and early 1890s, R. F. Rogers was born in Darlington, South Carolina, on May 30, 1846. His parents were John J. and Julia Farrell Rogers. He arrived at Lake City, Florida, with his parents in 1857, and he married Sarah J. Robertson there in 1863. Rogers represented Suwannee County in Florida's constitutional convention of 1885 and the Seventeenth District in the Florida Senate during 1889–1891. He sat in the Florida House of Representatives from Marion County in 1911–1912. From 1897 to 1900 Rogers presided as Lake City's mayor. He died in Ocala on December 29, 1933.[239]

Rose, Marquise de Lafietty. Information not available.

Rosenthal, Joseph. Born in Wurtemburg in 1831, Joseph Rosenthal lived for a short time during the 1850s at Lake City, Florida. By 1860 the merchant kept a store at Fernandina. Apparently he departed Florida with the outbreak of the Civil War. The date and place of his death are not known.[240]

Ross, William B. Second Seminole War volunteer officer and Whig political leader William B. Ross was born in North Carolina about 1809. He married Honora (or Honorie) G. Gautier in Duval County, Florida, on March 6, 1834. By 1850 Ross was established as one of Columbia County's leading planters. He represented the county in the Florida House of Representatives in 1845 and represented both Columbia and Suwannee Counties in 1862–1864. He sat in the Florida Senate in 1865–1866. Ross died in Columbia County on March 24, 1870.[241]

Russell, Green. Information not available. But see also Burwell K. Greene.

Rutledge, John T. John T. Rutledge was born July 28, 1810 [1815?], in Wayne County, Georgia. He married Sevilla Keen, daughter of Theophilus Keen and cousin of George G. Keen, in Columbia County, Florida, in 1844. Rutledge died in Manatee County, Florida, on March 31, 1894.[242]

Sandlin [Sanderlin], Robert. The son of John Sandlin, Robert Sandlin was born in Duplin County, North Carolina, on April 3, 1790. He married Zilpha Hicks on December 12, 1822, before moving to present-day Columbia County, Florida, in 1826. He died in that county on June 24, 1864.[243]

Sapp, Elisha. Born November 22, 1823, in Tattnall County, Georgia, Elisha Sapp was the son of Shadrick Sapp Jr. and Nancy Ann Parker Sapp. Apparently he married Sarah Moody, daughter of Gabriel Moody, in Columbia County, Florida. Elisha remained alive in Columbia County until at least 1853, but according to family report, he was murdered prior to the Civil War by a business partner.[244]

Sapp, John. Georgia native John Sapp was born about 1801. With his wife Hannah he lived by 1850 in that portion of Madison County, Florida, that would become Lafayette County. He died there in March 1860.[245]

Sapp, Newton. John Sapp's son Newton was born in Columbia County, Florida, on May 20, 1843. He served during the Civil War with the Fourth Florida

Infantry (CSA) before enlisting in the Second Florida Cavalry (USA). On November 12, 1875, Sapp was married in Lafayette County to Mary J. Harrell. From March 1875 to October 1877 he held office as county sheriff. Afterward Sapp farmed in Lafayette County, but by the century's end he operated a grocery store at Lake City. Newton Sapp died in Lafayette County on November 20, 1923.[246]

Scarborough, Mathew M. Born July 26, 1844, in Columbia County, Florida, M. M. Scarborough was the son of Stirling and Susan Brooks Scarborough. On February 15, 1869, he married Fannie E. Charles. An attorney by profession, Scarborough died at Lake City on September 22, 1909.[247]

Scarborough, Stirling. Georgian Stirling Scarborough was born April 3, 1801. He immigrated with his wife Susan Brooks Scarborough to Columbia County, Florida, from Decatur County, Georgia, during the 1840s. On October 6, 1845, he was elected clerk of the circuit court for Columbia County, and he served in that capacity until December 15, 1857. He died in the county on September 27, 1859.[248]

Sheffield, Kesiah Cone. See Kesiah Cone Sheffield Hagan.

Sheffield, William A. Born in Bulloch County, Georgia, on August 22 or 23, 1830, William A. Sheffield was the son of Simon and Kesiah Cone Sheffield. He arrived in Florida in 1849 as a teacher, and in 1853 or 1858 in Columbia County he married Mary Jones, daughter of John W. Jones. At various times Sheffield was sheriff and superintendent of public instruction for Columbia County and mayor of Lake City. He died at Lake City on April 7, 1903.[249]

Simmons, William Hayne. Physician, poet, and land speculator William Hayne Simmons was born in Charleston, South Carolina, in January 1784. He never married. Simmons moved to St. Augustine, Florida, in 1821 and launched himself into territorial affairs. The next year he published his *Notices of East Florida,* and in 1823 he and John Lee Williams decided upon Tallahassee as the site for Florida's capital. That year he also represented East Florida on the territorial council. Afterward Simmons returned to Charleston, where he died on October 4, 1870.[250]

Slade, John Gideon. See John Gideon Bell.

Slade, Nancy. See Nancy Slade Douglass.

Slade, Stephen F. Born about 1816 in Georgia, Stephen F. Slade may have been a son of Nancy Slade. By 1850 he was living with his wife Mary (also referred to as Margaret and Peggy) in that portion of Madison County, Florida, that became Lafayette County. Apparently he died there in 1870 or 1871.[251]

Smiley, Andrew Jackson ("Jack"). Lake City merchant and saloon keeper Jack Smiley was born in Florida about 1835, the son of J. M. and Nancy Sykes Smiley.

His father, a lieutenant of volunteers during the Second Seminole War, was murdered by Indians near his home five miles from Mineral Springs on January 24, 1837. Jack Smiley remained unmarried in 1860. He died at Lake Butler on November 16, 1860.[252]

Smith, George Washington. George W. Smith was one of Hamilton County, Florida's earliest pioneer settlers and a Second Seminole War captain. He married Harriet Oglesby in Hamilton County on November 13, 1831. A deputy United States marshal in the early 1840s, he was known as "Snorting Smith" because of the considerable difficulty he had breathing. Smith resided in Hamilton County until 1842 and may have lived in Columbia County in 1847. His whereabouts thereafter are not known with certainty.[253]

Smith, Henry C. North Carolina native Henry C. Smith was born about 1804. He was in Florida by 1837 and was living in 1850 in present-day Lafayette County with his wife Nancy. Available evidence suggests that he died there before 1858.[254]

Smith, Martha Jane. Born in Georgia about 1829, Martha Jane Smith was the wife of Matthew Whit Smith. She moved with him to Lake City during the 1850s. Although the couple lived for a time in Tampa and Jacksonville, Martha Jane Smith died in Columbia County circa August 1883.[255]

Smith, Matthew Whit. Lawyer, editor, Methodist preacher, and entrepreneur M. Whit Smith was born in Tennessee on October 7, 1814. In the 1850s he lived with his wife Martha Jane at present-day Lake City. By 1855 he edited and published the *Alligator Advertiser* there. Later he also published the *Tampa Herald* and the *St. Johns Mirror.* Briefly during the Civil War, Smith served as lieutenant colonel of the Fourth Florida Infantry (CSA). He died at Lake City on August 31, 1866.[256]

Smith, Thomas Williford. Born in Marlboro District, South Carolina, about 1813, Thomas Williford Smith was the son of William W. Smith.[257]

Smith, Virginia C. See Virginia C. Smith Curtis.

Sparkman, Stephen. Columbia County planter Stephen Sparkman was born about 1782 in North Carolina. He married Elsa Keightley. Sparkman died at Lake City in 1873.[258]

Sparkman, Stephen. An antebellum Columbia County planter, Stephen Sparkman was born in 1826 in Georgia. His first wife was named Francis. On May 20, 1885, he was married in Volusia County to Josephine E. M. Hall, having moved from Columbia County about 1874. Sparkman died in Volusia County on March 4, 1897.[259]

Stallings, Eliza Jane Hooker. The daughter of William B. Hooker and Mary Amanda Hair Hooker, Eliza Jane was born in Hamilton County, Florida, on December 25, 1833. On April 18, 1850, she married William W. Stallings in Tampa. Eliza Jane died about 1858 in Hillsborough County.[260]

Stallings, William Walker. North Carolinian William W. Stallings was born November 4, 1820, the son of Wiley and Susanna Mugby Stallings. He arrived in Hillsborough County, Florida, in the 1840s and married Eliza Jane Hooker there on April 18, 1850. Stallings died in the Confederate army on September 15, 1862, at Warrenton, Virginia.[261]

Staten, Barzilla. The son of John and Penelope Staten, Barzilla Staten was born in Georgia (likely Effingham County) about 1791. In 1817 he married Catherine Watson, daughter of James and Catherine Watson. Staten settled in present-day Lanier County in the early 1830s. He was wounded badly on August 27, 1836, in the Second Seminole War engagement at Cow Creek but served again in 1838 as a first lieutenant. Staten died in (then) Lowndes County, Georgia, in 1846.[262]

Stephens, Henry Monroe ("Hamp"). Born February 3, 1823, in Tattnall County, Georgia, Henry Monroe Stephens was the son of Henry and Elizabeth Stephens. The family moved to Hamilton County, Florida, in 1832. Hamp Stephens subsequently served in the Second Seminole War and the Civil War. He also held office as clerk of the circuit court for Hamilton County. Stephens married Maria Louisa Varns in 1844. In 1865 he married Elizabeth Dees, the mother of Worth Stephens. Henry M. Stephens died in Hamilton County on August 15, 1871.[263]

Stephens, Worth. Worth Stephens was born in Hamilton County, Florida, on January 12, 1857. His widowed mother was married in 1865 to Henry Monroe Stephens, who adopted her son. Worth lived in Hamilton and Suwannee Counties before dying in Live Oak on March 1, 1907.[264]

Stewart, Alexander T. Born in Ireland on October 12, 1803, Alexander T. Stewart was George G. Keen's vision of the preeminent millionaire. From a small dry goods store he opened in New York City in 1823, Stewart built an industrial, merchandising, and real estate empire. He died at his New York City home on April 10, 1876.[265]

Stewart, Asa A. Early Columbia County pioneer Asa A. Stewart was born in Georgia on April 18, 1813. On February 6, 1842, he married Nancy Tucker, the widow of John Edward Tucker. Following distinguished service as a captain in the Confederate army, Stewart died in Columbia County on September 2, 1880.[266]

Stewart, Daniel. Georgian Daniel Stewart was born about 1815. Present in Columbia County, Florida, by 1834, he married Nancy Emery. The couple lived for a time in Georgia before relocating by 1860 in Lafayette County, Florida. Daniel's whereabouts thereafter are not known.[267]

Stewart, Nancy Emery. Born in Georgia about 1811 (1816 according to George G. Keen), Nancy Emery married Daniel Stewart in Columbia County, Florida, during the mid 1830s. Following a return to Georgia for a decade or more after 1838, Nancy was living with Daniel in Lafayette County, Florida, in 1860. Her whereabouts thereafter are not known.[268]

Summerlin, Jacob, Sr. A native of Spanish Florida, Jacob Summerlin Sr. was born during 1792, the son of Joseph Summerlin [or Summerall]. He married Mary Ann Hagan, who died in Jefferson County on February 13, 1836. Jacob was then married in the county to a Miss Partridge. One of East Florida's leading Whig politicians, Summerlin served Columbia County in the territorial house of representatives in 1843 and East Florida in the territorial senate in 1845. He died at Lake City (then Alligator) on January 15, 1848.[269]

Summerlin, Louisa. See Louisa Summerlin Frink Purviance.

Summerlin, Rebecca B. See Rebecca B. Summerlin Steele Alexander.

Tecumseh [or Tekamthi]. One of the most outstanding Native American leaders in United States history, Tecumseh was born on the Little Miami River in present-day Ohio about 1768. His father was the Creek warrior Puckeshinwa, and his mother was a Shawnee, Methoastaske. Described by President William Henry Harrison as "one of those uncommon geniuses, which spring up occasionally to produce revolutions and overturn the order of things," Tecumseh organized a widespread coalition to resist white encroachments. His efforts resulted in warfare on November 7, 1811, with the Battle of Tippecanoe. Tecumseh died fighting with British forces during the War of 1812 at the Battle of the Thames, Ontario, Canada, on October 5, 1813. Many of those chiefs and warriors he influenced in the South eventually came to Florida as refugees after the War of 1812.[270]

Thomas, John G. Born May 2, 1807, in Georgia, John G. Thomas, with his wife Eliza (a relation of the Raulerson family), became a pioneer settler of Columbia and Hillsborough Counties in Florida. He died in Hillsborough County on July 21, 1865.[271]

Tillis, Richard. Apparently a son of Richard Tillis, Columbia County's Richard Tillis was born in Camden County, Georgia, on January 5, 1813. Richard was living in Columbia County by the 1830s. His first wife, whose name is not known, was killed by Indians on February 24, 1842, as described by George G. Keen. He was married in 1844 to Sarah (Johnson?). Sarah died in Suwannee County circa

July 25, 1885, after which Richard moved to Polk County. He died at Fort Meade on November 28, 1887.[272]

Todd, Samuel Bryant. Physician and planter Samuel B. Todd was born in Vermont about 1820. A graduate of Harvard University, he ministered as a Methodist and, after 1865, Baptist preacher. Present in Hillsborough County by the late 1840s, Todd was married there on December 25, 1849, to Martha Knight, daughter of the Reverend Samuel Knight and Mary Roberts Knight. Todd moved to Georgia in 1868 and died in Valdosta on May 1, 1870.[273]

Tompkins [Thompkins], Donald. Longtime Columbia County constable Donald Tompkins was born during 1830 in Camden County, Georgia. He was a butcher by trade, and he and his wife Ann continued to live in Columbia County after the Civil War. He remained alive there in 1874, but the date and place of his death are not known.[274]

Townsend, Horatio G. Methodist minister Horatio G. Townsend was born in South Carolina about 1831. By 1858–1859 he was at Lake City, Florida, editing the *Alligator Advertiser* and planning to establish a new journal, the *Eastern Herald.* George G. Keen stated that Townsend later practiced law. The date and place of his death are not known.[275]

Tracy, Erasmus Darwin. Prominent early Floridian Erasmus Darwin Tracy was born in Norwich, Connecticut, on September 22, 1810. His parents were Cyrus Tracy Jr. and Hannah Snow Tracy. E. D. Tracy represented Nassau County in the Florida House of Representatives in 1845–1846 and sat in the state senate during 1847–1848 and 1854–1856. He presided over the senate in 1854–1855 and over Florida's constitutional convention in 1865. Tracy died in Boulogne, Nassau County, on February 18, 1877. [276]

Vanzant [VanZandt], Garrett. Columbia County planter Garrett Vanzant was born in Spanish Florida (present-day Nassau County) on October 5, 1818. On December 30, 1841, he was married in Columbia County to Julia C. Goodbread, daughter of John Starling and Charity Crews Goodbread. During 1854–1855, 1860–1861, and 1865–1866 Vanzant represented Columbia County in the Florida House of Representatives. He died at Lake City on February 15, 1895. [277]

Waldron, George W. S. The son of Oliver Waldron, George W. S. Waldron was born in Bryan County, Georgia, on January 13, 1813. On September 5, 1833, he married Henrietta, daughter of Jacob Raulerson. She died in 1838, and Waldron then married Catherine, daughter of James B. Stewart. Following Catherine's death George married Rebecca Lane Raulerson. Waldron died in Columbia County, Florida, on May 24 [28?], 1895.[278]

Waldron, George Washington. George W. S. and Catherine Waldron's son George Washington Waldron was born in Columbia County, Florida, on February 18, 1847. He married Mary K. Green. George W. Waldron died at Lake City on October 11, 1910. Mary Green Waldron followed on October 28, 1924.[279]

Walker, Ansel. Born in Camden County, Georgia, in 1807, Ansel Walker was the son of Littleberry and Elizabeth McClain Walker. He married: Sabra Taylor (d. 1844); in 1852, Sallie Summerall (d. 1855); in 1855, Martha Jane Hatcher (d. 1863); and in 1864, Sabra J. Hatcher. Walker was an early pioneer of Columbia County, Florida. In the early 1870s he moved to Polk County, where he died on October 12, 1885.[280]

Walker, Elias. A brother to Ansel Walker, Elias Walker was born in Glynn County, Georgia, about 1805. He was a resident of Columbia County, Florida, by the mid 1830s, and he and his wife Elizabeth remained there until his death circa October 1874.[281]

Walker, P. K. Information not available.

Watts, Joseph B. Hamilton County pioneer Joseph B. Watts was born about 1798 in North Carolina. His wife Sarah was a native Floridian born about 1810. He represented Hamilton County in Florida's 1838–1839 constitutional convention and sat in the state senate during 1847–1848. Watts moved to Madison County in 1849 and eventually relocated in Orange County, where he died on August 23, 1870.[282]

Watts, William F. Kentucky native William F. Watts was born in January 1869. Apparently he and his wife Blanche moved to Lake City, Florida, in the 1890s. He remained alive there in 1910, but the 1920 census found Blanche a widow.[283]

White, John F., Sr. Son of the Reverend George White, John F. White was born in Rogersville, Hawkins County, Tennessee, on February 18, 1824. He married Sarah A. Latimer. A onetime Tennessee legislator, White moved to Florida late in the Civil War. In 1866 he received appointment as judge of the criminal court of Suwannee County. Afterward he served as a state attorney and circuit judge. He died in Live Oak on August 14, 1901.[284]

Wightman, Charles Christopher. The son of John Thomas Wightman, Christopher Charles Wightman was born in Charleston, South Carolina, on June 6, 1834. On January [February?] 27, 1858, he married Mary Victoria Miller. Wightman, considered a mechanical genius, died in Charleston on March 10, 1905.[285]

Wightman, Mary Victoria Miller. Born in Charleston, South Carolina, on July 28, 1837, Mary Victoria Miller was the daughter of James A. and Sarah M. Miller.

On January [February?] 27, 1858, she married Charles Christopher Wightman in Charleston. She died in Orangeburg, South Carolina, on July 24, 1879.[286]

Wilkerson, Joseph. Born during the 1810s, Joseph Wilkerson was living in Columbia County, Florida, by the early 1830s, if not earlier. According to George G. Keen, he married Sookie Morgan there about 1834. By 1850 Wilkerson resided in Levy County with his wife Charlotte Ann, born in North Carolina about 1828. He died in that county circa December 1873.[287]

Williams, John Lee. A native of Salem, Massachusetts, John Lee Williams was born in 1775. His family soon relocated to New York, where he attended Hamilton College. After achieving admission to the bar, Williams moved to Virginia. His first wife, Mary Irwin, died early, and in 1820 Williams moved to Pensacola in Spanish West Florida. In 1823 he and William Hayne Simmons of St. Augustine served as commissioners to locate the site for Florida's capital. Later Williams moved to St. Augustine and then to Bayard and Picolata on the St. Johns River. In 1827 he published his *A View of West Florida, Embracing its Geography, Topography, with an Appendix Treating of its Antiquities, Land Titles, and Canals,* which was followed after ten years by *The Territory of Florida.* In 1829 Williams married Martha Mackey Ives. He died in Picolata on November 7, 1856.[288]

Williams, Maria Mackey. See Maria Mackey Williams Burtchaell.

Williams, Martha Lockhart Mackey Ives. The daughter of John and Abagail Mills Mackey, Martha Lockhart Mackey was born in Louisville, Georgia, on August 16, 1795. In Charleston, South Carolina, on July 2, 1815, she married Capt. Jeremiah Ives, a native of Hartford, Connecticut. In 1824 the family relocated near New Smyrna, Florida, where Jeremiah died on June 15, 1827. On March 9, 1829, Martha was remarried in St. Augustine, to John Lee Williams. About 1847 they separated and she moved with her daughter, Sarah Pamela Williams, to Alligator (Lake City). She died there on March 8, 1872.[289]

Williams, Pink. Information not available.

Williams, Sarah Pamela. See Sarah Pamela Williams Niblack Kelly.

Wright, Arthur J. T. Lake City merchant A. J. T. Wright was born in Georgia on January 2, 1826 [1825?]. Wright was living in Columbia County by the 1840s and married Harriet Scarborough there on June 10, 1849. Wright served as one of Columbia County's delegates to Florida's secession convention in 1861 and later as lieutenant colonel in the Third Florida Infantry (CSA). He died in Columbia County on September 2, 1872.[290]

Wright, Harriet Scarborough. The daughter of Stirling S. and Susan Brooks Scarborough, Harriet Scarborough was born at Fort Gaines, Georgia, on September

4, 1826. She moved with her family to Lake City, Florida, in the 1840s. There on June 10, 1849, she married Arthur J. T. Wright. Harriet died at Lake City on November 4, 1909.[291]

Wright, Mitchell Edwin ("Ed"). The son of Arthur J. T. and Harriet S. Wright, Ed Wright was born at Lake City, Florida, on August 10, 1864. He died in Columbia County on November 18, 1911.[292]

Wright, Riley. Born about 1815 in Georgia, Riley Wright was living in Columbia County, Florida, prior to 1850. Soon thereafter he and his wife Mary Ann moved to Lafayette County. During 1864 Wright served in William White's Band, Union Rangers, operating out of Cedar Keys. His whereabouts thereafter are not known.[293]

Young, Alexander. A native of Scotland, Lake City merchant Alexander Young was born on April 9, 1822. He married Florida-born Serenah Clothilde Young. Alexander Young died at Lake City on June 9, 1879.[294]

Yulee, David Levy. The son of early Florida developer Moses Levy, David Levy Yulee was born in St. Thomas, West Indies, on June 12, 1810. He studied law at St. Augustine and achieved admission to the bar in 1836. He represented St. Johns County in the territorial council in 1837–1838 and in Florida's constitutional convention of 1838–1839. During 1841–1845 he sat in the United States Congress as delegate from Florida. In 1845 he became Florida's first United States senator, as well as the first Jewish man to enter that body. He held his seat from 1845 to 1851, then returned from 1855 to 1861. He died October 10, 1886, in New York City. [295]

Zolindi, Frederick. Information not available.

ABBREVIATIONS

FSA   Florida State Archives, Tallahassee

JFT-U   *Jacksonville Florida Times-Union*

LCC-R   *Lake City Citizen-Reporter*

LCFI   Lake City Florida Index

NA   National Archives, Washington, D.C.

PKY   P. K. Yonge Library of Florida History, University of Florida, Gainesville

RG   Record Group

SLF   State Library of Florida, Tallahassee

TFP   *Tampa Florida Peninsular*

TST   *Tampa Sunland Tribune*

TP   *Territorial Papers of the United States, Florida*

NOTES

INTRODUCTION

1. On Florida's historical diversity, see Greenberg, Rogers, and Brown, eds., *Florida's Heritage of Diversity.*

2. On the origin of the name Cracker and on Florida's Cracker population generally, see Lewis, "Cracker—Spanish Florida Style," and Denham, "Florida Cracker Before the Civil War."

3. On southern women see McMillen, *Southern Women;* Cashin, *Family Venture;* Fox-Genovese, *Within the Plantation Household;* Clinton, *Plantation Mistress;* Drew Gilpin Faust, *Mothers of Invention;* Bleser, ed., *In Joy and Sorrow;* Boles, *South Through Time,* 220–30; Wolfe, *Daughters of Canaan;* Wyatt-Brown, *Southern Honor.* On Florida women see Denham, "Cracker Women and Their Families," and Revels, "Grander in Her Daughters."

4. The principal work on Columbia County's history is Keuchel, *History of Columbia County, Florida.*

5. See Smith, *Slavery and Plantation Growth in Antebellum Florida;* Paisley, *Red Hills of Florida.*

6. The principal work on the Second Seminole War is Mahon, *History of the Second Seminole War.*

7. Brown, *Florida's Peace River Frontier,* 63–136.

8. Patrick, *Florida Fiasco;* Brown, *Ossian Bingley Hart,* 18–41.

9. Keuchel, *History of Columbia County,* 17–32; F. A. Walker, *Ninth Census—Volume I,* 18–19, 97–98.

10. Keuchel, *History of Columbia County,* 59–82; F. A. Walker, *Ninth Census—Volume I,* 97–98; Washington M. Ives Journal, entry of March 14, 1860, Florida State Archives.

11. The migratory nature of the cattle culture, especially the tendency to affect settlement patterns in Florida and other sections of the South, has been chronicled in Brown, *Florida's Peace River Frontier;* Jordan, *Trails to Texas;* and McWhiney and McDonald, "Celtic Origins of Southern Herding Practices," among others. On herding on Florida's open ranges, see Akerman, *Florida Cowman;* Otto, "Hillsborough County"; idem, "Florida's Cattle-Ranching Frontier"; idem, "Florida Cattle-Ranching Frontier"; and idem, "Open Range Ranching in Southern Florida." See also Elliott and Knetsch, eds., *Proceedings of the Florida Cattle Frontier Symposium.*

12. On attitudes toward law and order and Florida's antebellum system of justice, frontier and otherwise, see Denham, *"Rogue's Paradise."* On nose biting, see Greenberg, "The Nose, the Lie, and the Duel in the Antebellum South."

13. Augustus Baldwin Longstreet, *Georgia Scenes* (1835); Johnson J. Hooper, *Adventures of Captain Simon Suggs, Late of the Tallapoosa Volunteers* (1845); Joseph G. Baldwin, *Flush Times of Alabama and Mississippi* (1853); Joel Chandler Harris, *Uncle Remus: His Songs and Sayings* (1880); and idem, *Nights with Uncle Remus* (1880). For a general overview of other southern humorists and postbellum southern literary traditions, see

Rubin, *Edge of the Swamp;* Cohen and Dillingham, eds., *Humor of the Old Southwest;* Ridgely, *Nineteenth-Century Southern Literature;* Price, "Stories with a Moral"; and Cooper and Terrill, *American South,* 257–58, 641–42. On southern autobiography see Watkins, ed., *Southern Selves.*

14. Cohen and Dillingham, eds., *Humor of the Old Southwest,* xxiv.

15. For comments regarding the racist and sexist characteristics of much of southwestern humor, see ibid., xiii.

16. For more on plain folk and Crackers, see Owsley, *Plain Folk in the Old South;* McWhiney, *Cracker Culture;* Newby, *Plain Folk in the New South;* Denham, "Florida Cracker Before the Civil War"; idem, "Cracker Women and Their Families"; Ste. Claire, *Cracker: The Cracker Culture in Florida History;* Hyde, *Plain Folk of the South Revisited;* Flynt, *Poor But Proud;* and idem, *Dixie's Forgotten People.*

17. Denham, "Florida Cracker Before the Civil War," 454.

PART ONE

1. On the early history of Columbia County and the town of Alligator (Lake City), see Keuchel, *History of Columbia County,* 1–32. For general information on the Florida frontier during the early nineteenth century, see Brown, *Florida's Peace River Frontier,* 3–33, 63–74. Regarding the lifestyle of Florida Cracker families, see Denham, "Florida Cracker Before the Civil War." Florida's antebellum judicial system is explored in Denham, *"Rogue's Paradise."*

2. Principal sources on the Second Seminole War are: Mahon, *History of the Second Seminole War;* Sprague, *Origin, Progress, and Conclusion of the Florida War;* and Peters, *Florida Wars.*

3. Confirming this incident, the *St. Augustine Florida Herald* of July 1, 1835, reported: "We understand a rencontre took place between a party of Indians, in the neighborhood of the Hogtown [present-day Gainesville] settlement on the 18th ult. in which one of the Indians was killed and another so severely wounded that he was not expected to live. Three of the white men were badly wounded. The circumstances so far as we have ascertained are as follows:—It appears that a party of seven Indians went out of their bounds clandestinely for the purpose of hunting. After a short time they separated and agreed to meet again at a certain spot. Five of them had assembled when they were met by the party of white men, who disarmed four of them and flogged them with their cow-whips. They were in the act of whipping the fifth when the other two Indians made their appearance, who seeing what was going on, raised the war whoop and fired upon the whites. The fire was returned which killed one and wounded the other fatally." See Mahon, *History of the Second Seminole War,* 98–99.

4. Wright, *Creeks & Seminoles,* 209.

5. Likely Keen refers to attacks on the plantations of Thomas Randall and John Gamble in Jefferson County that occurred in late April and early May 1836. *St. Augustine Florida Herald,* May 6, 1836; Shofner, *History of Jefferson County,* 73–74. For background on these attacks, see Brown, "Florida Crisis of 1826–1827."

6. On June 18, 1836, the Suwannee River plantation of A. Watson was destroyed. See *St. Augustine Florida Herald,* July 9, 1836.

7. As early as February–March 1836 the military situation in Florida appeared grim for frontier settlers. Regular and volunteer forces had met with defeat, and

Middle Florida soldiers under Gov. Richard Keith Call had withdrawn to protect their home areas. Call remembered the situation this way: "The sparseness of the population of East Florida, settled in single families or small neighborhoods, often fifteen or twenty miles from any other settlement, and the local situation of the country, intersected with swamps and hammocks, afforded every facility for the approach and concealment of the enemy, while it exposed the defenceless inhabitants to the most fearful destruction. There was not a family in that whole region of country which was not placed in utmost peril." See *Jacksonville Florida Republican,* February 1, 1849.

8. A brief report of the attack on Joseph Howell's family and subsequent events was carried in the *Tallahassee Floridian* on August 28, 1840.

9. No independent report verifies the number of Indian casualties reported by Keen, and the editors consider them unlikely.

10. Apparently Fort Jinks was the homestead of a family named Jinks, located at present-day Wellborn, Suwannee County. See *Lake City Florida Index,* December 22, 1899.

11. The *Apalachicola Gazette* published details on the attack upon Roanoke, Georgia, in its issue of May 28, 1836. That account listed casualties as seven whites, five blacks, and three Indians. See also Motte, *Journey into Wilderness,* 10–13, 251–52.

12. For more details, see *Apalachicola Gazette,* September 24, 1836; Huxford, *Pioneers of Wiregrass Georgia,* I, 261–63.

13. See *Savannah Georgian,* November 13, 1838.

14. Gen. Charles R. Floyd's report of his reconnaissance of the Okefenokee Swamp was published in the *St. Augustine News* on December 3 and 22, 1838.

15. On November 23, 1838, a band of Indians attacked and killed members of the John Tippins family, who were traveling to visit Mrs. Tippins's father, David Mizell. The incident occurred near Ocean Pond, ten miles east of Lake City. Keen apparently confused this occurrence with the attack on the Higginbotham and Johns families at their homes about seven and ten miles west of Jacksonville, respectively, on September 15, 1836. See *St. Augustine Florida Herald and Southern Democrat,* November 29, 1838; L. S. Walker, *History of Ware County,* 67; *Apalachicola Gazette,* October 8, 1836; Davis, *History of Jacksonville,* 78–79.

16. Details of the attack on the Gillett family can be found in *Tallahassee Floridian,* April 7, 1838; *Tallahassee Floridian* (Supp.), February 9, 1839; Keuchel, *History of Columbia County,* 44; and L. S. Walker, *History of Ware County,* 66–67.

17. Several sources contain information about the attack on the Richard Tillis family: *Niles Register,* April 9, 1842; *Army and Navy Chronicle,* March 26, 1842; *St. Augustine News,* March 5, 1842; John S. Purviance to Gen. Alexander McRae, March 3, 1842, Purviance Letters, PKY.

18. See Col. William J. Worth's report, February 28, 1842, in House Document No. 262, 27th Cong., 2d sess., 13.

19. This engagement is not independently substantiated.

20. Brown, *Florida's Peace River Frontier,* 67–68, 79–80, 92.

21. Apparently at least one of George G. Keen's letters was published in an issue of *The Florida Index* that no longer is available. Sheffield may be referring here to Hillsborough and Polk County pioneer Silas McClelland. See McClelland, *Silas and*

Penelope (Anderson) McClelland, 21–26; Brown, *Florida's Peace River Frontier,* 69, 92, 143, 354–55, 358, 379, 390, 394.

22. For a recent summary of current scholarship on Florida's Indian populations, see Gannon, *New History of Florida.*

23. Keen visited South Florida, if not before, as a soldier in Capt. J. J. Knight's volunteer company during the Indian crisis of 1849–1850. See Indian War pension record #WC-5899, NA; *Jacksonville Florida Republican,* September 13, 1849.

24. The Second Seminole War fort at Alligator was called Fort Lancaster. The legislature subsequently renamed the town accordingly, but before 1842 it again went by the name Alligator. See Keuchel, *History of Columbia County,* 75.

25. Historian Edward F. Keuchel relates a separate tradition that the name was changed to Lake City in December 1858 "at the insistence of Mrs. William B. Ross who feared her daughter's friends at the school she was to attend would ridicule her if she was from a town called Alligator." Keuchel, in *History of Columbia County,* 75, notes that state representative John Frink of Hamilton County unsuccessfully attempted at the time to gain legislative approval, presumably tongue in cheek, to change the name to Crocodile.

26. Florida House of Representatives, Office of the Clerk, *People of Lawmaking in Florida,* 13; Huxford, *Pioneers of Wiregrass Georgia,* VI, 334.

27. Florida House of Representatives, Office of the Clerk, *People of Lawmaking in Florida,* 48, 65.

28. *Jacksonville Florida Times-Union and Citizen,* November 27, 1901; *Jacksonville Evening Metropolis,* November 26 and 27, 1901; *Tampa Tribune,* November 27, 1901.

29. Yulee was David Levy's paternal grandfather's name, according to Yulee family notes, collection of Samuel Proctor, Gainesville.

30. See returns of elections in Benton County, 1850, in Election Returns, RG 156, series 21, box 3, FSA.

31. See Brown, *Florida's Peace River Frontier,* 80–86; Schene, "Not a Shot Fired."

32. Brown, *Florida's Peace River Frontier,* 106–20. For general information on the Third Seminole or Billy Bowlegs War, see Covington, *Billy Bowlegs War.*

33. Jacksonville historian T. Frederick Davis suggests that Lewis Z. Hogans, rather than Arch Hogans, was the early settler in question. See Davis, *History of Jacksonville,* 53.

34. Isaiah David Hart died at Jacksonville on September 4, 1861. His second son, Ossian Bingley Hart, served as governor of Florida from January 1873 until his death at Jacksonville on March 18, 1874. See Brown, *Ossian Bingley Hart,* 118–28, 294–96.

35. William G. Dawson and Stephen E. Buckles are credited with opening Jacksonville's first store, probably doing so in 1819. See Davis, *History of Jacksonville,* 52.

36. Returns of the election of October 7, 1850, Benton County, in Election Returns, RG 156, series 21, box 3, FSA.

37. On October 6, 1845, Thomas B. Fitzpatrick defeated Charles F. Fitchett and William H. Rousseau for sheriff of Columbia County. In the same election Silas Scarborough bested Levi Carter for clerk of the circuit court. See returns of the election of October 6, 1845, Columbia County, in Election Returns, RG 156, series 21, box 6, FSA.

38. Keuchel, *History of Columbia County,* 92–93; Hartman and Coles, *Biographical Rosters,* I, 362, and II, 478.

39. Records of Commissions, Columbia County, RG 156, series 259, vols. 28 and 30, and Records of Appointments, Columbia County, RG 156, series 1284, vol. 2, FSA; Brown, *Ossian Bingley Hart,* 283–84, 286–87; *New York Sun,* March 17, 1873; Keuchel, *History of Columbia County,* 128. Representing him as a "good Republican and efficient man," a Lake City man recommended Keen for the Columbia County board of commissioners. See E. S. Johnson to Harrison Reed, November 19, 1870, RG 101, series 577, box 1, FSA. Keen's resignation as sheriff can be found in Keen to Marcellus L. Stearns, July 4, 1873, RG 151, series 1326, box 1, FSA.

40. Morris, *Florida Handbook,* 426, 433.

41. Affidavit of William F. Bynum, July 22, 1859, in Comptroller vouchers, 1846–1862, RG 350, series 565, box 7, folder 3, FSA.

42. Ibid. See Coroner's Inquest, July 18, 1859. Though county court records are unavailable, state prosecution records reveal that Noah Cason was indicted for the murder of Locklear (or Locklier) and tried and acquitted in the Suwannee County Court in 1859. The next year William and Noah Cason were indicted again, this time in Lafayette County, and then convicted, fined, and imprisoned. See Ibid., *State vs Noah Cason,* box 4, folder 1, and Ibid., *State vs William Cason and Noah Cason,* box 6, folder 2.

43. Troupville, Georgia, lay on the banks of the upper Withlacoochee River. Laid out in 1836 on the line of the Brunswick and Chattahoochee Railroad, it became the Lowndes County seat in 1837 and by 1842 contained a population of five hundred. See Shelton, *Pines and Pioneers,* 95.

PART TWO

1. John Lee Williams family notes, collection of Helen Ives, St. Petersburg, Florida.

2. Covington, "Armed Occupation Act"; Brown, *Florida's Peace River Frontier,* 63–68.

3. Martin, *Florida During the Territorial Days,* 51.

4. An interesting story with, no doubt, some basis in truth. Still, Williams has confused events. Joseph B. Lancaster was elected speaker of the territorial house of representatives as a Whig in 1843–1844. So the placard she mentions represents his victory but not the naming of Alligator as Lancaster. The latter event grew out of the naming of the village's Second Seminole War outpost as Fort Lancaster in 1835. Before 1842 the name had reverted to Alligator. See Florida House of Representatives, Office of the Clerk, *People of Lawmaking in Florida,* 55; Keuchel, *History of Columbia County,* 54, 75; Doherty, *The Whigs of Florida,* 13.

5. Mrs. S. B. Bowman conducted the Female Department of the Quincy Male and Female Academy in the late 1840s. See *Tallahassee Floridian & Journal,* January 3, 1849.

6. Kennedy, *Population of the United States in 1860,* 54.

7. P. L. Faust, ed., *Historical Times Illustrated Encyclopedia of the Civil War,* 398–99.

APPENDIX

1. Population census, 1850, Columbia County, Florida.

2. Population census, 1860, Duval County, Florida; *Bartow Polk County Democrat,* January 27, 1972; *St. Augustine Examiner,* May 18, 1867; Duval County probate records,

packet 1916-D (Holmes Steele); 1880 population census, Liberty County, Georgia; Liberty County, Georgia, litigation files; Summerlin family files, Polk County Historical and Genealogical Library, Bartow; *Bartow Courier-Informant,* August 8, 1900.

3. Sprague, *Origin, Progress, and Conclusion of the Florida War,* 97–98; Keuchel, *History of Columbia County,* 13–14; Brown, *Florida's Peace River Frontier,* 371–72; Mahon, *History of the Second Seminole War,* 127; Coe, *Red Patriots,* 174.

4. *JFT-U,* June 21, 1892; James McNair Baker biographical file, Florida Supreme Court Historical Society, Tallahassee.

5. David St. John, Baker County Historical Society, to Canter Brown, Jr., n.d., collection of Canter Brown, Jr.

6. Hartman and Coles, *Biographical Rosters,* II, 471; Confederate Pension Application #11748, FSA; 1860 population census, Columbia County, Florida.

7. Population censuses, 1850 and 1860, Austin County, Texas; Haskew, *Historical Records of Austin and Waller Counties,* 25; *LCFI,* November 8, 1901.

8. Indian War pension records #WC-3510 and WC-4603, NA; *Members of the Texas Legislature 1846–1980.* Austin: Secretary of State, 1980, 55.

9. Frizzell, *Bellville,* 9–10; Haskew, *Historical Records of Austin and Waller Counties,* 25; Alice Heisch, Bellville, Texas, Public Library, to Canter Brown, Jr., January 3 and 17, 1996, collection of Canter Brown, Jr.

10. Population censuses, 1850 and 1860, Columbia County, Florida; *Jacksonville Florida Republican,* June 28, 1855; *LCFI,* May 13, 1904; *LCC-R,* May 13, 1904.

11. Edwards, Lucy Ames. *Grave Markers of Duval County, 1808–1916.* Jacksonville: Privately published, 1953, 143; *JFT-U,* June 19, 1889; Davis, *History of Jacksonville,* 87, 90.

12. Edwards, *Grave Markers of Duval County,* 143; *Jacksonville Daily News-Herald,* April 26, 1888.

13. Wright, *Creeks & Seminoles,* 209, 243, 274–75; Covington, *Seminoles of Florida,* 310.

14. Westergard and VanLandingham, *Parker & Blount in Florida,* 224–27; Brown, *Florida's Peace River Frontier,* 91.

15. Population censuses, 1850 and 1860, Columbia County, Florida.; Bonnell family biographical materials, collection of Wanda De Montmollin, Plant City; Columbia County Deed Records, Book G, 832, L, 699–700; White, *Index to Indian Wars Pension Files,* I, 148; *LCC-R,* August 26, 1910.

16. Population censuses, 1850 and 1860, Columbia County, Florida.

17. Cutler, *History of Florida,* II, 331; *JFT-U,* November 17, 1948.

18. *Tallahassee Floridian & Journal,* January 3, 1849.

19. Population census, 1850, Benton County, Florida; Hernando County historical materials, collection of Virginia Jackson, Brooksville, Florida; Florida House of Representatives, Office of the Clerk, *People of Lawmaking in Florida,* 10; Covington, *Billy Bowlegs War,* 48, 53–54; White, *Index to Indian Wars Pension Files,* I, 163.

20. Raulerson, comp., *Raulerson Documents 1800–1900,* n.p.; election returns, election at house of Joseph Dyalls, November 1831, Alachua County, RG 156, series, 21, box 1, FSA; 1880 population census, Columbia County, Florida.

21. Columbia County tax rolls, 1845.

22. "Burris Brewer Bounty Land Application"; Warren, ed., *Georgia Marriages,* 35; 1830 population census, Alachua County, Florida; 1840 population census, Camden

County, Georgia; *Georgia Genealogical Magazine* 1 (July 1961): 32, and 22 (October 1966): 1500.

23. "Bounty Land Application of James Brewer, Florida Seminole Wars"; Hartman and Coles, *Biographical Roster,* IV, 1360; election returns, election at Sapp's precinct, Columbia County, October 9, 1837, RG 156, series 21, FSA; 1860 population census, Columbia County, Florida; 1870 population census, Polk County, Florida; 1864, 1866 Columbia County tax rolls.

24. Hartman and Coles, *Biographical Rosters,* I, 18; 1860 population census, Nassau County, Florida; Columbia County probate records, Book A2, 164; 1869–1875 Columbia County tax rolls.

25. Rerick, *Memoirs of Florida,* I, 457; Hartman and Coles, *Biographical Rosters,* I, 397; *LCC-R,* November 24, 1905.

26. Florida State Genealogical Society Florida Pioneer Certification Publications, M84-13, box 57, FSA; *TST,* October 26, 1878.

27. Hartman and Coles, *Biographical Rosters,* I, 163; 1860 population census, Columbia County, Florida.

28. Florida State Genealogical Society State Pioneer Certification Publications, M84-13, box 57, FSA; *TFP,* February 15, 1871; 1860 population census, Hillsborough County, Florida; Florida House of Representatives, Office of the Clerk, *People of Lawmaking in Florida,* 13; *TST,* October 26, 1878; Brown, *Florida's Peace River Frontier,* 67–68, 79–80.

29. Huxford, *Pioneers of Wiregrass Georgia,* IV, 35–36; Florida House of Representatives, Office of the Clerk, *People of Lawmaking in Florida,* 13.

30. Huxford, *Pioneers of Wiregrass Georgia,* V, 51; Hamilton County Bicentennial Committee, *Early History,* 32, 37, 145; Florida House of Representatives, Office of the Clerk, *People of Lawmaking in Florida,* 13.

31. Huxford, *Pioneers of Wiregrass Georgia,* VI, 30; 1860 population and agricultural censuses, Columbia County, Florida; tombstone inscription, Bethel Cemetery, Columbia County, Florida.

32. Huxford, *Pioneers of Wiregrass Georgia,* VI, 30; *LCC-R,* June 7, 1907; tombstone inscription, Bethel Cemetery, Columbia County, Florida.

33. *Biographical Souvenir of the States of Georgia and Florida,* 107.

34. Williams and Burtchaell family notes, collection of Helen Ives, St. Petersburg, Florida.

35. Ibid.; 1860 population census, Columbia County, Florida.

36. Rerick, *Memoirs of Florida,* I, 467–68; *JFT-U,* June 6, 1902, February 27, 1923.

37. Rerick, *Memoirs of Florida,* I, 468–69; *JFT-U,* December 16, 1927.

38. Population censuses, 1860 and 1885, Lafayette County, Florida.

39. Hartman and Coles, *Biographical Rosters,* IV, 1387.

40. Population census, 1850, Columbia County, Florida; 1870 population census, Suwannee County, Florida; Suwannee County probate records, Order Book B (1869–1877), 278.

41. Baxley, Gordon, and Rodriguez, *Oaklawn Cemetery and St. Louis Catholic Cemetery,* I, 178; Carruth family materials, collection of Julius J. Gordon, Tampa.

42. Population census, 1850, Columbia County, Florida; Huxford, *Pioneers of Wiregrass Georgia,* VIII, 399; *Jacksonville Florida News,* October 25, 1851; 1848–1851

Columbia County tax rolls; Suwannee County deed records, Book A, 293–94; Madison County deed records, Book F, 546.

43. Huxford, *Pioneers of Wiregrass Georgia*, II, 58; 1850 population census, Columbia County, Florida; 1858–1860 Lafayette County tax rolls.

44. Hartman and Coles, *Biographical Rosters*, II, 763; Confederate pension files, file #D1146, roll 97, RG 137, series 587, FSA.

45. Population census, 1850, Columbia County, Florida; 1860 population census, Lafayette County, Florida.

46. Henderson et al., comps., *Group of Genealogical Records*, 39; *LCFI*, August 9, 1907; *LCC-R*, August 2, 1907.

47. Hartman and Coles, *Biographical Rosters*, III, 1245; Hodges, *Cemeteries of Hamilton County*, 261; Hamilton County Bicentennial Committee, *Early History*, 17, 33, 93.

48. Columbia County deed records, Book B, 414; 1880 population census, Echols County, Georgia; Huxford, *Pioneers of Wiregrass Georgia*, IX, 406.

49. *JFT-U*, November 22, 1890; Florida House of Representatives, Office of the Clerk, *People of Lawmaking in Florida*, 21; *Jacksonville Florida Union*, February 11, 1869; *Savannah Daily Republican*, March 18, 1867; *Savannah Daily Advertiser*, February 19, 1869; *Tallahassee Sentinel*, March 25, 1871.

50. Vocelle, *History of Camden County*, 67–74; Huxford, *Pioneers of Wiregrass Georgia*, II, 66–67; *Tallahassee Floridian & Journal*, September 5 and October 10, 1857.

51. Population censuses, 1850, Columbia and Madison counties, Florida; 1860 population census, Lafayette County, Florida; Lafayette County marriage records, Book A, 13; Hartman and Coles, *Biographical Rosters*, V, 1832.

52. Population census, 1850, Columbia County, Florida; 1860 population census, Lafayette County, Florida; 1873–1874 Lafayette County tax rolls.

53. Population censuses, 1870 and 1885, Lafayette County, Florida; Lafayette County marriage records, Book A, 15.

54. Hooker family notes, collection of Kyle S. VanLandingham, Kerrville, Texas.

55. Columbia County tax rolls, 1845–1850.

56. Population censuses, 1860, 1870, and 1880, Columbia County, Florida.

57. Kaiser, "My Family," n.p.; Hartman and Coles, *Biographical Rosters*, V, 1989. Hartman and Coles place Dancy's death in 1896.

58. Harold B. Bennett to Canter Brown, Jr., January 26, 1996, collection of Canter Brown, Jr.; 1870 population census, Suwannee County, Florida; tombstone inscriptions, Mt. Beulah Church Cemetery, Suwannee County, Florida.

59. Indian War pension records, file #WC-3996, NA.

60. Population censuses, 1850 and 1860, Columbia County, Florida; Warren, ed., *Georgia Marriages*, 74; *TP*, XXV, 374; 1861–1862 Columbia County tax rolls.

61. Population census, 1860, Columbia County, Florida; *Jacksonville Florida Sun*, August 22, 1876; *Gainesville Times*, August 3, 1876; Columbia County probate records, Order Book B, 46.

62. Tombstone inscriptions, Oak Lawn Cemetery, Lake City, Florida; 1860 population census, Columbia County, Florida; Hartman and Coles, *Biographical Rosters*, V, 2251.

63. Population censuses, 1850 and 1860, Columbia County, Florida; 1870 population census, Levy County, Florida; 1878–1879 Levy County tax rolls; Levy County deed records, Book D, 11.

64. *Tallahassee Sentinel,* February 10, 1872; 1860 population census, Columbia County, Florida; *Jacksonville Florida Union,* March 3, 1874; Morris, *Florida Handbook,* 327–28; *Jacksonville Weekly Sun & Press,* January 10, 1878.

65. Population censuses, 1840, 1850, and 1870, Columbia County, Florida; 1854–1858 Columbia County tax rolls.

66. Population censuses, 1840 and 1850, Columbia County, Florida; 1845–1847 Columbia County tax rolls; Pulaski County, Georgia, will records, 1810–1816, 12–15; return of election held at North Prong precinct, Columbia County, on May 25, 1845, in election returns, RG 156, series 21, folder: 1845, FSA.

67. Huxford, *Pioneers of Wiregrass Georgia,* IX, 137–38; *Jasper News,* September 29, 1899.

68. Hartman and Coles, *Biographical Rosters,* II, 853.

69. Population census, 1860, Hillsborough County, Florida; Hillsborough County marriage records; Hartman and Coles, *Biographical Rosters,* II, 696; DeShong family notes, collection of Julius J. Gordon, Tampa, Florida.

70. DeShong family notes, collection of Julius J. Gordon, Tampa, Florida.

71. Population census, 1830, Alachua County, Florida; Huxford, *Pioneers of Wiregrass Georgia,* III, 109–10; 1860 population census, Lafayette County, Florida; return of election held at Newnansville, Alachua County, on November 7, 1848, election returns, RG 156, series 21, FSA; 1876–1877 Lafayette County tax rolls.

72. Population census, 1860, Lafayette County, Florida.

73. Morris, *Florida Handbook,* 318; Florida House of Representatives, Office of the Clerk, *People of Lawmaking in Florida,* 29. On DuVal, see also Snyder, "William Pope DuVal," and "Nancy Hynes DuVal."

74. Huxford, *Pioneers of Wiregrass Georgia,* V, 136 and VI, 334.

75. 1860 population census, Columbia County, Florida; Hartman and Coles, *Biographical Rosters,* I, 164.

76. Bunch, "Ellis Family in Florida," 7–9; Florida House of Representatives, Office of the Clerk, *People of Lawmaking in Florida,* 30.

77. Population census, 1860, Alachua County, Florida; Alachua County marriage records, Book 2, 58; Alachua County tax rolls, 1855–1867.

78. Huxford, *Pioneers of Wiregrass Georgia,* II, 102 and VI, 82–84; 1830, 1840, 1850 population censuses, Columbia County, Florida; 1845–1847 Columbia County tax rolls.

79. Population census, 1860, Alachua County, Florida; Alachua County marriage records, Book 2, 58; 1866–1867 Alachua County tax rolls; Hartman and Coles, *Biographical Rosters,* III, 980.

80. *JFT-U,* November 5, 1885; Hartman and Coles, *Biographical Rosters,* V, 2084–85.

81. Population census, 1850, Alachua County, Florida; Alachua County tax rolls, 1849–1853; returns of elections, Columbia County, November 15, 1843, and October 6, 1845, RG 156, series 21, box 6, FSA; *TFP,* October 11, 1856.

82. *TP,* XXVI, 431; return of election, Columbia County, October 6, 1845, RG 156, series 21, box 6, FSA; *Roster of State and County Officers Commissioned by the Governor of Florida 1845–1868,* 73; *Jacksonville Florida Republican,* May 31, 1849.

83. Fleming, *Memoirs,* Intro., 17, 64; "In Memorium: Francis Philip Fleming," 3–4.

84. Floyd family notes, Huxford Genealogical Library, Homerville, Georgia; Vocelle, *History of Camden County,* 69–74.

85. Population census, 1850, Columbia County, Florida; 1860 and 1870 population censuses, Clay County, Florida; Hartman and Coles, *Biographical Rosters,* III, 993.

86. Raulerson, comp., *Raulerson Documents 1800–1900,* n.p.; Wiggins, *History of the Absolute Mt. Enon Association,* 3–4; Brown, *Florida's Peace River Frontier,* 68–69; *TFP,* March 29, 1871.

87. Population censuses, 1850 and 1860, Hillsborough County, Florida; Stanaback, *History of Hernando County,* 17; Hartman and Coles, *Biographical Rosters,* V, 2206.

88. *Tallahassee Floridian,* April 7, 1838, February 9, 1839.

89. Gillett family notes, Huxford Genealogical Library, Homerville, Georgia; 1850 population census, Columbia County, Florida; 1860 population census, Alachua County, Florida.

90. Snell, *Testimony to Pioneer Baptists,* 4–6; Huxford, *Pioneers of Wiregrass Georgia,* VI, 91.

91. Gillett family notes, Huxford Genealogical Library, Homerville, Georgia; Alachua County probate records, Administrator's Bonds Book B (1857–1864, 1869), 157.

92. Huxford, *Pioneers of Wiregrass Georgia,* III, 109–10; *Tallahassee Floridian,* April 7, 1838, February 9, 1839.

93. Hartman and Coles, *Biographical Rosters,* III, 881; Westergard and VanLandingham, *Parker & Blount in Florida,* 58; 1900 population census, Pasco County, Florida.

94. Hair family notes, collection of Kyle S. VanLandingham, Kerrville, Texas; Snell, *Testimony to Pioneer Baptists,* 4–6; Manasota Genealogical Society, *Tombstone Inscriptions,* 70.

95. Huxford, *Pioneers of Wiregrass Georgia,* III, 109–10; *Tallahassee Floridian,* April 7, 1838, February 9, 1839.

96. Population census, 1850, Madison County, Florida; Madison County marriage records, Book A, 50; Madison County deed records, Book F, 222.

97. *History of Lowndes County, Georgia,* 247; Shelton, *Pines and Pioneers,* 116; *Jacksonville News,* September 29, 1849; vouchers for criminal prosecutions, Columbia County, December Term 1849, Comptroller's Vouchers, 1846–1862, RG 350, series 565, box 1, folder 5, FSA.

98. Huxford, *Pioneers of Wiregrass Georgia,* V, 171; Goodbread, *Cemeteries of Columbia & Hamilton Counties,* 83; Florida House of Representatives, Office of the Clerk, *People of Lawmaking in Florida,* 38.

99. *Register of Columbia County, Florida, Cemeteries,* 21–23; Goodbread, *Cemeteries of Columbia & Hamilton Counties,* 33; Keuchel, *History of Columbia County,* 60–61.

100. Huxford, *Pioneers of Wiregrass Georgia,* VI, 92.

101. Population census, 1850, Columbia County, Florida; 1855–1856 Columbia County tax rolls.

102. *Register of Columbia County, Florida, Cemeteries,* 68; 1880 population census, Columbia County, Florida; Florida House of Representatives, Office of the Clerk, *People of Lawmaking in Florida,* 39.

103. Hartman and Coles, *Biographical Rosters,* IV, 1389; Confederate pension application #A1437, FSA.

104. *Jacksonville East Florida Advocate,* May 12, 1840; 1846 Duval County tax rolls; *Jacksonville Florida News,* November 1, 1851, and January 8, 1853.

105. Cone, *Some Account of the Cone Family,* 484.

106. Gordon, *Biographical Census of Hillsborough County,* 233–34; Hooker family notes, collection of Kyle S. VanLandingham, Riverview, Florida; *TFP,* August 4, 1866; 1885 population census, Hillsborough County, Florida.

107. Population census, 1850, Columbia County, Florida; Hair family notes, collection of Kyle S. VanLandingham, Riverview, Florida; *Jacksonville Florida News,* May 28, 1853.

108. Population census, 1840, Duval County, Florida; 1850 and 1870 population censuses, Alachua County, Florida; 1878 Alachua County tax rolls; records of appointments, RG 156, series 1284, vol. 2, and records of commissions, RG 156, series 259, vols. 28 and 30, FSA.

109. Population census, 1860, Columbia County, Florida; *LCFI,* June 23, 1899; 1857–1861 Columbia County tax rolls.

110. Population censuses, 1860 and 1900, Columbia County, Florida; Confederate pension application #A11824, FSA; Columbia County probate records, Order Book B, 131; Goodbread, *Cemeteries of Columbia & Hamilton Counties,* 4; pension warrants paid, vols. 6 and 7, RG 350, series 476, FSA.

111. John M. Hanson biographical file, St. Augustine Historical Society Research Library.

112. Huxford, *Pioneers of Wiregrass Georgia,* IX, 238–39.

113. Raulerson, comp., "Raulerson Allied Families Group Sheet #2," n.p.

114. Ibid.

115. Huxford, *Pioneers of Wiregrass Georgia,* IX, 238–39; *LCFI,* April 19, 1907.

116. Brown, *Ossian Bingley Hart,* 7–120; Hart family Bible.

117. Brown, *Ossian Bingley Hart.*

118. Telephone interview, Mrs. William O. Baker, Atlanta, Georgia, by Canter Brown, Jr., October 8, 1991, notes in collection of Canter Brown, Jr.

119. George L. Hartsuff biographical materials in Hartsuff Family Collection, Bentley Historical Library, University of Michigan; Covington, *Billy Bowlegs War,* 35–36.

120. Population census, 1840, Duval County, Florida; 1850 and 1870 population censuses, Monroe County, Florida; file on estate of Chauncey L. Hatch, filed December 18, 1872, Monroe County probate records.

121. *LCFI,* March 15 and October 6, 1907; tombstone inscription, Bethel Cemetery, Columbia County, Florida.

122. *LCFI,* October 11, 1907; tombstone inscription, Bethel Cemetery, Columbia County, Florida.

123. Population census, 1850, Duval County, Florida; Duval County probate records, packet #850 (Joshua Hickman); 1846 Duval County tax roll; *Jacksonville Florida News,* October 11, 1851.

124. Population census, 1860, Columbia County, Florida; Hartman and Coles, *Biographical Rosters,* I, 262.

125. Florida State Genealogical Society State Pioneer Certificate Publications, M84-13, box 37, #1468, FSA; Davis, *History of Jacksonville,* 51.

126. Population census, 1850, Alachua County, Florida.

127. Population census, 1800, Pendleton District, South Carolina; 1840 population census, Columbia County, Florida; 1850 population census, Alachua County, Florida;

Columbia County election returns, September 1, 1834, and October 2, 1835, RG 156, series 21, box 5, FSA; 1847–1848 Alachua County tax rolls.

128. Hartman and Coles, *Biographical Rosters,* II, 709; Alachua County marriage records, vol. 2, 27.

129. Population census, 1850, Alachua County, Florida; 1846–1847 Columbia County tax rolls; 1847–1860 Alachua County tax rolls; Alachua County deed records, Book E, 10, 12, 127; 1870 population census, Harris County, Texas; Anne Douglass, Houston (Texas) Public Library, to Canter Brown, Jr., January 21, 1966, collection of Canter Brown, Jr.

130. Hooker family notes, collection of Kyle S. VanLandingham, Kerrville, Texas.

131. VanLandingham, "William Brinton Hooker"; Hooker family notes, collection of Kyle S. VanLandingham, Kerrville, Texas; *TFP,* June 17, 1871.

132. Huxford, *Pioneers of Wiregrass Georgia,* VIII, 167–69; Warren, ed., *Georgia Marriages,* 148; 1840 population census, Alachua County, Florida; 1860 population census, Colorado County, Texas; Bill Stein, Archives of the Nesbitt Memorial Library (Columbus, Texas), to Canter Brown, Jr., January 31, 1996, collection of Canter Brown, Jr.; *JFT-U,* January 4, 1891.

133. Gordon, *Biographical Census,* 281; Joseph Howell notes, collection of Julius J. Gordon, Tampa, Florida; *Jacksonville Florida Herald,* March 25, 1836; *Tallahassee Floridian,* August 28, 1840; Brown, *Fort Meade,* 28–29; Joseph Howell Bounty Land Records, NA.

134. Population census, 1850, Levy County, Florida; Hartman and Coles, *Biographical Rosters,* III, 920.

135. Population census, 1860, Lafayette County, Florida; Hartman and Coles, *Biographical Rosters,* III, 920 and V, 1834.

136. Population census, 1860, Columbia County, Florida; tombstone inscription, Oak Lawn Cemetery, Lake City, Florida; Confederate Pension Application #A12981, FSA; Florida House of Representatives, Office of the Clerk, *People of Lawmaking in Florida,* 48.

137. Population census (mortality schedule), 1850, Columbia County, Florida; A. J. T. Wright to Thomas Brown, February 15, 1850, Correspondence of Gov. Thomas Brown, RG 101, series 755, box 1, folder 6, FSA; *Roster of State and County Officers,* 68.

138. Tombstone inscription, Bethel Cemetery, Columbia County, Florida; 1860 population census, Columbia County, Florida; Hartman and Coles, *Biographical Rosters,* I, 350; *LCFI,* March 15, 1907.

139. Population census, 1860, Columbia County, Florida; tombstone inscription, Bethel Cemetery, Columbia County, Florida.

140. Goodbread, *Cemeteries of Columbia & Hamilton Counties,* 5; tombstone inscription, Bethel Cemetery, Columbia County, Florida; 1860 population census, Columbia County, Florida.

141. Hartman and Coles, *Biographical Rosters,* I, 349–50; 1860 population census, Columbia County, Florida; tombstone inscription, Bethel Cemetery, Columbia County, Florida.

142. Confederate Pension Application #A01343, FSA; Hartman and Coles, *Biographical Rosters,* II, 528.

143. Hunter, *William Miles Hunter Family History,* 15.

144. Tombstone inscription, Bethel Cemetery, Columbia County, Florida; 1870 population census, Columbia County, Florida; Columbia County probate records, Order Book B, 142.

145. Ives family notes, collection of Helen Ives, St. Petersburg, Florida.

146. Ibid.

147. Ibid.; *JFT-U,* April 13, 1891; *LCFI,* June 6, 1902; *Biographical Souvenir of the States of Georgia and Florida,* 444.

148. Rerick, *Memoirs of Florida,* I, 587–88; *JFT-U,* October 18, 1921.

149. Population censuses, 1840 and 1850, Columbia County, Florida; 1845–1853 Columbia County tax rolls; voucher of James H. Johnson for serving as a jail guard at Lake City, Florida, May 1855, Comptroller Vouchers, Criminal Prosecutions, RG 350, series 565, box 1, folder 6, FSA.

150. Population census, 1850, Columbia County, Florida; Petition of citizens of Columbia County, August 18, 1846, in Correspondence of Gov. William D. Moseley, RG 101, series 679, box 2, FSA; Florida House of Representatives, Office of the Clerk, *People of Lawmaking in Florida,* 51; Grismer, *Tampa,* 122; 1860 population census, Escambia County, Florida; *TFP,* June 20, 1868; *TST,* January 15 and February 5, 1880; 1880 population census, Sumter County, Florida.

151. Population census, 1860, Columbia County, Florida; Hartman and Coles, *Biographical Rosters,* III, 935; Columbia County probate records, Order Book A, 33 and Order Book A2, 226.

152. *Register of Columbia County, Florida, Cemeteries,* 32; 1860 population census, Columbia County, Florida; Goodbread, *Cemeteries of Columbia & Hamilton Counties,* 80; Florida House of Representatives, Office of the Clerk, *People of Lawmaking in Florida,* 52.

153. Keen family notes, collection of Mrs. Doyle Chancey, Palmetto, Florida; Hartman and Coles, *Biographical Rosters,* II, 729.

154. Indian War pension record, widow's pension #WC-5899, NA.

155. Population census, 1900, Columbia County, Florida; Keen family notes, collection of Wanda De Montmollin, Plant City, Florida; *LCC-R,* February 14, 1902; Stella and Aaron L. Rutledge to Mrs. Hazel Keen, June 8, 1984, collection of James D. Keen, Columbia City, Florida.

156. Keen family notes, collection of Wanda De Montmollin, Plant City, Florida; Keen family notes, collection of Mrs. Doyle Chancey, Palmetto, Florida; Hartman and Coles, *Biographical Rosters,* II, 478; Keen, *My Autobiography,* 4.

157. Keen family notes, collection of Wanda De Montmollin, Plant City, Florida; Keen family notes, collection of Mrs. Doyle Chancey, Palmetto, Florida; 1845 Columbia County tax roll; *Jacksonville Florida News,* January 8, 1853.

158. Keen family notes, collection of Wanda De Montmollin, Plant City, Florida; 1850 population census, Columbia County, Florida; Huxford, *Pioneers of Wiregrass Georgia,* III, 109–10; 1856–1857 Columbia County tax rolls.

159. Keen family notes, collection of Virgil E. Raulerson, Jacksonville, Florida; Hartman and Coles, *Biographical Rosters,* II, 478.

160. Keen family notes, collection of Wanda De Montmollin, Plant City, Florida; 1850 population census, Columbia County, Florida.

161. Keen family notes, collection of Wanda De Montmollin, Plant City, Florida; Keen family notes, collection of Mrs. Doyle Chancey, Palmetto, Florida; Hartman and Coles, *Biographical Rosters,* II, 478.

162. Keen family notes, collection of Mrs. Doyle Chancey, Palmetto, Florida; 1850 population census, Columbia County, Florida; 1852–1853 Columbia County tax rolls.

163. Population census, 1870, Columbia County, Florida; Keen family notes, collection of Wanda De Montmollin, Plant City, Florida; *JFT-U,* February 28, 1889; *Madison Recorder,* March 8, 1889; J. A. Bethea to Francis P. Fleming, March 25, 1889; John F. White to Francis P. Fleming, June 19, 1889; A J. Henry to Francis P. Fleming, July 19/30, 1889. Correspondence of Governors. RG 101, series 580, box 18, folder 3. FSA.

164. Kelly family notes, collection of Helen Ives, St. Petersburg, Florida.

165. William, Niblack, and Kelly family notes, collection of Helen Ives, St. Petersburg, Florida.

166. Kelly family notes, collection of Helen Ives, St. Petersburg, Florida.

167. Brown-Hazen, *Blue Book,* 13; Kendrick family notes, collection of Joseph (Pat) Adams, Tampa, Florida; Huxford, *Pioneers of Wiregrass Georgia,* VI, 160; *JFT-U,* February 19, 1894; *Jacksonville Florida Times-Union and Citizen,* November 27, 1901; Accounts books "3rd Qr. 1837" and "Oct. 10–Dec. 27, 1838," Records of the St. Augustine Land Office, Florida Department of Environmental Protection.

168. Brown-Hazen, *Blue Book,* 13–14; Kendrick family notes, collection of Joseph (Pat) Adams, Tampa, Florida; William H. Kendrick Indian War pension file, NA; *Jacksonville Florida Times-Union and Citizen,* November 27, 1901; Florida House of Representatives, Office of the Clerk, *People of Lawmaking in Florida,* 53.

169. *Biographical Souvenir of the States of Georgia and Florida,* 491; *JFT-U,* December 25, 1895.

170. May, "Zephaniah Kingsley," 147–49, 155–57; Schafer, *Anna Kingsley,* 7–8.

171. Population census, 1900, Columbia County, Florida.

172. Population census, 1860, Columbia County, Florida; 1854–1864 Columbia County tax rolls.

173. Gordon, *Biographical Census,* 328–29; Brown, "Ossian Bingley Hart," 55–56, 139–41; *TFP,* December 27, 1856.

174. Population census, 1850, Benton County, Florida; 1870 population census, Hillsborough County, Florida; Hartman and Coles, *Biographical Rosters,* V, 2066.

175. Population census, 1850, Madison County, Florida; 1860 population census (mortality schedule), Lafayette County, Florida; affidavit of William F. Bynum, July 18, 1859, regarding postmortem examination of Elijah Locklier, in Comptroller's Vouchers, 1846–1862, RG 350, series 565, box 7, FSA.

176. Population census, 1860, Lafayette County, Florida; Lafayette County marriage records, Book A, 29; Hartman and Coles, *Biographical Rosters,* IV, 1389.

177. Population census, 1850, Madison County, Florida; 1860 population census, Lafayette County, Florida; Hartman and Coles, *Biographical Rosters,* V, 1850; Livingston, "William Henry Locklear," 10–12.

178. Tombstone inscription, Oak Grove cemetery, Columbia County, Florida; Huxford, *Pioneers of Wiregrass Georgia,* V, 195; 1840 population census, Nassau County, Florida.

179. Population census, 1860, Nassau County, Florida; 1870 population census, Columbia County, Florida; 1880 population census, Bradford County, Florida; *Jacksonville Florida Republican,* March 21, 1850; Thomas T. Long grave registration card in Department of Military Affairs Veterans' Graves Registration Cards, FSA; Hartman and Coles, *Biographical Rosters,* V, 1988; Durbin, *Glynn County, Georgia, Marriage Index,* 8; Florida House of Representatives, Office of the Clerk, *People of Lawmaking in Florida,* 58; *Tallahassee Weekly Floridian,* April 28, 1874. For an account of Long's early life and political career, see *Savannah Morning News,* May 21, 1874.

180. Wessels, *Born To Be a Soldier,* 2–4; 1850 population census, St. Johns County, Florida.

181. Population censuses, 1840 and 1850, Columbia County, Florida; returns of elections, Columbia County, 1843, in Election Returns, RG 156, series 21, box 6, FSA; 1855–1856 Columbia County tax rolls.

182. Population census, 1870, Columbia County, Florida; baptismal record, St. James Episcopal Church, Lake City, Florida; *Tallahassee Weekly Floridian,* May 2, 1871; *Tallahassee Sentinel,* April 29, 1871

183. Marcum family notes, collection of Aleene Havird, Lake City, Florida; Taylor, *Florida Pioneers,* 33–34, 138–39; Taylor and Barnes, *Florida Connections,* 268.

184. McAuley family notes, collection of Harold B. Bennett, Live Oak, Florida; *JFT-U,* November 24, 1883.

185. McClellan family notes, collection of Harold B. Bennett, Live Oak, Florida; Suwannee County probate records, files 29 and 30; tombstone inscriptions, McClellan cemetery, Suwannee County.

186. McClelland, *Silas and Penelope (Anderson) McClelland,* 30–31.

187. Ibid., 21–26.

188. Stone, "William McCullough."

189. Gordon, *Biographical Census,* 410–11; 1880 population census, Manatee County, Florida; Florida House of Representatives, Office of the Clerk, *People of Lawmaking in Florida,* 65; 1876–1880 tax rolls, Manatee County, Florida.

190. Huxford, *Pioneers of Wiregrass Georgia,* III, 210–11; Stirk, *Tombstone Registry,* 73; Florida House of Representatives, Office of the Clerk, *People of Lawmaking in Florida,* 68.

191. Livingston, "Enoch Everett Mizell," 13–17; Florida *Senate Journal* (1865), 211.

192. Florida State Genealogical Society State Pioneer Certificate Publications, #1524, M84-13, box 38, FSA; Huxford, *Pioneers of Wiregrass Georgia,* VII, 506; returns from Alligator precinct, Columbia County, Florida, October 9, 1837, Election Returns, RG 156, series 21, FSA; Brown, *Florida's Peace River Frontier,* 143; 1862–1863 Polk County tax rolls.

193. Huxford, *Pioneers of Wiregrass Georgia,* IX, 305.

194. Hartman and Coles, *Biographical Rosters,* I, 166.

195. Livingston, "Benjamin Moody 1811–1896."

196. Population census, 1850, Benton County, Florida; *TFP,* September 10, 1859.

197. Hartman and Coles, *Biographical Rosters,* I, 161; Gordon, *Biographical Census,* 448–50; *Savannah Morning News,* February 12, 1881; 1850 and 1860 population censuses, Columbia County, Florida; Florida House of Representatives, Office of the Clerk, *People of Lawmaking in Florida,* 69; *Jacksonville Florida Times-Union and Citizen,* October 11, 1898.

198. Population censuses, 1870 and 1880, Columbia County, Florida.

199. Florida State Genealogical Society State Pioneer Certificate Publications, #1632, M84-13, box 41, FSA; 1860 population census, Levy County, Florida.

200. Westergard and VanLandingham, *Parker & Blount in Florida,* 58.

201. Morgan, "Ancestors of Leo E. Morgan"; affidavit of William F. Bynum, July 22, 1859, for postmortem examination of James Munden, Comptroller Vouchers, RG 350, series 565, box 7, FSA.

202. Niblack family notes, collection of Helen Ives, St. Petersburg, Florida.

203. Population census, 1880, Columbia County, Florida; *LCC-R,* November 12, 1909; Columbia County probate records, Order Book B, 345.

204. Population census (slave schedule), 1860, Columbia County, Florida; 1870 population census, Manatee County, Florida; 1880 and 1885 population censuses, Hillsborough County, Florida; 1866 Columbia County tax rolls; 1868–1869 Manatee County tax rolls; Gordon, *Afro-Americans,* 99.

205. Huxford, *Pioneers of Wiregrass Georgia,* VI, 196; tombstone inscriptions, Bethel Cemetery, Columbia County, Florida.

206. Ibid.; Goodbread, *Cemeteries of Columbia & Hamilton Counties,* 5.

207. Population censuses, 1870, 1880, 1900, and 1910, Columbia County, Florida.

208. *Biographical Directory of the American Congress 1774–1949,* 1615; Rerick, *Memoirs of Florida,* II, 637; *JFT-U,* February 16, 1883; *TST,* February 22, 1883.

209. Niblack family notes, collection of Helen Ives, St. Petersburg, Florida.

210. Huxford, *Pioneers of Wiregrass Georgia,* I, 212; 1830 population census, Ware County, Georgia; Compiled Service Records of Volunteer Soldiers Who Served in Organizations from the State of Florida During the Florida Indian Wars, M-1086, NA (RG 1025, series 608, roll 45, at FSA); North family notes, collection of Aleene Havird, Lake City, Florida.

211. Boyd, "Asi-Yaholo or Osceola," 252–53; Brown, *Florida's Peace River Frontier,* 9–14, 19–26, 34–50.

212. Osteen family notes, collection of Aleene Havird, Lake City, Florida.

213. Columbia County election returns, February 1834, RG 156, series 21, box 5, FSA; Compiled Service Records of Volunteer Soldiers Who Served in Organizations from the State of Florida During the Florida Indian Wars, M-1086, NA (RG 1025, series 608, roll 22 at FSA).

214. Huxford, *Pioneers of Wiregrass Georgia,* VII, 304–5; 1858–1859 Columbia County tax rolls; 1850 population census, Columbia County, Florida; Madison County deed records, Book E, 372–73; 1866–1867 Madison County tax rolls.

215. *LCFI,* June 6, 1902; *JFT-U,* April 4, 1916; tombstone inscription, Oak Lawn Cemetery, Lake City, Florida; Florida House of Representative, Office of the Clerk, *People of Lawmaking in Florida,* 73.

216. Population census, 1860, Suwannee County, Florida; 1880 and 1885 population censuses, Levy County, Florida; "Persons Subject to Military Duty, Levy County 1876," 43.

217. Population censuses, 1860 and 1880, Lafayette County, Florida; Hartman and Coles, *Biographical Rosters,* V, 1851; Lafayette County marriage records, Book A, 70.

218. Goodbread, *Cemeteries of Columbia & Hamilton Counties,* 4; 1860 population census, Columbia County, Florida.

219. Huxford, *Pioneers of Wiregrass Georgia,* IX, 329–30; Florida State Genealogical Society Pioneer Certificate Publications #57, M84-13, box 1, FSA; 1830 and 1850 population censuses, Columbia County, Florida.

220. Payne family notes, collection of Aleene Havird, Lake City, Florida.

221. Population census, 1850, Columbia County, Florida; Livingston, "Levi Pearce," 38; Pasteur, "John J. Pearce," 9; returns of elections at Alligator precinct, Columbia County, Florida, October 9, 1837, Election Returns, RG 156, series 21, FSA; Covington, *Story of Southwestern Florida,* I, 442; Columbia County probate records, Will Book A, 76–79.

222. Peeples family notes, collection of Vernon E. Peeples, Punta Gorda, Florida.

223. Livingston, "Willoughby Whidden," 8–10; 1860 population census, Manatee County, Florida; Pulaski County, Georgia, probate records, Will Book (1810–1816), 7–9.

224. Population census, 1860, Lafayette County, Florida; *TFP,* October 21, 1871; *Savannah Morning News,* July 25, 1873.

225. Henderson et al., comps., *Group of Genealogical Records,* 44; 1860 population census, Columbia County, Florida; Florida House of Representatives, Office of the Clerk, *People of Lawmaking in Florida,* 78.

226. Hodges, *Cemeteries of Hamilton County,* 109; Confederate pension application #A00076, FSA; *Bartow Polk County Democrat,* December 6, 1971; 1860 population census, Escambia County, Florida; Hartman and Coles, *Biographical Rosters,* II, 522.

227. "Biographical Notes," 50–51.

228. Raulerson family notes, collection of Virgil E. Raulerson, Jacksonville, Florida; *JFT-U,* April 14, 1912; tombstone inscriptions, Oak Law Cemetery, Lake City, Florida; Hamilton County Bicentennial Committee, *Early History,* 29, 103.

229. Raulerson, comp., "Raulerson Group Sheet #1," n.p.; Hillsborough County Probate Records, Old Administration Record (1845–1908), 13.

230. Huxford, *Pioneers of Wiregrass Georgia,* IX, 357–58; 1830 population census, Alachua County, Florida; 1840 population census, Columbia County, Florida; 1845–1848 Columbia County tax rolls.

231. Taylor, *Florida Pioneers,* 171.

232. Population census, 1850, Columbia County, Florida; Hartman and Coles, *Biographical Rosters,* I, 363.

233. Population census, 1850, Columbia County, Florida; Taylor, *Florida Pioneers,* 171; Raulerson, comp., "Raulerson Group Sheet #1," n.p.

234. Huxford, *Pioneers of Wiregrass Georgia,* V, 356–57; Raulerson, comp., "Raulerson Group Sheet #1," n.p.; *LCFI,* July 31, 1903.

235. *Tallahassee Floridian* (Supp.), February 9, 1839.

236. Raulerson, comp., "Raulerson Group Sheet #1," n.p.; Indian War pension record #WC-5899, NA.

237. Foster and Foster, "Chloe Merrick Reed"; Morris, *Florida Handbook,* 326–27; Florida House of Representatives, Office of the Clerk, *People of Lawmaking in Florida,* 80.

238. Roberts family notes, collection of Aleene Havird, Lake City, Florida.

239. Rerick, *Memoirs of Florida,* I, 669–70; *LCFI,* June 6, 1902; Florida House of Representatives, Office of the Clerk, *People of Lawmaking in Florida,* 83; *JFT-U,* December 31, 1933.

240. Population census, 1860, Nassau County, Florida.

241. Population censuses, 1850 and 1860, Columbia County, Florida; *St. Augustine Florida Herald,* March 15, 1834; *Jacksonville Florida Republican,* May 23, 1850; Keuchel, *History of Columbia County,* 60; Florida House of Representatives, Office of the Clerk, *People of Lawmaking in Florida,* 83; Columbia County probate records, Order Book A-2, 307.

242. Rutledge and Keen family notes, collection of James D. Keen, Columbia City, Florida; Manasota Genealogical Society, *Tombstone Inscriptions;* Hartman and Coles, *Biographical Rosters,* III, 924.

243. Huxford, *Pioneers of Wiregrass Georgia,* V, 377–78 and VII, 539; Hamilton County Bicentennial Committee, *Early History,* 152–53; telephone interview, Kyle S. VanLandingham by Canter Brown Jr., July 28, 1996 (notes in collection of Canter Brown Jr.).

244. Sapp, "Shadrick Sapp, Jr.," 14–15; Huxford, *Pioneers of Wiregrass Georgia,* I, 194; 1853–1855 Columbia County tax rolls.

245. Population census, 1850, Madison County, Florida; 1860 population census (mortality schedule), Lafayette County, Florida.

246. Hartman and Coles, *Biographical Rosters,* I, 411 and V, 1841; Lafayette County marriage records, Book B, 50; appointments records, RG 156, series 1284, vol. 2, 132–33; 1885 population census, Lafayette County, Florida; 1900 population census, Columbia County, Florida.

247. Hartman and Coles, *Biographical Rosters,* III, 1053; tombstone inscription, Oak Lawn Cemetery, Lake City, Florida.

248. Henderson et al., comps., *Group of Genealogical Records,* 48; *Roster of State and County Officers,* 66; 1850 population census, Columbia County, Florida; *LCC-R,* November 12, 1909.

249. *LCFI,* January 5, 1900, and February 13, 1903; *LCC-R,* April 10, 1903; tombstone inscription, Oak Lawn Cemetery, Lake City, Florida; Hartman and Coles, *Biographical Rosters,* I, 397.

250. Simmons, *Notices of East Florida,* xi, xxxix; Buker, "Americanization of St. Augustine," 154–55, 160–61.

251. Population census, 1850, Madison County, Florida; 1860 and 1870 population censuses, Lafayette County, Florida; 1871–1873 Lafayette County tax rolls.

252. Population census, 1860, Columbia County, Florida; *LCFI,* June 23, 1899; *Apalachicola Gazette,* February 25, 1837; Washington M. Ives Journal, entries of November 16–18, 1860, FSA.

253. Population censuses, 1830 and 1840, Hamilton County, Florida; Hamilton County marriage records; Hamilton County Bicentennial Committee, *Early History,* 32, 123; 1847 Columbia County tax rolls.

254. Population census, 1850, Madison County, Florida; return of election at Sapp's Precinct, Columbia County, October 9, 1837, in Election Returns, RG 156, series 21, FSA; Madison County Deed Records, Book D, 364.

255. Population census, 1860, Columbia County, Florida; *Tampa Herald,* December 6, 1854; *Tallahassee Floridian & Journal,* June 2, 1860; Columbia County probate records, Book A2, 164, Book B, 130.

256. Tombstone inscription, Oak Lawn Cemetery, Lake City, Florida; 1860 population census, Columbia County, Florida; *TFP,* August 25, 1855; *Tampa Herald,*

December 6, 1854; Hartman and Coles, *Biographical Rosters,* I, 367; *Tallahassee Florida Sentinel,* October 15 and 29, 1850; *Tallahassee Floridian & Journal,* June 2, 1860.

257. Florida State Genealogical Society State Pioneer Certificate Publications, #962, M84-13, box 26, FSA.

258. Taylor, *Florida Pioneers,* 199–200; 1860 population census, Columbia County, Florida; *Savannah Morning News,* April 3, 1873.

259. Population census, 1860 and 1870, Columbia County, Florida; Hartman and Coles, *Biographical Rosters,* III, 940; Confederate pension application #A00999, FSA; 1874–1875 Columbia County tax rolls.

260. Hooker family notes, collection of Kyle S. VanLandingham, Riverview, Florida.

261. Ibid.; Gordon, *Biographical Census,* 560; Hartman and Coles, *Biographical Rosters,* II, 871.

262. Huxford, *Pioneers of Wiregrass Georgia,* I, 261–63.

263. Hartman and Coles, *Biographical Rosters,* III, 1003; Hamilton County Bicentennial Committee, *Early History,* 136.

264. Population census, 1900, Suwannee County, Florida; Suwannee County cemetery records, Book III, 36, at Suwannee County Public Library, Live Oak, Florida; Hamilton County Bicentennial Committee, *Early History,* 136.

265. *New York Times,* April 12, 1876.

266. Goodbread, *Cemeteries of Columbia & Hamilton Counties,* 7; Hartman and Coles, *Biographical Rosters,* III, 927; 1850 population census, Columbia County, Florida.

267. Population census, 1860, Lafayette County, Florida; returns of elections in Columbia County, September 1834, Election Returns, RG 156, series 21, box 5, FSA.

268. Population census, 1860, Lafayette County, Florida.

269. *Jacksonville News,* January 29, 1848; Work Projects Administration, *Spanish Land Grants in Florida,* I, 299 and II, 60; *Tallahassee Floridian,* February 20, 1836; *Bartow Polk County Democrat,* December 6, 1971; Florida House of Representatives, Office of the Clerk, *People of Lawmaking in Florida,* 93. On Jacob Summerlin, Sr.'s well-known son, cattleman Jacob Summerlin, Jr., see Akerman, "Jacob Summerlin."

270. Gilbert, *God Gave Us This Country,* 2, 53–54, 324; Tindall, *America,* I, 363–64.

271. Bruton and Bailey, *Plant City,* 30–33.

272. Livingston, "Willoughby Tillis," 4–5; Department of Military Affairs Veterans' Grave Registration Cards, roll 7, FSA; *St. Augustine News,* March 5, 1842; 1850 population census, Columbia County, Florida; Suwannee County probate records, file 38 (Sarah Ann Tillis).

273. Population census, 1860, Hillsborough County, Florida; Gordon, *Biographical Census,* 591; Osborn and Dalton, "South Florida Baptist Association," 53; DeVane, "Jacob Summerlin, Jr.," n.p.; *Jacksonville News,* October 20, 1849; *TFP,* December 5, 1868, and July 20, 1870.

274. Population census, 1870, Columbia County, Florida; Hartman and Coles, *Biographical Rosters,* V, 2081; 1874–1875 Columbia County tax rolls.

275. Population census, 1860, Columbia County, Florida; *TFP,* January 15 and August 13, 1859.

276. Tracy family notes, collection of Tracy Danese, Tallahassee, Florida; Florida House of Representatives, Office of the Clerk, *People of Lawmaking in Florida,* 97.

277. Tombstone inscription, Oak Lawn Cemetery, Lake City, Florida; Hartman and Coles, *Biographical Rosters*, II, 471; Florida House of Representatives, Office of the Clerk, *People of Lawmaking in Florida*, 99.

278. Huxford, *Pioneers of Wiregrass Georgia*, V, 484–85; Hartman and Coles, *Biographical Rosters*, VI, 2349.

279. Population censuses, 1850 and 1900, Columbia County, Florida; tombstone inscriptions, Oak Lawn Cemetery, Lake City, Florida.

280. Huxford, *Pioneers of Wiregrass Georgia*, V, 488; Indian War pension records, #WA-10659, NA.

281. Huxford, *Pioneers of Wiregrass Georgia*, V, 488; Columbia County probate records, Order Book A-2, 493.

282. Population census, 1860, Madison County, Florida; Florida House of Representatives, Office of the Clerk, *People of Lawmaking in Florida*, 101; Joseph B. Watts to W. D. Moseley, July 20, 1849, Governor's Correspondence, RG 101, series 679, box 2, FSA; Hamilton County probate records, file #6B (est. of J. B. Watts).

283. Population censuses, 1900, 1910, and 1920, Columbia County, Florida.

284. *Biographical Souvenir of the States of Georgia and Florida*, 835–36; Chapin, *Florida*, II, 564; *Jacksonville Florida Times-Union and Citizen*, August 15, 1901; *LCFI*, August 16, 1901.

285. Wightman, John Pinckney. "A Sketch of the Wightmans of Charleston, S.C., And of the Related New-England and Canadian Branches." Typescript. Richmond, VA, 1928, 24 [copy in collection of the South Carolina Historical Society, Charleston); Miller family notes, collection of Helen Ives, St. Petersburg, Florida.

286. Ibid.

287. Population census, 1840, Columbia County, Florida; return of Columbia County elections, February and September 1834, Election Returns, RG 156, series 21, box 5, FSA; 1850 and 1860 population censuses, Levy County, Florida; Levy County probate records, Book C, 212–13.

288. Williams family notes, collection of Helen Ives, St. Petersburg, Florida; *Jacksonville Florida Republican*, November 19, 1856; Williams, *Territory of Florida*, ix, xii–xiii.

289. Mackey, Ives, and Williams family notes, collection of Helen Ives, St. Petersburg, Florida.

290. Henderson et al., comps., *Group of Genealogical Records*, 17; tombstone inscription, Oak Lawn Cemetery, Lake City, Florida; Keuchel, *History of Columbia County*, 87; Hartman and Coles, *Biographical Rosters*, I, 261.

291. *LCC-R*, November 5 and 12, 1909; Confederate pension application #A11143, FSA; tombstone inscription, Oak Lawn Cemetery, Lake City, Florida.

292. Henderson et al., comps., *Group of Genealogical Records*, 17–18.

293. Population census, 1850, Columbia County, Florida; 1860 population census, Lafayette County, Florida; 1863–1865 Lafayette County tax rolls; Hartman and Coles, *Biographical Rosters*, V, 1853.

294. Goodbread, *Cemeteries of Columbia & Hamilton Counties*, 22; 1860 population census, Columbia County, Florida; tombstone inscriptions, Oak Lawn Cemetery, Lake City, Florida.

295. *Biographical Directory of the United States Congress*, 2102–3.

BIBLIOGRAPHY

MANUSCRIPTS

Hart Family Bibles. Xerographic copies in Florida Collection, Hayden Burns Public Library, Jacksonville.

Hartsuff Family Collection. Bentley Historical Library, University of Michigan, Ann Arbor.

Howard, O. O. Papers. Bowdoin College Library, Brunswick, Maine.

Ives, Washington M. Journal. FSA.

Purviance, John S. Letters. PKY.

St. James Episcopal Church. Baptismal Records. Lake City, Florida.

PUBLIC DOCUMENTS AND PUBLIC RECORDS

Alachua County, Florida. Deed Records. Alachua County Courthouse, Gainesville.

———. Marriage Records. Alachua County Courthouse, Gainesville.

———. Probate Records. Alachua County Courthouse, Gainesville.

———. Tax rolls, 1849–1880. Available at FSA.

Biographical Directory of the American Congress 1774–1949. Washington, D.C.: U.S. Government Printing Office, 1950.

Bounty Land Records. NA.

Carter, Clarence E., ed. *Territorial Papers of the United States,* vols. XXII–XXVI, *Florida Territory.* Washington, D.C.: U.S. Government Printing Office, 1956–1962.

Columbia County, Florida. Deed Records. Columbia County Courthouse, Lake City.

———. Probate Records. Columbia County Courthouse, Lake City.

———. Tax Rolls, 1845–1880. Available on microfilm at FSA.

Department of War. Compiled Service Records of Confederate Soldiers Who Served in Organizations from the State of Florida. Microcopy No. M-251, NA.

———. Compiled Service Records of Volunteer Soldiers Who Served in Organizations from the State of Florida During the Florida Indian Wars, 1835–1858. Microcopy M-1086, NA. Available at FSA as RG 1025, series 608.

Duval County, Florida. Probate Records. Duval County Courthouse, Jacksonville.

———. Tax Rolls, 1845–1880. Available on microfilm at FSA.

Florida. Department of Environmental Protection. St. Augustine Land Office Records.

Florida. House of Representatives, Office of the Clerk. *People of Lawmaking in Florida 1822–1991.* Tallahassee: Florida House of Representatives, 1991.

———. *Senate Journal,* 1865.

Florida State Archives. Comptroller's Records of Pension Warrants Paid. RG 350, series 476.

————. Comptroller's Vouchers, 1846–1862. RG 350, series 565.

————. Confederate Pension Applications. RG 137, series 587.

————. Decennial Census, 1885.

————. Elections, Division of. Appointments. RG 156, series 1284.

————. Elections, Division of. Commissions, 1827–1978. RG 156, series 259 and 259A.

————. Elections, Division of. Election Returns, 1824–1970. RG 156, series 21 and 1258.

————. Florida State Genealogical Society State Pioneer Certificate Publications. M84-13.

————. Secretary of State, Resignations and Removals from Office, 1844–1904, RG 151, series 1326.

————. State Board of Pensions. Confederate Pension Files, 1885–1954. RG 137, series 587.

————. Territorial and State Governors' Papers. RG 101.

Hillsborough County, Florida. Probate Records. Hillsborough County Courthouse, Tampa.

Indian War Pension Files, 1892–1926. NA.

Kennedy, Joseph C. G. *Population of the United States in 1860; Compiled from the Original Returns of the Eighth Census.* Washington, D.C.: Government Printing Office, 1864.

Lafayette County, Florida. Deed Records. Lafayette County Courthouse, Mayo.

————. Marriage Records. Lafayette County Courthouse, Mayo.

————. Tax Rolls, 1858–1880. Available on microfilm at FSA.

Levy County, Florida. Deed Records. Levy County Courthouse, Bronson.

————. Probate records. Levy County Courthouse, Bronson.

————. Tax Rolls, 1878–1880. Available on microfilm at FSA.

Liberty County, Georgia. Litigation Files. Office of the Probate Judge, Liberty County Courthouse, Hinesville.

Madison County, Florida. Deed Records. Madison County Courthouse, Madison.

————. Marriage Records. Madison County Courthouse, Madison.

————. Tax Rolls, 1866–1868. Available on microfilm at FSA.

Manatee County, Florida. Tax Rolls, 1868–1880. Available on microfilm at FSA.

Monroe County, Florida. Probate Records. Monroe County Courthouse, Key West.

Polk County, Florida. Tax Rolls, 1861–1867. Available on microfilm at FSA.

Pulaski County, Georgia. Probate Records. Pulaski County Courthouse, Hawkinsville.

Roster of State and County Officers Commissioned by the Governor of Florida 1845–1868. Jacksonville: Florida Historical Records Survey, 1941.

Suwannee County, Florida. Cemetery Records. Suwannee County Public Library, Live Oak.

———. Deed Records. Suwannee County Courthouse, Live Oak.

———. Probate Records. Suwannee County Courthouse, Live Oak.

United States Decennial Censuses, 1820–1920. Manuscript returns. Available on microfilm at FSA.

United States House of Representatives. House Document No. 262, 27th Cong., 2nd sess. "Correspondence—Secretary of War and Commanding Officer in Florida."

Walker, Francis A. *Ninth Census—Volume I: The Statistics of the Population of the United States.* Washington, D.C.: Government Printing Office, 1872.

Work Progress Administration. *Spanish Land Grants in Florida.* 5 vols. Tallahassee, Fla.: Historical Records Survey, 1940.

NEWSPAPERS AND PERIODICALS

Apalachicola Gazette, 1836–1837.

Army and Navy Chronicle, 1842.

Bartow Courier-Informant, 1900.

Bartow Polk County Democrat, 1971–1972.

Gainesville Times, 1876.

Jacksonville Daily News-Herald, 1888.

Jacksonville East Florida Advocate, 1840.

Jacksonville Evening Metropolis, 1901.

Jacksonville Florida News, 1851–1853.

Jacksonville Florida Republican, 1849–1855.

Jacksonville Florida Sun, 1876.

Jacksonville Florida Times-Union, 1883–1896, 1902–1927.

Jacksonville Florida Times-Union and Citizen, 1898–1901.

Jacksonville Florida Union, 1874.

Jacksonville News, 1848–1849.

Jacksonville Tri-Weekly Florida Union, 1873.

Jacksonville Weekly Sun & Press, 1878.

Jasper News, 1899.

Lake City Citizen-Reporter, 1901–1912.

Lake City Florida Index, 1899–1910.

Madison Recorder, 1889.

New York Sun, 1873.

New York Times, 1876.

Niles' Register, 1842.

St. Augustine Examiner, 1867.

St. Augustine Florida Herald, 1834–1836.

St. Augustine Florida Herald and Southern Democrat, 1838.

St. Augustine News, 1842.

Savannah Daily Advertiser, 1869.

Savannah Daily Republican, 1867.

Savannah Georgian, 1838.

Savannah Morning News, 1873–1881.

Tallahassee Florida Sentinel, 1850.

Tallahassee Floridian, 1836–1840.

Tallahassee Floridian & Journal, 1849–1857.

Tallahassee Sentinel, 1871–1874.

Tallahassee Weekly Floridian, 1871–1874.

Tampa Florida Peninsular, 1855–1861, 1866–1871.

Tampa Herald, 1854.

Tampa Sunland Tribune, 1878–1883.

Tampa Tribune, 1901.

SECONDARY SOURCES

Akerman, Joe. *Florida Cowman: A History of Florida Cattle Ranching.* Kissimmee: Florida Cattleman's Association, 1976.

————. "Jacob Summerlin: King of the Crackers." In *Florida Pathfinders,* edited by Lewis N. Wynne and James J. Horgan. Saint Leo, Fla.: Saint Leo Press, 1994, 105–26.

Baxley, John Hood, Julius J. Gordon, and Diane Moore Rodriguez. *Oaklawn Cemetery and St. Louis Catholic Cemetery: Biographical & Historical Gleanings.* 2 vols. Tampa, Fla.: Baxley, Gordon & Rodriguez, 1991.

"Biographical Notes." *Florida Historical Quarterly* 19 (July 1940): 50–51.

Biographical Souvenir of the States of Georgia and Florida. Chicago: F. A. Battey & Company, 1889.

Bleser, Carol, ed. *In Joy and Sorrow: Women, Family, and Marriage in the Victorian South.* New York: Oxford University Press, 1990.

Boles, John B. *The South Through Time: A History of an American Region.* Englewood Cliffs, N.J.: Prentice Hall, 1995.

Boyd, Mark F. "Asi-Yaholo or Osceola." *Florida Historical Quarterly* 33 (January–April 1955): 249–305.

Brown, Canter, Jr. "The Florida Crisis of 1826–1827 and the Second Seminole War." *Florida Historical Quarterly* 73 (April 1995): 419–42.

————. *Florida's Peace River Frontier.* Orlando: University of Central Florida Press, 1991.

————. *Fort Meade, 1849–1900.* Tuscaloosa: University of Alabama Press, 1995.

————. "Ossian Bingley Hart: Florida's Loyalist Reconstruction Governor." Ph.D. dissertation, Florida State University, 1994.

————. *Ossian Bingley Hart: Florida's Loyalist Reconstruction Governor.* Baton Rouge: Louisiana State University Press, 1997.

Brown-Hazen, Pauline. *The Blue Book and History of Pioneers, Tampa, Fla., 1914.* Tampa, Fla.: Tribune Publishing Co., 1914.

Bruton, Quintilla Geer, and David E. Bailey, Jr. *Plant City: Its Origin and History.* St. Petersburg, Fla.: Valkyrie Press, 1977.

Buker, George E. "The Americanization of St. Augustine 1821–1865." In *The Oldest City: St. Augustine, Saga of Survival,* edited by Jean Parker Waterbury. St. Augustine, Fla.: St. Augustine Historical Society, 1983.

Bunch, James H. "The Ellis Family in Florida." Typescript in biographical files, Florida Collection, SLF.

"Burris Brewer Bounty Land Application." *Georgia Genealogical Magazine* 20 (April 1966): 1334.

Cashin, Joan E. *A Family Venture: Men and Women on the Southern Frontier.* New York: Oxford University Press, 1991.

Chapin, George M. *Florida, 1513–1913 Past, Present and Future; Four Hundred Years of Wars and Peace and Industrial Development.* 2 vols. Chicago: S. J. Clarke Publishing Co., 1914.

Clinton, Catherine. *The Plantation Mistress: Woman's World in the Old South.* New York: Pantheon, 1982.

Coe, Charles H. *Red Patriots: The Story of the Seminoles.* Cincinnati: The Editor Publishing Co., 1898. Reprint ed., Gainesville: University of Florida Press, 1974.

Cohen, Hennig, and William B. Dillingham, eds. *Humor of the Old Southwest.* Athens: University of Georgia Press, 1994.

Cone, William Whitney, comp. *Some Account of the Cone Family in America.* Topeka, Kans.: Crane & Company, 1903.

Cooper, William J., and Thomas E. Terrill. *The American South: A History.* New York: McGraw-Hill, 1991.

Covington, James W. "The Armed Occupation Act of 1842." *Florida Historical Quarterly* 40 (July 1961): 51–52.

————. *The Billy Bowlegs War, 1855–1858: The Final Stand of the Seminoles Against the Whites.* Chuluota, Fla.: Mickler House Publishers, 1982.

————. *The Seminoles of Florida.* Gainesville: University Press of Florida, 1993.

————. *The Story of Southwestern Florida.* 2 vols. New York: Lewis Historical Publishing Co., 1957.

Cutler, Henry Gardner. *History of Florida Past and Present.* 3 vols. Chicago: Lewis Publishing Co., 1923.

Davis, Thomas Frederick. *History of Jacksonville, Florida and Vicinity 1513 to 1924.* Jacksonville: Florida Historical Society, 1925. Reprint ed., Jacksonville: San Marco Bookstore, 1990.

Denham, James M. "Cracker Women and Their Families in Nineteenth-Century Florida." In *Florida's Heritage of Diversity: Essays in the Honor of Samuel Proctor,* edited by Mark I. Greenberg, William Warren Rogers, and Canter Brown Jr. Tallahassee: Sentry Press, 1997, 15–27.

————."The Florida Cracker Before the Civil War as Seen Through Travelers' Accounts." *Florida Historical Quarterly* 72 (April 1994): 453–62.

————.*"A Rogue's Paradise": A History of Crime and Punishment in Antebellum Florida, 1821–1861.* Tuscaloosa: University of Alabama Press, 1997.

DeVane, Albert. "Jacob Summerlin, Jr." In *DeVane's Early Florida History, Volume One.* Sebring, Fla.: Sebring Historical Society, 1978.

Doherty, Herbert J. *The Whigs of Florida, 1845–1854.* Gainesville: University of Florida Press, 1959.

Durbin, Larry, comp. *Glynn County, Georgia, Marriage Index 1818–1867.* Jacksonville, Fla.: Southern Genealogists' Exchange Society, 1993.

Elliott, Brenda J., and Joe Knetsch, eds. *Proceedings of the Florida Cattle Frontier Symposium.* Kissimmee: Florida Cattlemen's Association and the Florida Cracker Cattle Breeders Association, 1995.

Faust, Drew Gilpin. *Mothers of Invention: Women of the Slaveholding South in the American Civil War.* Chapel Hill: University of North Carolina Press, 1996.

Faust, Patricia L., ed. *Historical Times Illustrated Encyclopedia of the Civil War.* New York: Harper & Row, 1986.

Fleming, Francis P. *Memoirs of Capt. C. Seton Fleming of the Second Infantry, C.S.A.* Jacksonville, Fla.: Times-Union Pub. House, 1881. Reprint ed., Alexandria, Va.: Stonewall House, 1985.

Flynt, Wayne. *Dixie's Forgotten People: The South's Poor Whites.* Bloomington: Indiana University Press, 1980.

————. *Poor But Proud: Alabama's Poor Whites.* Tuscaloosa: University of Alabama Press, 1989.

Foster, Sarah Whitmer, and John T. Foster, Jr. "Chloe Merrick Reed: Freedom's First Lady." *Florida Historical Quarterly* 71 (January 1993): 279–99.

Fox-Genovese, Elizabeth. *Within the Plantation Household: Black and White Women of the Old South.* Chapel Hill: University of North Carolina Press, 1988.

Frizzell, Isabel. *Bellville: The Founders and Their Legacy.* New Ulm, Tex.: New Ulm Enterprise, n.d.

Gannon, Michael. *The New History of Florida.* Gainesville: University Presses of Florida, 1996.

Gilbert, Bil. *God Gave Us This Country: Tekamthi and the First American Civil War.* New York: Athenaeum, 1989.

Goodbread, James Piper Taliaferro. *Cemeteries of Columbia & Hamilton Counties, Florida.* N.p., n.d.(Publication is available in Columbia County Public Library, Lake City.)

Gordon, Julius J. *Afro-Americans of Hillsborough County, Florida 1870–1890.* Tampa, Fla.: Privately published, 1993.

————. *Biographical Census of Hillsborough County, Florida 1850.* Tampa, Fla.: Privately published, 1989.

Greenberg, Kenneth. "The Nose, the Lie, and the Duel in the Antebellum South." *American Historical Review* 95 (February 1990): 57–74.

Greenberg, Mark I., William Warren Rogers, and Canter Brown Jr., eds. *Florida's Heritage of Diversity: Essays in the Honor of Samuel Proctor.* Tallahassee: Sentry Press, 1997.

Grismer, Karl H. *Tampa: A History of the City of Tampa and tha Tampa Bay Region of Florida.* St. Petersburg: St. Petersburg Printing Co., 1950.

Hamilton County Bicentennial Committee. *An Early History of Hamilton County, Florida,* 2nd ed. Live Oak, Fla.: Miles Printing, 1990.

Hartman, David W., and David J. Coles. *Biographical Rosters of Florida's Confederate and Union Soldiers 1861–1865.* 6 vols. Wilmington, N.C.: Broadfoot Publishing Company, 1995.

Haskew, Corrie Pattison. *Historical Records of Austin and Waller Counties.* Bellville, Tex.: Premier Printing & Letter Service, 1969.

Henderson, Mrs. J. D., Mrs. J. Q. Howell, Mrs. John McConnaughhay, Mrs. D. H. Means, and Miss Merrill Willey, comps. *A Group of Genealogical Records from Columbia County, Florida.* Lake City, Fla.: Edward Rutledge Chapter, Daughters of the American Revolution, 1951–1952.

History of Lowndes County, Georgia 1825–1941. Valdosta, Ga.: Gen. James Jackson Chapter, D.A.R., 1942.

Hodges, Winnie Smith. *Cemeteries of Hamilton County, Florida.* Jasper, Fla.: Privately published, n.d.

Howard, Oliver O. *Autobiography of Oliver Otis Howard, Major General United States Army.* 2 vols. New York: Baker & Taylor Co., 1907. Reprint ed., New York: Books for Libraries Press, 1971.

Hunter, William K. *William Miles Hunter Family History.* Live Oak, Fla.: William Miles Hunter Assoc., 1981.

Huxford, Folks. *Pioneers of Wiregrass Georgia.* 9 vols. Homerville, Ga.: Folks Huxford and the Huxford Genealogical Society, 1951–1993.

Hyde, Samuel C. *Plain Folk of the South Revisited.* Baton Rouge: Louisiana State University Press, 1997.

"In Memorium [*sic*]: Francis Philip Fleming." *Florida Historical Quarterly* 2 (April 1909): 3–8.

Jordan, Terry. *Trails to Texas: Southern Roots of Western Cattle Ranching.* Lincoln: University of Nebraska Press, 1981.

Kaiser, Sarah Margaret. "My Family." Typescript at St. Augustine Historical Society Research Library.

Keen, John Wesley. *My Autobiography.* Frostproof, Fla.: Betty Jane Keen Fulton, 1992.

Keuchel, Edward F. *A History of Columbia County, Florida.* Tallahassee: Sentry Press, 1981.

Lewis, James A. "Cracker—Spanish Florida Style." *Florida Historical Quarterly* 63 (October 1984): 184–204.

Livingston, Richard. "Benjamin Moody 1811–1896." *South Florida Pioneers* 8 (April 1976): 9–11.

———. "Enoch Everett Mizell 1806–1887." *South Florida Pioneers* 3 (January 1975): 14–17.

———. "Levi Pearce 1806–1874." *South Florida Pioneers* 21/22 (July/October 1979): 38–41.

———. "William Henry Locklear 1845–1923." *South Florida Pioneers* 23/24 (January/April 1980): 10–12.

———. "Willoughby Tillis 1808–1895." *South Florida Pioneers* 39/40 (January/April 1984): 4–11.

———. "Willoughby Whidden 1799–1861." *South Florida Pioneers* 11 (January 1977): 8–11.

Lossing, Benson J. *Memoir of Lieut.-Col. John T. Greble, of the United States Army.* Philadelphia: Privately published, 1870.

Mahon, John K. *History of the Second Seminole War.* Gainesville: University of Florida Press, 1967.

Manasota Genealogical Society. *Tombstone Inscriptions in Cemeteries of Manatee County, Florida 1850–1980.* Bradenton, Fla.: Manasota Genealogical Society, 1982.

Martin, Sidney Walter. *Florida During the Territorial Days.* Athens: University of Georgia Press, 1944.

May, Philip S. "Zephaniah Kingsley, Nonconformist (1765–1843)." *Florida Historical Quarterly* 23 (January 1945): 145–59.

McClelland, Clifton A. *Silas and Penelope (Anderson) McClelland, and Some Descendants 1790–1987.* Baltimore: Gateway Press, 1987.

McMillen, Sally G. *Southern Women: Black and White in the Old South.* Arlington Heights, Ill., 1992.

McWhiney, Grady. *Cracker Culture: Celtic Ways in the Old South.* Tuscaloosa: University of Alabama Press, 1986.

McWhiney, Grady, and Forrest McDonald. "Celtic Origins of Southern Herding Practices." *Journal of Southern History* 51 (May 1984): 165–82.

Morgan, Leo E. "Ancestors of Leo E. Morgan." *'Latchua Country News* 9 (September 1990): 19.

Morris, Allen. *The Florida Handbook 1991–1992.* Tallahassee: Peninsular Publishing Company, 1991.

Motte, Jacob Rhett. *Journey into the Wilderness: An Army Surgeon's Account of Life in Camp and Field during the Creek and Seminole Wars, 1836–1838.* James F. Sunderman, ed. Gainesville: University of Florida Press, 1953.

Newby, I. A. *Plain Folk in the New South: Social Change and Persistence, 1880–1915*. Baton Rouge: Louisiana State University Press, 1989.

Osborn, George C., and Jack P. Dalton. "The South Florida Baptist Association." *Tequesta* 14 (1954): 51–60.

Otto, John S. "Florida Cattle-Ranching Frontier: Manatee and Brevard Counties (1860)." *Florida Historical Quarterly* 64 (July 1985): 48–61.

———. "Florida's Cattle-Ranching Frontier: Hillsborough County." *Florida Historical Quarterly* 63 (July 1984): 71–83.

———. "Hillsborough County (1850): A County in the South Florida Flatwoods." *Florida Historical Quarterly* 62 (October 1983): 180–93.

———. "Open Range Ranching in Southern Florida." *Florida Historical Quarterly* 65 (January 1987): 317–34.

Owsley, Frank L. *Plain Folk in the Old South*. Baton Rouge: Louisiana State University Press, 1949.

Paisley, Clifton. *The Red Hills of Florida, 1528–1865*. Tuscaloosa: University of Alabama Press, 1989.

Pasteur, Margaret Pearce. "John J. Pearce 1808–1878." *South Florida Pioneers* 14 (October 1977): 9–10.

Patrick, Rembert W. *Florida Fiasco: Rampant Rebels on the Georgia-Florida Border 1810–1815*. Athens: University of Georgia Press, 1954.

"Persons Subject to Military Duty, Levy County 1876." *'Latchua Country News* 4 (May 15, 1986): 43.

Peters, Virginia Bergman. *The Florida Wars*. Hamden, Conn.: Archon Books, 1979.

Price, Michael E. "Stories With a Moral: Augustus Baldwin Longstreet, William Tappan Thompson, and Other Literary Defenders of Plantation Society in Antebellum Georgia." *Atlanta History: A Journal of Georgia and the South* 39 (Summer 1995): 23–45.

Raulerson, Virgil E., comp. "Raulerson Group Sheet #1." Typescript and manuscript available at Huxford Genealogical Library, Homerville, Georgia.

———. "Raulerson Allied Families Group Sheet #2." Typescript and manuscript available at Huxford Genealogical Library, Homerville, Georgia.

———. *Raulerson Documents 1800–1900*. Jacksonville, Fla.: Privately published, 1986.

A Register of Columbia County, Florida, Cemeteries. Lake City, Fla.: Columbia County Historical Society Productions, 1988.

Rerick, Rowland H. *Memoirs of Florida*. 2 vols. Atlanta: Southern Historical Association, 1902.

Revels, Tracy J. "Grander in Her Daughters: Florida's Women During the Civil War." *Florida Historical Quarterly* 78 (Winter 1999): 261–82.

Ridgely, J.V. *Nineteenth-Century Southern Literature*. Lexington: University of Kentucky Press, 1980.

Rubin, Louis D., Jr. *The Edge of the Swamp: A Study in Literature of the Old South*. Baton Rouge: Louisiana State University Press, 1989.

Sapp, Mitchell. "Shadrick Sapp, Jr.—1793–Circa 1872." *'Latchua Country News* 14 (September 1995): 14–15.

Schafer, Daniel L. *Anna Kingsley.* St. Augustine, Fla.: St. Augustine Historical Society, 1994.

Schene, Michael G. "Not a Shot Fired: Fort Chokonikla and the 'Indian War' of 1849–50." *Tequesta* 37 (1977): 19–37.

Shelton, Jane Twitty. *Pines and Pioneers: A History of Lowndes County, Georgia 1825–1900.* Atlanta: Cherokee Publishing Co., 1976.

Shofner, Jerrell H. *History of Jefferson County.* Tallahassee: Sentry Press, 1976.

————. *Nor Is It Over Yet: Florida in the Era of Reconstruction 1863–1877.* Gainesville: University of Florida Press, 1974.

Simmons, William Hayne. *Notices of East Florida.* Charleston, S.C.: A. E. Miller, 1822. Reprint ed., Gainesville: University of Florida Press, 1973.

Smith, Julia Floyd. *Slavery and Plantation Growth in Antebellum Florida 1821–1860.* Gainesville: University of Florida Press, 1973.

Snell, Marvis R. *Testimony to Pioneer Baptists: The Origin and Development of the Gillette First Baptist Church.* DeLeon Springs, Fla.: E. O. Painter Printing Co., 1974.

Snyder, Frank L. "Nancy Hynes DuVal: Florida's First Lady, 1822–1834." *Florida Historical Quarterly* 72 (July 1993): 19–34.

————. "William Pope DuVal: An Extraordinary Folklorist." *Florida Historical Quarterly* 69 (October 1990): 195–212.

Sprague, John T. *The Origin, Progress, and Conclusion of the Florida War.* New York: Doubleton, Appleton & Co., 1848. Reprint ed., Gainesville: University of Florida Press, 1964.

Stanaback, Richard J. *A History of Hernando County 1840–1976, Bicentennial Edition.* Brooksville, Fla.: Action '76 Steering Committee, 1976.

Ste. Claire, Dana. *Cracker: The Cracker Culture in Florida History.* Daytona Beach, Fla.: Museum of Arts and Sciences, 1998.

Stirk, Kathryn London. *Tombstone Registry of Central Florida, Volume I: Orange County (part).* Orlando, Fla.: Privately published, 1984.

Stone, Spessard. "William McCullough—Polk County Unionist." *Polk County Historical Quarterly* 20 (March 1994): 6.

Taylor, Anne Wood. *Florida Pioneers and Their Descendants.* Vol. 1. Tallahassee: Florida State Genealogical Society, 1992.

Taylor, Anne Wood, and Mary Lee Barnes. *Florida Connections Through Bible Records.* Vol. 1. Tallahassee: Florida State Genealogical Society, 1993.

Tindall, George Brown. *America: A Narrative History.* 2 vols. New York: W. W. Norton, 1988.

VanLandingham, Kyle S. "William Brinton Hooker 1800–1871." *South Florida Pioneers* 5 (July 1975): 6–12.

Vocelle, James T. *History of Camden County, Georgia.* Brunswick, Ga.: James T. Vocelle, 1914.

Walker, Laura Singleton. *History of Ware County, Georgia*. Macon, Ga.: J. W. Burke Co., 1934.

Warren, Mary Bondurant, ed. *Georgia Marriages 1811 Through 1820*. Danielsville, Ga.: Heritage Press, 1988.

Watkins, James. H., ed. *Southern Selves: From Mark Twain and Eudora Welty to Maya Angelou and Kaye Gibbons, A Collection of Autobiographical Writing*. New York: Vintage, 1998.

Wessels, William L. *Born To Be a Soldier: The Military Career of William Wing Loring of St. Augustine, Florida*. Fort Worth: Texas Christian University Press, 1971.

Westergard, Virginia W., and Kyle S. VanLandingham. *Parker & Blount in Florida*. Okeechobee, Fla., 1983.

White, Frank L. "Macomb's Mission to the Seminoles: John T. Sprague's Journal Kept During April and May, 1839." *Florida Historical Society* 35 (October 1956): 130–93.

White, Virgil D., trans. *Index to Indian Wars Pension Files 1892–1926*. 2 vols. Waynesboro, Tenn.: National Historical Publishing Co., 1987.

Wiggins, Early I. *History of the Absolute Mt. Enon Association*. Plant City, Fla.: Mt. Enon Cemetery Memorial, 1975.

Williams, John Lee. *The Territory of Florida*. New York: A. T. Goodrich, 1837. Reprint ed., Gainesville: University of Florida Press, 1962.

———. *A View of West Florida, Embracing its Geography, Topography, with an Appendix Treating of its Antiquities, Land Titles, and Canals*. Philadelphia: L. R. Bailey, 1827.

Wolfe, Margaret Ripley. *Daughters of Canaan: A Saga of Southern Women*. Lexington: University of Kentucky Press, 1995.

Wright, J. Leitch, Jr. *Creeks & Seminoles: The Destruction and Regeneration of the Muscogulge People*. Lincoln: University of Nebraska Press, 1986.

Wyatt-Brown, Bertram. *Southern Honor: Ethics and Behavior in the Old South*. New York: Oxford University Press, 1982.

INDEX

Crackers, 101; characteristics of, xviii,
xvi–xviii, xix, 87–97; origins of
term, 8. *See also* Scotch-Irish
Creeks (Indians), xv; burn town of
Roanoke, Ga., 35, 37. *See also*
Seminoles
Crews family: attacked by Indians, 36
crime, 3–6
Curry, Bill, 71
cursing, 23; in ragtown, 83
Custer, Gen., 86
Cuthbert, Ga., 123
Czar (slave), 91–92

Dade City, 67
Dalgreen Lake, 110
Dancy, Colonel [Francis Littlebury], 66
Daniels, Aaron, 71
Daniels, Elam, 23, 71; threatens Charles
Fitchett, 23–24
Daniels, Isaac [Squire], 18, 20, 21, 23
Daniels, [J. E.] Berry, 18
Daniels, Jeff, 71
Daughtrey, [Arthur], 47, 55
Daughtrey, Lewis, 93
David (biblical prophet), 60
Day, Dr. S[amuel] T., 76
Deadman's Bay, 42
D[ean], widow Rhoda, 47, 49, 51, 54
Deese, James, 28
Deese, Melton: marriage to Mary
Sistrunk, 22; death of, 22
DeLeon, Ponce, 81
Delilah (biblical figure), 54
Deloch [DeLoach], Edmond J., 55
Democratic Party, 57, 65–67, 71, 110;
absorbs Whigs after Civil War, 58
Demosthenes, 49
Deshong, Caroline C., 54
DeShon[g], Edna, 54
DeSoto County, xvii
DeSoto Lake, 81, 110
Didwell, Josiah, 42–44
Doggett (widow): marries Tom Holder,
93
Douglas, Tasset, 14

Douglas[s], James, 12, 83; George G.
Keen's stepgrandfather, 95
drinking, 3, 5, 13, 20, 22, 45, 72; attitutes
toward, 29; at Christmas, 106; "kiss-
ing Hanner," 62; in ragtown, 83
dueling, 73–74
DuPre, Madame, 115
DuVal, Gov. William Pope, 101
Duval County, xv
Dyal[l], Joseph, 61

East Florida: characteristics of, xv–xvi,
xvii
education: need for, 13; building of
schools, 29–30; school at Jacob Sum-
merlin's house, 110; in Quincy, 110.
See also Gillett, Daniel
Edwards family: as dish rag aristocray of
LaFayette County, 83
Edwards, William, 28
elections, 66–68, 70, 71–73, 110. *See also*
politics
Ellaville, 20
Ellinger, Abe, 3–6; killed in battle of
Williamsburg, 6
Ellis, Betsy: marries Tom Holder, 92
Ellis, Lydia, 92
Ellis, Q. W. [Giles U.], 66, 70
Ellis, Tommy, 92
Emery, Nancy, 17; marries Daniel Stew-
art, 15
Enterprise, 110
Everglades, 68

Fayetteville: as county seat of LaFayette
County, 84
F. C[.] & P. Railroad, 37
Fernandina, 58, 59
fighting, 11–13, 20–22, 45, 82–86. *See
also* violence; dueling
Finnegan, General [Joseph J. Finegan],
106
Fitchet[t], Charles, 72; as Columbia
County sheriff, 23–24
Fitchpatrick [Fitzpatrick], old Tom B.,
56; wins sheriff election, 72–73

www.ingramcontent.com/pod-product-compliance
Lightning Source LLC
Chambersburg PA
CBHW050648270326

41927CB00012B/2923